Get Sober Stay Sober

Get Sober
Stay Sober

The Truth About Alcoholism

Cynthia Perkins, M.Ed.

Published by Cynthia A. Perkins, USA

© 2009 by Cynthia A. Perkins

Printed in the United States of America

ISBN: 978-0-9841446-0-0

Edited by Brenda Judy
www.publishersplanet.com

Cover Design by Andrew Perkins
www.andrewscustomwebdesign.com

Bullseye with checkmark artwork by
www.iStockphoto.com/enot-poloskun

This book is printed on acid-free paper.

.

Disclaimer

The information in this book has not been evaluated by the Food and Drug Administration. The author is not a medical doctor and any information in this book is not intended to diagnose, treat, cure or prevent any disease.

The information shared in this book is designed for educational purposes only, based on the personal and professional experiences and opinions of the author, and should not be taken as professional medical advice or used as a substitute for medical care or psychological counseling. With all medical or mental health conditions, you should consult a qualified medical or mental health professional before making changes in your diet, adopting an exercise regimen or taking nutritional supplements and/or other natural remedies.

You agree the author is not responsible for any adverse affects or consequences that may result, either directly or indirectly, from the suggestions contained herein and are aware that the author makes no guarantees on the outcome of recovery. Results and benefits may vary from person to person.

Some of the author's family members deny some of the events that took place in the author's childhood; however, it is the author's position that every word is the absolute truth. The real names of other individuals in the author's life have been changed to protect their identities.

Contents

Acknowledgements

A deep heartfelt thank you to:

Andrew, my beloved son and anchor, for loving me, forgiving me, enriching my life and being such a great trooper through it all.

Daryl, my mentor, and Scott, my friend, for your encouragement and support through the process of writing and publishing this book.

All those who touched my life and contributed to my healing.

One

The Truth

Most alcoholics do not recover from their disease, they die. Their death certificate may read cirrhosis, suicide, fatal car accident, pancreatitis, gun shooting, etc., but the underlying cause is alcoholism. Not only that, they usually die about 26 years before their non-drinking counterparts. Alcohol consumption is the third leading preventable cause of death in the U.S.[1]

Those who do recover with a 12 step program fight constant cravings to drink and suffer with a variety of other symptoms like irritability, anxiety, tension, fatigue and depression that has a deep impact on the quality of their life and forces them to be dependent upon attending Alcoholics Anonymous (AA) meetings the rest of their life. Staying sober is a constant battle and they continue to be addicted to a variety of other substances and activities like sugar, caffeine, sex and cigarettes.

Even Bill Wilson (aka Bill W.), the founder of Alcoholics Anonymous, was plagued with symptoms like depression and fatigue and remained an incurable addict in more ways than one until the day he died. I point this out not to discredit Bill, he was doing the best he could with what he had to work with at the time. I believe he had a true desire to help people and was a man in search of the truth; however, he did not have all the pieces of the puzzle.

Unfortunately, he didn't have at his disposal the knowledge we have today about genetics and biochemistry. I believe if he had, that he would have been a man who accepted and embraced this life-changing truth rather than walk away because, as you'll learn later in this book, Bill was actually one of the first people to learn a small piece of information about the biochemistry of addiction and he attempted to inform the members of AA but was promptly silenced.

AA has contributed to saving the lives of many people, including myself, however, we need to be honest about what AA does and does not achieve. We need to recognize its limits and be realistic about its effectiveness. Bill W. is a portrait of the typical member in Alcoholics Anonymous and sadly this is not a picture of a person that is free from addictions.

It's crucial that we take a look at Bill W.'s life because he is responsible for creating a phenomenon that has been adopted by our society as the main treatment method for not only alcoholism, but addiction in general. A program that is falsely believed to be successful and based on sound principles, when what we really have is an entire medical society and justice system demanding attendance in a program that emerged from the mind of a man that was consumed with sexual obsession and crippling depression and heavily influenced by the brainwashing of a religious cult.

Before getting sober, Bill was repeatedly admitted to a hospital that was famous for treating alcoholics, called Town's Hospital, where he met a wise doctor named Dr. Silkworth. Dr. Silkworth believed that alcoholism was caused by an allergy to alcohol, not a lack of willpower, and it was the allergy that created the cravings for alcohol. He shared this belief with Bill W. and told him that once you have the allergy, you can never drink again because it results in the inability to control your drinking. This theory made great sense to Bill W. and he embraced it thoroughly; and this is where the whole "alcoholism is a disease" concept originated.

Bill tried over and over and over again not to drink, but couldn't succeed. Unfortunately, during this time he had another alcoholic friend who had joined the Oxford Group, an evangelical Christian cult, and he tried to convince Bill that this was the path to sobriety. Initially Bill was resistant, but as his drinking grew more and more out of control and he was facing the possibility of being committed to an insane asylum, he grew increasingly desperate and started to be influenced by the teachings of the Oxford Group, which included admitting defeat, taking personal inventory of sins, confession, making restitution, helping others, prayer and passing the message on.

During one of his many hospitalizations for alcoholism, after a visit from his friend from the Oxford Group, while he was experiencing severe delirium tremors and highly sedated with a mixture of morphine, psychoactive drugs and belladonna (a hallucinogen), Bill experienced what he described as an intense religious experience where he came to believe that God was now his higher power as he had been taught by the Oxford Group. When in reality, what Bill was probably experiencing were hallucinations.

The primary concept of the Oxford Group was called "God Control." They believed that human beings were powerless and that the only way to solve our problems was to submit our will completely to God. They also believed that all human problems were a result of sin, so Bill had adopted this concept as well. Frank Buchman, the leader of the group, had an obsession with sexual matters—he liked to focus on and pry sexual information out of his followers. He had a particular fondness for spending time with young men and talking about sexual matters like masturbation. Buchman was asked to leave and even banned from more than one institution for inappropriate behaviors of a sexual nature with young students that sounded an awful lot like sexual abuse; and if we really had all the facts, we would probably learn it actually was.

Buchman was a very unreliable person who didn't show up for appointments and would simply state that God had guided him to miss the appointment. He encouraged others to engage in irresponsible behavior and just trust that God would provide. At one point, he actually "publicly thanked God for the existence of Adolph Hitler and said he thought Hitler would make a great key person for the Oxford Group."[2] So this tells you just a little bit about where their head was.

Bill W. introduced Dr. Bob (co-founder of AA) to the Oxford Group and convinced him that this was the path to sobriety, and the two of them began to carry the message to other alcoholics. The Oxford Group held meetings around town in hotels or member's homes and targeted the educated and elite. It used elder members of the group to teach the newer members. The very first AA meeting was a group of alcoholics who were members of the Oxford Group that Bill pulled together.

Eventually, the Oxford Group grew intolerant of the untidy drunks because they didn't fit in with the wealthy bunch they catered to, so they stopped allowing them to attend their meetings. Bill W. and Dr. Bob left and formed their own Oxford Group, called Alcoholics Anonymous, where they brought all their teachings with them. The 12 Steps of Alcoholics Anonymous are taken directly from the teachings of the Oxford Group. In the Oxford Group, the steps were used to cure sin; but in AA, they are used to cure alcoholism. Bill Wilson tells us this directly on page 39 in his book, *Alcoholics Anonymous Comes of Age.*

> Early AA got its ideas of self-examination, acknowledgement of character defects, restitution for harm done, and working with others straight from the Oxford Group and directly from Sam Shoemaker, their former leader in America, and nowhere else.

The tragedy in this story is that Dr. Silkworth was absolutely right. We now know that allergy is one of the most powerful roots in the cause and perpetuation of alcoholism and that alcoholism is most definitely a physical disease. However, although Dr. Silkworth knew the cause, he didn't yet know what to do about it other than tell Bill not to drink ever again. Dr. Silkworth and Bill W. were on the right track, but because they didn't yet have enough knowledge about what they had discovered, they weren't able to find a solution and stop the cravings.

It is unfortunate that out of his desperation Bill W. turned to the Oxford Group and ended up combining the whole "alcoholism is a disease" concept with the "religious sin" concept; thus, in the process, we really ended up losing the truth about alcoholism in the 12 Step Program. It is apparent when we look at the 12 Steps of Alcoholics Anonymous that although Bill believed in his mind that alcoholism is a physical disease, in his heart he felt it was a spiritual disease that emerged from sin, and he was not able to break free from the hold that the Oxford Group had instilled in him.

Additionally, Bill struggled with depression that was so severe at times that he would hold his head in his hands and weep, he wasn't able to respond to questions and he couldn't get out of bed. It, at times, was accompanied by heart palpitations, a stomachache and feeling sick all over. His wife, Lois, often referred to him as "almost a hypochondriac" and he sometimes experienced hysteria and breathing problems that he felt he couldn't control.[3]

Bill's behavior indicated that he also had a very active sex addiction that completely ruled his life and often threatened to destroy everything he had worked for. Bill's sex life is not well known or talked about because people of AA "shrouded it in secrecy."[4] It was intentionally kept out of official AA literature and archives because it would have a negative impact on the AA movement.

Bill Wilson was the original 13 stepper. It is where the term was coined. If you're unfamiliar with what a 13 stepper is, it is an elder member in AA who takes advantage of the newer and vulnerable members to meet their sexual needs. Although Bill was married, he engaged in numerous affairs over the years with AA members, particularly the newcomers, and is said to have had an eye for the younger ladies. The older he got, the younger he liked them. The sad truth of the matter is that Bill W. used his position as a leader in the AA community to use and sexually exploit young women who were new to the program.[5]

His behavior was so out of control that it is rumored that certain members of AA were actually delegated the responsibility of following Bill and working as "watch dogs" to keep vulnerable young women out of his grip. Whenever they saw him zeroing in on his prey, one person would distract Bill while another person took the young woman under their wing for protection.[6]

Later on he maintained a mistress with a woman who was 22 years younger than he was, Helen Wynn, and even left her 10 percent of earnings from the *Big Book* in his will.[7] He had wanted to leave her a much heftier amount, but the AA trustees wouldn't allow it. At more than one point Bill contemplated leaving his wife for Helen, but never went through with it out of fear for the controversy it would cause in AA.

Bill's sexual behavior with the women caused a great deal of controversy and concern throughout the AA community and even caused him loss of friendships. Tom Powers a long time close friend, colleague and editor actually left the fellowship and developed his own offshoot group as a result of his disappointment and disgust with Bill's inability to control his sexual urges. He didn't want to be publicly associated with Bill and is quoted as saying, "this sex thing ran through the whole business" and "Bill had to get this sex thing straightened out in program terms so he wasn't lying about it all the time."[8]

A lot of people, including trustees, worked very hard to keep Bill's big sexual secret hidden and actually devoted their life to protecting the image of Bill W. in order to prevent public embarrassment of AA. Even his wife, Lois, accepted his infidelities, kept quiet and participated in the cover up.

Friends who were close to Bill W. would try and talk to him about the sex issue and he would acknowledge that they were right and try to mend his ways, but he just couldn't do it. They report that it was a source of great inner conflict and agony for him. In Bill's writings he often referred to the sex drive as a "natural human trait that could at times rage out of control."[9] His friends tell us he was tortured by his behavior that violated his own values and morals; however, he vacillated back and forth between attempting to change and then rationalizing and justifying his behavior when he fell backwards.

In a program that Bill himself designed to demand rigorous honesty and unselfishness, Bill was living a lie and a very poor example of a man who was supposed to be living an unselfish, spiritual life. He was constantly cheating, lying and sneaking around on his wife and exploiting vulnerable women in the program with no regard for the impact it had on their life. His friends say he was consumed with remorse, self-loathing, guilt, despair and shame as a result of his inability to live up to his own expectations as well as others, and often felt he wasn't worthy of leading AA.[10]

Sex was not the only addiction Bill W. was still struggling with. He was also a heavy chain-smoker and caffeine consumer. It is reported that his wife, Lois, often complained of these behaviors and accused him of being addicted to them, but Bill brushed it off by referring to her as an overreacting nag. This is Bill rationalizing his behavior in the *Big Book*.[11]

> One of our friends is a heavy smoker and coffee drinker. There was no doubt he over-indulged. Seeing this, and meaning to be helpful, his wife commenced to admonish him about it. He admitted he was overdoing these things, but frankly said that he was not ready to stop. His wife is one of those persons who really feels there is something rather sinful about these commodities, so she nagged, and her intolerance finally threw him into a fit of anger. He got drunk.
>
> Of course our friend was wrong—dead wrong. He had to painfully admit that and mend his spiritual fences. Though he is now a most effective member of Alcoholics Anonymous, he still smokes and drinks coffee, but neither his wife nor anyone else stands in judgment. She sees she was wrong to make a burning issue out of such a matter when his more serious ailments were being rapidly cured.

Bill repeatedly struggled with a battle to give up cigarettes. He would give them up for a while and then drive other people crazy by begging for theirs. He was rarely seen without a cigarette in his hand. Papers on his desk were consistently covered with ashes and little burn holes, and the edges of tables and desks were scarred with long cigarette burns.

He was so addicted to nicotine that he continued to smoke even though he developed emphysema and became dependent upon an oxygen tank to get through the days. It was clear to Bill that smoking was the cause of his emphysema, but he couldn't quit. Those close to him report that he often struggled with making a decision about what he needed or wanted more—a cigarette or oxygen. More often than not the cigarette won out.

In 1969, as he got sicker and sicker, he pretended to quit smoking, but he kept cigarettes hidden in his car and would sneak out for a drive to have a secret smoke. Bill Wilson literally smoked himself to death. He died from emphysema and pneumonia.[12]

Bill also continued to fight intense cravings for alcohol until the moment he died. As he lay on his deathbed, he wanted a drink so badly that he asked his assistants to bring him one on at least five different occasions; but knowing the disastrous impact it would have on AA, they refused. His cravings were so intense that on one of these occasions he became belligerent and threatened to punch a nurse.[13]

These facts about Bill W., although disturbing, are important, because all concepts, beliefs, values and methods in AA and the 12 Step Program are a reflection of what was going on in Bill W.'s mind and life. Bill Wilson did not discover a "cure" or "great secret" for alcoholism or any other addiction. He was very clearly still a full-blown addict and just switched his substance of choice and replaced his cravings for alcohol with women, sex, cigarettes, caffeine and cult-like religious fanaticism.

Bill Wilson was projecting his struggles, feelings of powerlessness, depression, inadequacy and shame over his inability to control his sexual compulsions and nicotine addiction and his religious beliefs into the principles and methods, which became the 12 Step Program of Alcoholics Anonymous. One only needs to look at the words in the 12 Steps, the *Big Book* and the *Twelve Steps and Twelve Traditions* to see that this is true. Here are just a few examples straight out of Bill's mind:

> Our next thought is that you should never tell him what he must do about his drinking. If he gets the idea that you are a nag or a killjoy, your chance of accomplishing anything useful may be zero. He will use that as an excuse to drink. He will tell you that he is misunderstood. This may lead to lonely evenings for you. He may seek someone else to console him—not always another man.[14]

> When and how and in just what instances did my selfish pursuit of the sex relation damage other people and me? Just how did I react? Did I burn with a guilt that nothing could extinguish? [15]

> We cannot for example unload a detailed account of extramarital adventuring upon the shoulders of the unsuspecting wife or husband.[16]

> Since most of us are born with an abundance of natural desires, it isn't strange that we often let these far exceed their intended purpose.[17]

God alone can judge our sex situation. Counsel with persons is often desirable, but we let God be the final judge. We realize that some people are as fanatical about sex as others are loose. We must avoid hysterical thinking or advice.[18]

Perhaps he is having a secret and exciting affair with the girl who understands. In fairness we must say that she may understand, but what are we going to do about a thing like that? A man so involved often feels very remorseful at times, especially if he is married to a loyal and courageous girl who has literally gone through hell for him.[19]

In *Twelve Steps and Twelve Traditions*, many of the discussions revolve around sex and sexual needs. These are not the words of a man who was divinely guided by God, as he so often claimed, and people still believe to this day. These are the words of a man struggling with shame, self-loathing, guilt and remorse and trying to find a way to deal with them and explain his behaviors. Unfortunately, all he had to turn to at the time was the teachings he had learned from the religious cult, the Oxford Group. Like all religions, they attempted to control behavior through shame and guilt and this is the method that Bill adopted and passed along.

I do not sit in judgment of Bill Wilson. I have compassion and complete understanding for his plight. Like most addicts, I too have struggled with most of the same or similar issues. Unlike me, he did not have the good fortune available to him that we now know about the biochemistry of addiction. Bill was not aware that his addiction to cigarettes, caffeine and sex were all interconnected to his alcoholism or have the means to learn about it. He didn't understand that when his mother and father abandoned him as a child, it too had a profound impact on his addictive biochemistry. If Bill were alive today and could take advantage of the knowledge we've gained, we would probably be telling a very different story.

However, the problem is that Bill W. had not yet conquered these problems and his mind was not physically, emotionally or spiritually healthy. Although he had good intentions, the message he was carrying was tainted with dysfunction and half-truths. Thus, we ended up with a treatment program for alcoholism and addictions that is based on Christian evangelical cult beliefs and attempts to control people's behavior through guilt and mind control and shaming them into submission rather than a real medical treatment that focuses on the true physiological roots of alcoholism. These distasteful practices have resulted in the largest part of the addicted population to fail to maintain sobriety and/or take issue with the current treatment approach and often walk away.

The even bigger tragedy in this story is the fact that the medical community embraced this irrational way of thinking. Unfortunately, that is probably due to the fact that Bill had buddied up with Dr. Bob, a medical doctor, which gave him a foot in the door to the medical society and added credibility to his approach. However, you would think that somewhere along the line someone would have questioned the methods or suggested we grow with the times instead of engaging in mass delusion for over 70 years.

Alcoholics Anonymous was formally developed in 1935. Since that time we have learned an astounding amount of information and have a much better understanding of the addiction process. Scientific evidence now tells us that alcoholism, or any addiction, has its roots in an imbalance of the neurotransmitters in the brain, nutritional deficiencies and allergies.[20] Yet AA and 12 step programs have not grown or expanded their treatment approach in any way. With all other physical diseases, we consistently update and change our treatment approaches as we learn more information about the terrain; but that is not the case with alcoholism or addiction, it remains stubbornly stuck in the past.

AA and 12 step treatment programs refuse to even look at new scientific evidence, listen to new insights or hear anything that contradicts the original AA principles, and continue to treat addiction with an outdated model that, besides being sexist, shaming, abusive, cult like and patriarchal, isn't and never has been very successful. What's even worse is that they rationalize and justify their failure by blaming the victim.

Alcoholics Anonymous and 12 step programs are in denial. They are in denial about what they are and what they achieve. In spite of all the evidence to the contrary, AA and 12 step treatment programs insist they are not a religious program, that they do not engage in brainwashing or cult-like behaviors and claim to be successful in maintaining sobriety. When in reality their practices exude shame, religious fanaticism and cult-like/brainwashing practices, and the statistics for success are extremely low.

Here's a fine example of their blaming and shaming attitude taken directly from page 58 of the *Big Book* and recited out loud at the beginning of most AA meetings.

> RARELY HAVE we seen a person fail who has thoroughly followed our path. Those who do not recover are those who cannot or will not give themselves completely to this simple program, usually men and women who are constitutionally incapable of being honest with themselves. There are such unfortunates. They are not at fault; they seem to have been born that way.

Another very popular slogan in AA and 12 step programs is the following: "The program never fails anyone. People just fail the program."

Wow, excuse me, but that is the biggest crock of bull I have ever heard. Millions of people walk out the doors of Alcoholics Anonymous or 12 step treatment programs and return to drinking. Most people do not succeed in a 12 step program, but AA does not consider that as a failure of the program. Instead they blame the alcoholic with statements like "they haven't hit their bottom yet," "they're in denial," or "they didn't work the program." When in reality, that has nothing to do with it.

Yes, some people are in denial and it is true that you must be ready and willing to change; but if we had an effective treatment program that actually addressed the physiological disease of addiction rather than the so-called "spiritual disease," that wouldn't be much of an issue. People leave or don't succeed with AA and 12 step treatment programs for a variety of very valid and healthy reasons such as they are uncomfortable with: the powerlessness concept; the "group think" mentality; the religious aspect; the abusive aspect; the rigid, dogmatic structure; the shaming; the blaming; the sexist aspect; the patriarchal aspect; the archaic aspect; the demeaning aspect; the abusive criticizing on the hot seat; and the cult-like brainwashing methods to name a few. Then since there are no other treatment options available to them, they return to drinking.

The truth is that our current treatment approach for alcoholism, the 12 Steps of Alcoholics Anonymous, is basically a failure. The success rate of sobriety is poor at best. Accurate statistics are hard to come by because of many factors like anonymity and dishonesty, but most studies reveal that AA only has about a 2.5 percent success rate for over five years of sobriety. Some statistics have it as low as 1 percent. Experts report that spontaneous remission of alcoholism will occur about 5 percent of the time, so treatment and Alcoholics Anonymous actually have a lower success rate than doing it alone.[21]

It's entirely possible that the percentage of AA people who stayed sober are actually people who would have stayed sober anyhow because they fall within that spontaneous remission percentage. Maybe they just finally had enough, but AA is where they happened to be when something finally clicked. Perhaps after one attempt after another of failure, by the time they made it to the doors of AA, they were just so desperate and in enough pain they would have gotten sober with anything.

Ending an addiction is a process. The individual usually goes through many phases and bounces back and forth between abstinence and using. They usually have to endure a great deal of emotional pain and reach desperation before being ready. Rarely does someone just wake up one day a changed person. It's a slow transformation and there may be many different paths they follow before arriving. Some people end up in a church, some people do it themselves, some people end up in AA, but wherever it is they arrive when the final break happens, they then attribute their success to whatever program they are in at the time.[22]

Many AA people will attempt to challenge these truths by saying that they have a lot more sober members than this, but it's important to keep in mind here that we're not talking about members of Alcoholics Anonymous; we're talking about people who have attempted to stay sober through AA and have not succeeded. The ones who have walked out the door. They are not sitting in the seats of a meeting to be counted. Another important point to remember is that an active alcoholic is notoriously dishonest about their drinking behavior and AA is full of people claiming to be sober when in truth they only attend meetings as a smoke screen to deceive spouses, employers or the judicial system, because they have been sentenced to attend against their will.

Additionally, we're talking about long-term sobriety, not short-term. Sure, a good deal of people can get a few months of sobriety or a year under their belt with some serious white knuckling, but in the overall picture of life, one year is not a long time. That does not constitute stable sobriety. Not only that, continuously fighting overwhelming cravings to drink does not constitute success.

Another important fact to keep in mind is that almost all alcoholism treatment centers are based on the 12 Step Program and demand that all patients attend Alcoholics Anonymous. AA meetings are built into the treatment curriculum and the 12 steps and serenity prayer are recited several times a day. So that means that treatment centers are having about the same success rate and failures as AA. Alcoholics Anonymous and traditional treatment are basically one in the same.

If we put the religious, cult-like, shame-based principles aside, we can say that AA is a support group and, like most support groups, it has a variety of aspects that are beneficial to the recovering person.

AA offers the following great benefits:

- emotional support
- people you can relate to
- a place to go to fill your time
- helps you reconnect with your morals and values which have most often been obliterated by drunkenness
- challenges denial

- enables you to build a new social life that takes you away from the old places and friends
- educates
- gives people something to hang onto
- a place to belong
- connections to others
- ability to develop a new lifestyle
- people who understand what you're going through and talk your language
- learn you're not alone and not feel so isolated
- hope and inspiration

When you go into a treatment center, in addition to all the above, you also have the benefit of the following aspects:

- a protected environment
- counseling
- education
- addressing psychological and emotional issues like child abuse
- coping skills
- personal growth

If someone just goes to AA as their only treatment choice, the only thing they get is the 12 steps and the support group aspects; so not only are they missing the biochemical aspect, but other emotional and psychological issues like dysfunctional relationships, child abuse, sex, social skills, coping skills, communication, etc., are never addressed either. The person who has nothing but AA is at a real disadvantage. Unfortunately, there are many people floating around out there in 12 step programs like this, where no real recovery takes place at all.

When I was in rehab, I had a superb counselor who was able to identify precisely my emotional, social and psychological issues, and guide me competently to all the appropriate sources I needed to heal in these areas. I, like many alcoholics, needed help with a lot more than just not drinking or drugging. There were child abuse issues, parenting, self-esteem, assertiveness, social, communication, sex and relationship issues, etc., that I needed help with desperately and they were essential components of my recovery. These are all great aspects and an important part of staying sober. I'm grateful that I had such a capable and caring teacher to get me on the right track, but the physiological or biochemical piece was unknowingly missing and that left me suffering and struggling needlessly for a long time.

We had only dealt with half the story. In no way do I intend to demean, belittle or minimize the benefits one can acquire when they attend a high-quality, competent treatment center. There are many beautiful and helpful people in treatment centers, AA and the world of psychology that intend well, have good hearts and make a difference in people's lives, but their approach is not complete and does not address the true root of alcoholism. AA, the 12 Step Program and psychology are a support group and a means for personal growth and emotional healing, but not a complete treatment for a powerful and complex medical condition like alcoholism.

Alcoholism is a physiological disease. Even traditional treatment centers acknowledge this fact to some degree; however, they continue to treat it as if it were a spiritual or psychological disease. Why is that? We don't send people with cancer or heart disease to meetings and suggest they work on their character flaws as their primary method of treatment. We may suggest a person with cancer or other chronic health conditions attend a support group or get some psychological counseling to help them cope and provide emotional support throughout the treatment process, but that would be in addition to treatment, not in place of it. To use a support group or psychological counseling as the sole source of treatment for a physical disease is absurd.

We don't tell anyone with cancer, diabetes, multiple sclerosis, arthritis or cardiovascular disease to get right with God or blame their condition on the state of their morality or spirituality. When was the last time anyone with one of the aforementioned conditions or any other physical disease besides alcoholism or addiction was told they must give their will and life over to a higher power, make a list of their sins, confess them to a group member, make restitution and engage in community service if they want to heal their health issues? When was the last time any of them were told the treatment protocol did not work because they are incapable of being honest, just not sick enough or in denial?

When AA does work, which is rare, it is largely because it always feels better to have others who are like you to support, accept and encourage you. This is true of any challenge or hurdle in life. We can overcome many things with love and support from others who understand us. However, like any physical disease, since the physiological aspect of addiction has never been addressed, relapse is almost certain.

Additionally, AA sometimes works because it provides someone whose life has been shattered by alcoholism with structure and direction. It's similar to the placebo effect, in that it doesn't really matter what the program consists of, it could be 3 steps, 2 steps, or whatever, it's simply a matter of being given a clear-cut path to follow that instills a false sense of protection and certainty in an unsafe and uncertain world.

People who are in severe emotional distress, personal or physical crises, or an extreme state of desperation will radically change their belief systems and grasp at straws by adopting views they normally consider irrational or ridiculous and may experience a religious conversion.[23] However, once the immediate crises pass and the desperation weakens, it's difficult to continue to justify their participation in the activity and they drift away. Which is why we see so many people come into the program who initially look like they will make it, or "get the program," but then walk out the door. Some people are able to be shamed and guilted into staying sober for a period of time, but since shame is also at the root of perpetuating addiction, this method does not work in the long run.

Regardless of how defiantly AA denies it, the bottom line is that AA and all 12 step programs are religious programs that employ the use of a variety of cult-like practices that drive many people out the door and back to the bottle. As we pointed out earlier, all the principles of AA came directly from the evangelical Christian cult, the Oxford Group. The word "sin" was replaced with "shortcomings," "wrongs" and "character defects." Additionally, in the original 12 steps, the word God is used four times. However, God is referenced to three other times in the term of him, his or power greater than ourselves. In some other versions, modified as they see fit, and used in treatment centers, the word God is used eight times. It would take too long to go through the *Big Book* and count all the references to God, but in chapter five alone I counted it 27 times and in chapter six I counted 20. Basically it is another version of the Bible. Here are just a couple examples taken directly from the *Big Book*:[24]

> We had to have God's help.

> Next we decided that hereafter in this drama of life, God was going to be our director.

> Without help it is too much for us. But there is ONE who has all power—that one is God. May you find him now!

The messages in AA and 12 step programs tell us we're powerless, we're full of character defects, we're helpless and defective, and we're spiritual derelicts not worthy of the love of God. We're subjected to abusive, angry, confrontational methods to break down denial. We're belittled and bullied by elder members. We're told the only way to get better is to get right with God. We are sinful wretches who should grovel humbly at the feet of a higher power.

In the 12 steps, you admit you're powerless, you give your power to God, list your sins, confess your sin, make restitution, engage in prayer, meditation and service to the program. We're very clearly talking about a religious conversion here—not a treatment for addiction. The sole purpose of the 12 steps is to induce guilt and shame in an attempt to change and control behavior; which is another contributing factor to why so many people can't succeed through the 12 steps. Shame and guilt only produce low self-esteem and encourage self-destructive behavior like drinking and drugs rather than healthy, loving behavior towards self.

The whole powerlessness concept came from two places. It was a core concept of the Oxford Group that Bill had internalized and, therefore, it became one of his core feelings. There is no scientific evidence or even common sense that says admitting we're powerless is effective in healing any physical health disease. Quite the contrary—it is counterproductive. The powerlessness concept was what the Oxford Group (cult) used to control, manipulate and retain members by making them completely dependent upon the group and that's what it ended up doing in AA as well.

Instilling a sense of powerlessness in an individual is destructive to self-esteem, teaches and perpetuates learned helplessness, perpetuates hopelessness, prevents one from taking personal responsibility and encourages a self-fulfilling prophecy that in the case of alcoholism or addiction often leads to binge drinking and justification for the binge. "If I'm powerless, I guess there's nothing I can do about it, so I might as well drink myself to death," is what the alcoholic mind concludes. Some studies indicate that the powerlessness concept actually increases binging behavior and relapse.[25]

It is completely disempowering, which is insane, because what the alcoholic or addict needs more than anything is to feel empowered. They need to feel capable of changing their life. Not only that, it's a complete lie. When the alcoholic understands that the true root of alcoholism lies in biochemistry and there are ways to correct it, they are given all the tools needed to overcome their addiction and the shame so often associated with being an alcoholic. Being an alcoholic is no longer a moral issue, a character flaw, a spiritual illness, a defect in spirit or a personality disorder. It frees them.

Does an alcoholic have to admit they have a problem? Absolutely, but there is a very big difference between admitting you have a problem and submitting to complete powerlessness. It's impossible to overcome any problem if one does not admit it exists, so yes it is a crucial first step. However, powerlessness is not an essential component of that first step.

It is the moral, religious attachment to the steps that makes them inappropriate, inaccurate and ineffective. Some of the steps could actually work if this element was removed. For example: After we admit we have a problem, if we do a personal inventory (but not a moral inventory) of why we drink, the impact it has on our lives, what needs to change, etc., this can be very helpful. It's always necessary to access the damage in order to know what steps to take to fix it.

I am certainly not opposed to living a moral life. I believe it's something we should all strive to do our best at and I practice it in my life daily, but requiring moral inventory as a treatment for alcoholism is absurd. This is not the place it belongs. You did not become an alcoholic because of your morality. Your morals became obliterated because you're under the influence of alcohol, and you're an alcoholic because of biochemical reasons.

Another one of the steps that could be helpful when used appropriately is the "pass it along to others." When you help others, it boosts your self-esteem, gives you something to invest your time in, gives you meaning and purpose in your life, and keeps the reality of how destructive alcoholism is in the forefront of your mind—which makes it more likely you'll continue to take care of yourself. However, many people get carried away with this step and inject themselves too deeply into other people's lives. They get wrapped up in other people's problems and stop focusing on their own issues. Additionally, the desire to help others usually occurs naturally as one learns, changes and grows, so it shouldn't be something that is pushed upon you or a requirement to stay sober. It should emerge on its own. However, again it's not likely to keep you sober for the long term when intense physiological cravings occur.

Is there anything wrong with honesty? Absolutely not, I subscribe whole heartedly to the rigorously honest concept, and practice so much honesty in my own life that people are often uncomfortable with me and I get accused of being too honest for my own good; however, it is not the root of alcoholism. Will it help keep you sober and should you practice it? Yes, because when you're not honest you feel guilt and shame. If you feel guilt and shame, you may drink to deal with your feelings. However, it's not likely to keep you sober for too long when the real cause of the addiction is not addressed. It is a very tiny fish in a large sea and being dishonest did not make you an alcoholic, being an alcoholic made you dishonest.

There is nothing fundamentally wrong with using spirituality to assist in the recovery of any illness. As a matter of fact, it is an essential component of my life; but not many people can make a full recovery with spirituality alone, regardless of the diagnosis, and not everyone can embrace this concept. Many people with alcoholism are too damaged physically and emotionally to begin working on their spiritual life, and some people are uncomfortable with the whole spiritual/religious aspect of AA and other people don't believe in a higher power. Even those individuals who already have strong religious or spiritual beliefs, most often do not succeed in sobriety by following AA and a

12 step program, and in all cases it is because spirituality it is not the root of the problem.

Another important point is that there is a very big difference between spirituality and religion and even though AA and 12 step treatment centers deny it vehemently, the 12 steps are a religious program, not a spiritual one. We'll go into more detail about this in Chapter 18, but for now we'll just suffice to say that spirituality is about the relationship you have with your core self and the world around you and finding meaning and purpose in your life, while religion is about beliefs and practices that involve God or a higher power. AA and the 12 steps clearly fall under the religion category.

Next, let's take a look at a few definitions of a cult:

"A cult typically refers to a cohesive social group devoted to beliefs or practices that the surrounding culture considers outside the mainstream, with a notably positive or negative popular perception."[26]

- followers of an exclusive system of religious beliefs and practices

- fad: an interest followed with exaggerated zeal;

- followers of an unorthodox, extremist, or false religion or sect who often live outside of conventional society under the direction of a charismatic leader[27]

Now let's take a look at some of the behaviors that cults engage in:

- use of mind control techniques and intimidation

- thrive on creating a sense of powerlessness in the member

- operate as a closed system with an authoritarian structure

- engage in elaborate religious rituals and emphasize prayer

- discourage skepticism and rational thought

- manipulate their members through guilt

- discourage independent thinking

- if you don't think like everyone else in the group, you're not accepted or welcomed until you do

- attempt to gain control of the members time and thoughts by controlling major aspects of a person's social and physical environment

- go to great lengths to retain members

- claim their way is the only path to salvation

- require complete submission to the will of God

- are hierarchical

- authoritarian structure that cannot be questioned

- built on a charismatic leader that is worshipped and revered

- espouse irrational and rigid beliefs

- claim to have the ultimate truth and embody dogmatism

- encourage separation from family and non-cult members.

AA and 12 step programs fit the definition of a cult like a glove and engage in each and every one of these cult-like behaviors. The program is based on the beliefs and values of their charismatic leader, Bill W., who is still seen as some kind of God today. AA is based on the "powerlessness concept," engages in a variety of religious rituals with strong emphasis on prayer, and you must follow the steps and believe completely to be accepted. AA uses thought-stopping techniques with slogan therapy, uses guilt and shame to control behavior, requires submission of will to a higher power, and is rigid, authoritarian and dogmatic. They believe AA is the one and only way and threaten that if you leave, you'll get drunk or die, and they encourage separation from society.

I'm not even saying that all these methods are a bad thing. In my early recovery I found some of them like the silly little chants, slogan therapy, rigid structure and separation from society to be helpful, however, many people don't. They feel uncomfortable with them. As I got more emotionally healthy, they became uncomfortable to me as well. Although AA and 12 step programs employ cult-like behaviors, I don't believe they do so with evil intentions. I believe that at the heart of AA and 12 step programs is a sincere desire to help others. The problem is that it is misguided and the end result is the same. Most alcoholics and addicts end up without getting the help they need because they have been driven away by these practices that feel frightening or uncomfortable and/or because they're simply ineffective for a powerful physiological disease like alcoholism and other addictions.

The other issue at hand in regard to cult-like behaviors and the religion issue is honesty. In a program that demands rigorous honesty, let's at least be honest about who and what we are and the methods we employ and not attack the people who are uncomfortable with these methods and call it like it is. AA is a religious program that uses cult-like practices; let's just admit that.

It's quite interesting that in spite of the fact that AA and 12 step treatment centers claim to be an open-minded and accepting group, everyone defends this program to the death with angry, defensive, sometimes hostile, vicious and vengeful attacks against people who dare say anything negative about the program, question any of its methods or beliefs or express any doubts or concerns whatsoever. If it's not angry attacks, it comes in the form of subtle, yet clear, rejection and disapproval. The message is very clear that if you do not believe 100 percent, you are not accepted. I have come face to face personally with this experience many times.

This illustrates one of the cult-like behaviors very clearly. Additionally, this behavior serves to protect their reality. They need to feel validated and certain that they are following the right path, so voices of the non-believers cannot be permitted because they threaten their sobriety.

Next, let's look at the definition of brainwashing:

> Brainwashing (also known as thought reform or as re-education) consists of any effort aimed at instilling certain attitudes and beliefs in a person—beliefs sometimes unwelcome or in conflict with the person's prior beliefs and knowledge, in order to affect that individual's value system and subsequent thought-patterns and behaviors.[28]

This is a clear definition of exactly what goes on in AA and 12 step treatment programs. The whole success of the program hinges on whether the alcoholic will buy their beliefs, adopt them as their own value system and think and behave in a particular manner. Just like prisoners of war or others subjected to brainwashing, when the alcoholic is resistant, they are confronted with hostile, angry confrontations, threats of relapse and failure, accusations of being in denial, not sick enough, or incapable of honesty, rejection and even death. Again, I don't believe members of Alcoholics Anonymous or mainstream treatment centers are evil or engaging in these practices with evil or harmful intentions. I believe they think they are doing something good, but then again, I'm sure that's what other brainwashers think. The fact remains that whether it is done with good intentions or not, brainwashing is occurring and many people are, rightfully so, uncomfortable with these methods.

Last but not least, every principle and technique used in AA and the 12 Step Program not only promote but also ensures dependence upon the program. It replaces one addiction with another—alcoholism for meetings. Instead of teaching the individual skills that they can apply to their life outside the program to live a full and productive life, they are brainwashed with fear tactics into believing they must attend Alcoholics Anonymous meetings for the rest of their life or they'll get drunk. They discourage independent thinking and, thus, the alcoholic becomes completely dependent upon the program and other members for not only their sobriety, but living in general. They look to AA for answers to managing all areas of their life.

AA and 12 step programs could be more beneficial if we removed the shaming, blaming, religious, cult-like/brainwashing practices and operated more like a traditional support group and then combined that with a real medical treatment plan that actually addresses the biochemical roots of alcoholism. Unlike other support groups, AA demands that you attend for the rest of your life and engage in a variety of religious practices to be an accepted member. Like other support groups, attendance in AA should be voluntary and used as a transitional phase for early stages of recovery, not something you're sentenced to for the rest of your life. AA should be like a parent—teach and raise the child and then release them into the world.

However, the real, the biggest and most important flaw with Alcoholics Anonymous and traditional 12 step treatment programs is that it is an incomplete approach. It's missing the most important component for recovery—the physiological or biochemical. It addresses the social, emotional, psychological and the spirit, but it does not address the root of alcoholism, which lies in biochemistry, and this is why relapse is so common and uncontrollable cravings to drink continue.

Scientific research tells us that the drive to self-medicate with alcohol, drugs, sex, food, etc., emerges from nutritional deficiencies, genetics, undiagnosed medical conditions, allergies and biochemical imbalances that result in an imbalance, deficiency or malfunctioning of neurotransmitters; not character flaws, mental disorders, weak will, personality disorders or spiritual deficits. Alcoholism is a physical disease with roots that lie in an imbalance of neurotransmitters in the brain.[29] When the alcoholic tries to stay sober without addressing the physiological or biochemical roots, then relapse is almost guaranteed, as the underlying biochemistry issues will perpetuate cravings and push the alcoholic to seek relief in a drink. If relapse does not occur, cravings are temporarily soothed by engaging in other addictive behaviors like sex, sugar, caffeine and cigarettes.

The biggest crime in this scenario is that there are actual treatment methods that are based on sound scientific evidence that can help the body repair these physiological or biochemical issues and ensure a much better chance of achieving sobriety. These methods come to us from the exciting fields of orthomolecular medicine and neuroscience and have a success rate of 74–80 percent, and yet are totally ignored and dismissed by AA and traditional treatment centers.[30]

Unfortunately, the truth of the matter is that alcoholics are being fed a pack of lies. Alcoholism is not a psychological problem, a spiritual disease or a personality disorder. You are not powerless over addiction. Your drinking does not occur as a result of character flaws, lack of willpower or your state of morality. You do not have to attend AA meetings the rest of your life. You do not have to fight constant cravings for a drink or a drug. You can get sober and stay sober for a lifetime without any cravings for alcohol or drugs at all. When you address alcoholism from the biochemical angle, drinking is no longer an issue in your life. I know for a fact that this is true because I have lived it. I have 21 years of uninterrupted sobriety and only attended AA for the first two years. I never experience cravings for alcohol or drugs. On the pages of this book I will share my journey with you from beginning to end and show you exactly how it can be done.

Two

My Story

Before we move on to the recovery process, it's important we take a look at where I came from, how I got broken and how much damage was done. So I'm going to give you a little background on my life and my journey through addiction. Throughout this book I use illustrations from my own life to provide you with an in-depth look at all the factors that contribute to setting the process of addiction into motion, the pain and struggles the addict endures, and the process of recovery. If you prefer to go straight to the meat and potatoes of staying sober, then you may want to skip the next two chapters and move on to chapter four; however, understanding my background will be helpful in understanding the principles for recovery more thoroughly.

I began drinking very early in life, around age nine or so. I lived with my father, stepmother and their four children—my two half brothers and two half sisters. My parents drank, of course, so there was always a bottle of something around the house. My father liked Black Velvet and Seagram's 7 and the image of these bottles stand out in my mind very clearly. Drinking, violence and all the insanity that accompanies it were a way of life in my household. My first memory of drinking was with my stepmother, who allowed me to put Black Velvet or Seagram's 7 in a cup of coffee. I got extremely ill and puked my guts out. You'd think that would have curbed my desire to continue, but it didn't.

Well let's back up a minute. Prior to the age of seven, I lived with my mother and her boyfriend. I guess my parents divorced when I was just a baby. I went with my mother to a tiny little town almost no one has ever heard of in Pennsylvania. My father lived just over the border in a little town in Ohio. I don't remember ever seeing my father during those seven years, but I am told that I did from time to time.

We were very poor and hardly had the basics. I was always cold, because we couldn't afford to turn up the heat. I remember hiding in the house with the door locked while bill collectors pounded on the door. Once I peeked out the curtain and the person pounding on the door saw me and he was yelling through the door that he saw me at the curtain. My mother still didn't answer and I got a good beating afterwards.

I also had to go hungry quite often because we didn't have very much money for food. However, there was always enough food for the boyfriend. I would be upstairs in my room aching with hunger and I could smell the food cooking downstairs for the boyfriend, but I wasn't allowed to come down and have any. Sometimes the smell of the food would draw me down the stairs and I would sit there on the steps and savor the aroma. I would peek around the corner and see them eating and enjoying themselves. If they noticed me, I would get a beating all the way back up the steps.

The boyfriend was crazy and violent and was handing out severe beatings to me quite regularly. Life was pretty wild with events like their drunken friends showing up in the middle of the night and tearing up our place. For some unknown reason the boyfriend and my mother would lock me in the basement, turn out the lights and tell me snakes were going to eat me. I would scream and cry in horror. It was a dirty, musty, cold basement and I was afraid there were actually snakes down there that were going to eat me. Sometimes I was left there for long periods and I cowered in the corner.

They would also make me stand behind an old grandfather clock in the corner of the room for hours and hours on end as a form of punishment. I remember being so tired and weak in the legs from standing that I couldn't stand anymore and would be falling down and then I would get beat for not standing up straight. Once, when we had company, they made me stand behind the grandfather clock and they displayed me to the company we had like I was an art exhibit. Pointing out how bad I was and totally humiliating me.

I had a bed-wetting problem and got severe beatings for this as well. Once when it occurred in the middle of winter, I was stripped down completely naked and tossed outside into a snowdrift and they locked the door and wouldn't let me in. I watched them through the window laugh at me. My bed-wetting didn't occur only at night, I apparently had a bladder problem and would sometimes pee my pants or shorts even during the day. So sometimes they made me wear diapers even though I was over the age of five. On one of these occasions, I was made to wear the pair of shorts that I had peed in continuously for months and months and months until they literally fell apart in shreds and there was nothing left of them and then I had to wear a diaper.

There were violent beatings from the boyfriend for every move I made. I can't even remember them all. Many of them are just a blur, except for the memories I've mentioned already stand out a little more clearly in my head. He did other cruel things like taking me to the county fair once and we got on the Ferris wheel. When we got to the top, he kept rocking the seat back forth pretending he was going to flip us upside down. I cried and begged him to stop, but he tortured me the whole time. He'd tell me to stop being a baby. I didn't think the ride would ever end and was so happy when I was able to get off. I'm still terrified of heights to this day.

I also have vague memories of sexual abuse with the boyfriend. It's very hazy and I have only pieces of it, but some of it took place outside in an area where he would carry me on his shoulders and there were cattails growing. He appears to be nuzzling his face in my crotch while I sat on his shoulders. He took me to this area with the cattails all the time and my mother didn't accompany us. He would also put his penis in my face, but I can't remember what happens after that.

Something horrific happened in an outhouse or shed too. I can't remember all the details. I only see me with the boyfriend's shadow hovering over me. It's dark, there's a horrible smell and I have the feelings, but no clear images. I feel feelings of terror, pain, humiliation, extreme violation, raw brutality and then it feels like I pass out.

In another fragmented memory, I think I'm about the age of four or five and I'm very little with a tiny skinny little frame, petite hips and groin. I'm naked from the waist down and wearing a sleeveless summer shirt. I have semen all over my belly and genital area. I feel very dirty and ashamed. A male is standing over me, but I can't see his face, so we can't say with certainty who this person is. There is more than one memory that is similar to this at a variety of different ages.

We had what I think was a small river stream that separated our house from downtown. There was a store across town that had penny candy that I loved to go to. The water was shallow enough that we could cut across it by foot to get to town, but there were some deeper spots and very muddy spots. I was afraid of the water, but the boyfriend and my mother would tell me I could go get some candy if I crossed the stream by myself. I would go down and attempt to cross, but would come home crying because I would get terrified and turn back around. Sometimes they would send me to the store, but I refused to cross, so they would give me a beating and send me to my room hungry. I got a very nasty cut in my foot once from stepping on a broken beer bottle in the stream and had to go to the doctor.

Once I had a friend spending the night and we were sleeping outside on the balcony, which was in front of my mother's bedroom. My friend and I were looking through the window and saw my mother and her boyfriend having sex, and we did some sexual exploration on each other. For some reason this little girl told her mother what we did and her mother told my mother and I got the living hell beat out of me. Part of this beating was focused on my hands, as a punishment for touching.

So this was life with the mother and boyfriend, day in and day out. My mother had a sister who lived down the road, my Aunt Patty. I remember feeling loved by her, and the only good memories I have during this part of my childhood are of the time I spent with her. She had a daughter, my cousin, that I was also close to as well. Sometimes I was allowed to go visit and I really looked forward to this. However, since my mother and her boyfriend knew this was pleasurable for me, it was also used as a source of punishment and cruelty. They would cancel plans I had to go for a visit for no reason at all at the last minute and wouldn't allow me to go. They held it over my head as a way to torture me. I was often denied a visit for not crossing the river.

I remember many fights between my mother and my aunt over why I wasn't allowed to go visit "this time." My aunt was aware of some of the crazy things going on in the household, although not all. She felt I wasn't being taken care of or fed properly and she knew the boyfriend was bad news. I was very skinny and dirty and she was worried about me. Eventually she decided to intervene and she secretly went to my father. She thought she was doing a good thing, and under the circumstances one would think that things could only get better, but they didn't.

Although life was no picnic with my mother, she was the only mother I knew, and naturally I loved her. I didn't even know my father and I was afraid of him. I hadn't spent almost any time with him. When I was seven, he showed up at our door one night with an attorney. It was dark and I remember standing in the doorway between my mother's legs and crying. Just like that, they packed up all my belongings and put them in the back of their car. It was a big dark car and I was terrified of these two scary men I didn't even know. It was very devastating being ripped away from my mother in the middle of the night. We pulled up to my new house in the middle of the night and were greeted by my stepmother.

What's very odd about this scenario is that I have a lot of memories from my childhood prior to the age of seven, but I have not one memory of my father during those years. He was a complete stranger to me when he showed up at the door to take me away and I was terrified of him. I was told by my stepmother that she and my father would come visit me during those first seven years, but I have no memory of that whatsoever.

I cried and cried and cried for what seemed an eternity. Every night for a long time I would wake up over and over in a fitful, fearful crying state. I felt lost, disconnected and terrified. My stepmother slept with me for a while, but she was a stranger to me and I didn't feel comforted by her.

We lived close to the train tracks and the train would blow its whistle in the middle of the night when I was up crying. To this day, when I hear a train whistle in the middle of the night, it instantly takes me back to those horrid nights and the overwhelming feeling of grief and displacement in my gut that I felt at that time. Eventually one day, the night crying stopped, but I carry the deep wound still to do this day. At age 46, right now as I write these words on this page and remember those days, I can still feel the pain, grief, fear and loss of that little girl inside me and I weep for her.

For a long time I cried for my mother even when I was in school. The other children would make fun of me because I was "crying for my mommy." This only intensified the pain and made me feel even more out of place. One of the children took pity on me and somehow turned into my best friend.

I never saw my mother again until I was 19 when I showed up at her door looking for some answers and trying to understand. She made no attempt to come after me and no attempt to come visit me, even though she lived less than two hours away. My father had no actual court order or anything. He simply used the attorney to intimidate her. I do remember talking to her on the phone when I was first taken away from her. She did seem to try and keep connected in that way, but then my stepmother started talking about her and convinced me that I shouldn't talk to her anymore since she didn't come and see me, and so we didn't speak again until I was 19.

However, her perverted boyfriend attempted to see me secretly. My father and stepmother were at the Indianapolis 500 races and we were with a babysitter for a weekend. I was at the city park with all my brothers and sisters and was climbing up the steps of the sliding board when I heard someone outside the fence call out, "Cindy Ann." Cindy Ann was what my birth mother, her boyfriend, my aunt and cousin called me. I turned around and there stood the boyfriend watching me. I can't remember what he said, but he tried to talk to me. I got scared, went down the slide, and tried to hide in the crowd in the water. I called our babysitter and told her what happened. So she came and got me and we called my father. Later on the boyfriend kept circling the house in a car. We called the cops and since we lived in a little town, you could actually get personal attention in that day and age. So they kept our house under watch overnight. He disappeared and I never saw him again.

Life with my father and stepmother turned out to be about as bad as it was with my mother, except I wasn't hungry or cold anymore. When my father took me from my mother, my understanding was that I was severely malnourished. I now had plenty of food. The only good thing I can say about my father was that he was a good provider and a hard worker. He was a truck driver and went to work faithfully every day. We always had a roof over our head, adequate clothing and enough food on our plates, but that's where the good stuff ends.

My father was a violent man. I came to understand in my later years that he didn't take me from my mother to rescue me. He took me because I was his property. It was about control, power and ownership. It had nothing to do with love. As a matter of fact, my father seemed to hold a deep hatred for me. He beat me violently with a thick black belt every chance he could. He created reasons to give me a beating. If I did something he felt I needed disciplined for, he would get a wicked grin on his face, and his eyes would light up like a Christmas tree and he would say, "Mmmm, I get to give you a beating for that." He truly and thoroughly enjoyed it. It seemed he would almost savor and salivate as he held that big, long, wide black belt in his hands and cracked it together. I can still see the glisten in his eyes.

I was left covered with severe bruises and welts more times than I can remember. It was a weekly ritual. I lived in constant fear of when the next beating would come. If I said the wrong words at the wrong time or did the wrong thing at the wrong time, those were good excuses for a beating. The problem was I didn't know what the right words or behavior were, because no matter what I did or said, it was wrong.

A beating could be provoked by the wrong look on my face, not moving fast enough, not doing the dishes good enough, not cleaning the house clean enough, talking about something that was forbidden or anything under the sun. No matter what I did, I couldn't get it right. Most of the time, I never even knew what I did wrong. Needless to say, I learned to pick my words very carefully and became quite a perfectionist.

My father was a black belt in Karate and once just for fun he gave me a Karate kick in the chest. I doubled over on the floor gasping for air, unable to breathe, while my father rolled with laughter on the couch and my stepmother had to give me mouth to mouth.

When I was nine or ten I had to get eyeglasses and shortly after getting them I lost them, a seemingly innocent mistake for a child. I remember this as the most brutal beating I ever received. My entire body was a black and blue mark. It was so intense, prolonged and violent that I thought I might pass out. I kept dropping to the floor and scooting away on my buttocks like a wounded animal and he kept picking me back up and beating more. I thought it would never end.

As I write these words and relive this brutal memory, I weep, my body quivers and I can feel the feeling that occurred in my brain at that time—the disbelief, the fear and a feeling of separation from my body. I showed the bruises to my best friend and her mother and they were horrified too, however, nothing was ever said to my father. I asked my stepmother to write a note to the school to have me excused from taking a shower in gym class so no one would see the bruises. I was so embarrassed and ashamed. I always had to hide my bruises in gym class behind my towel and shower very quickly, but these bruises were too plentiful and pronounced to cover.

When I arrived at my father's house, he and my stepmother had three other children and she was pregnant with another that arrived about a week or so after I did. I became the built-in babysitter, housekeeper and cook. My father and stepmother were very busy going to bars, having affairs, getting drunk, having vicious fights and being hungover. I took care of the other children all the time. I was basically their mother. They were with me at all times. I cooked, cleaned and cared for them on a daily basis. All the cooking and cleaning of the house were my responsibilities throughout my entire childhood. Friends and acquaintances often called me Cinderella through most of my life until I left home.

I almost never went anywhere alone. If I went swimming, I had to take all my brothers and sisters with me and take care of them. If I spent the night at a friend's, I frequently had to take one of them with me. My Aunt Patty and cousin from Pennsylvania would come and get me in the summer and take me to visit her for a week or two and I wasn't allowed to go by myself. She had to take all my brothers and sisters if she wanted to spend time with me. If she didn't take all of them, I wasn't allowed to go.

To make matters worse, I couldn't even escape the torment in school. I already felt like an outcast because the other children made fun of me for crying for my mother, but when my second teeth came in, I inherited my father's family teeth, which are quite large. As a little girl, the teeth were too big for my body and stuck out like a sore thumb. Now my classmates were making fun of my teeth. They called me Bucky Beaver, Bugs Bunny and bulldozer. It was devastating.

After a while I didn't want to go to school and wouldn't get out of bed. My stepmother called the principal of the school and he actually came to our house, into my bedroom, and got me out of my bed and made me go to school. I was totally mortified when he pulled my blanket off of me and saw me in my nightgown. He took me in his office and I finally spilled my guts on what the problem was. These children were called into the principal's office and the name calling stopped, however, the evil looks and snickers did not.

Talk about damaged self-esteem. Since there was no one at home to help me deal with any of these events in a loving manner, it was all internalized. I carried self-consciousness about my teeth for the rest of my life. I felt ugly and deformed. School was very painful in many ways all the way through high school. Classmates always seemed to dislike me, shun me or pick on me for one reason or another. Later on, in middle school, I was made fun of because I looked similar to another girl in our school that was labeled unattractive and they would call me by her name, and there were a variety of other similar events over the years. I never felt like I fit in anywhere and I always felt like I was on the outside looking in. Nobody really knew me or accepted me and I never felt like I had any true friends except for my best friend, but I often doubted that as well.

The message I received from everyone in the world was that there was something wrong with me. I was unacceptable, unlovable and no good. My mother didn't want me, my father and stepmother only wanted me to serve their needs, my father hated me and thought I was worthless, and my schoolmates thought I was ugly and weird. There was no escaping the abuse, torment and anguish.

Another important event going on in this mess was the presence of a cousin from my stepmother's side. A male in his early 20s I'm guessing. He was at our house all the time; sometimes he babysat us before I began babysitting, and even after I started babysitting, he was sometimes called in to check on me or be an additional babysitter. He also just hung out frequently when my parents were home.

Between the ages of seven and thirteen, he was sexually abusing me on an ongoing basis. He was forcing me to give him handjobs and perform oral sex on him. I remember one event of him attempting to have intercourse with me, but it hurt and I think he stopped, but I can't really remember. I also can't remember if intercourse attempts occurred again or not. I also witnessed him sexually abusing some of my siblings. I won't identify which ones, in case they prefer to keep this private. I later learned as an adult that he also abused a friend's brother. So I'm guessing there are a slew of people out there that he preyed on. Eventually I mentioned it to my best friend and she mentioned it to her mother, and then her mother told my stepmother; but I don't remember that anything was done about it. I just remember that there came a time when he no longer approached me.

There was other inappropriate and weird sexual interaction by my father and stepmother going on as well. I'm not saying that my father or stepmother actually molested me—because I have no recollection of that if they did—but there were quite a few events that really crossed the line into unacceptable sexual behavior between parent and child, which in itself was a violation of boundaries, filled me with discomfort and leaves me with many unanswered questions.

For example, my stepmother had breast implants when we were children and the stitches itched her. She used to lie on the living room floor with her shirt and bra off and have all of us children sit around her and scratch and rub her breasts. My father used to make fun of my breasts incessantly and laugh hysterically. I was a very late bloomer with breasts, and when they finally did arrive, I was very small breasted—or "flat chested"—as it was referred to by my father. He used to point at me, poke them with his finger or flick my nipples and call me Twiggy. Twiggy, I think was a model at the time that was not very well endowed and my father made fun of her. I felt so ashamed and inadequate and would cry. The more upset I got, the more he would instigate. For some reason vivid images of my father's manhood packed inside his briefs are deeply imprinted in my mind. It's not clear to me what this means, because there is no other memory connected to it.

My father would also tell me disrespectful stories about my birth mother and her breasts. He told me her breasts were only about two inches wide and hung all the way down to her knees and that my breasts would probably look like hers, then he would laugh hysterically. I didn't want to hear this, it made me very uncomfortable, and yet he told me this story over and over as a little girl.

Although I don't have any specific memories of sexual abuse with my father, my relationship with him felt emotionally incestuous because of the way he interacted with me. I often felt like he was an obsessive and jealous boyfriend, rather than a father, because he smothered me and wanted complete control and dominance over my every thought and move.

In another memory that comes to me periodically in the form of a very disturbing flashback, I see a man standing in front of me with his underwear pulled down and laughing a wicked laugh while swaying his hips back and forth from left to right and dangling his penis in my face. His white Fruit of the Loom briefs stand out very bright, like they were washed with too much bleach.

Sometimes when this flashback occurs, I feel like I'm being smothered and I literally whimper. I also quiver from head to toe and feel like I will lose my mind. I can't say with 100 percent certainty who this person is, because I can't see his face. I do recognize the body shape, the underwear, the laugh and the penis. However, since I can't see the face, and there were so many men sticking their penis in my face as a child, I think it would be inappropriate to say who I think it is, because there is no way to know for sure.

My father also liked to do other weird things to me to torture me and make me cry, like holding my head in his armpit to force me to smell his body odor and wrapping his legs around my neck and pulling my face into his buttocks while he farted on me. He would throw his head back and laugh his wicked laugh while I screamed and cried to be released. The harder I fought, the tighter his grip grew. He also teased me incessantly about my feet my entire life. I had big feet for a female and he would call me Bigfoot and roar with laughter. Then he'd stomp across the floor pretending he was Bigfoot and sway his arms back and forth like a monkey. "Look at her, here she comes, it's Bigfoot," he'd say. I was heartbroken and consumed with shame.

Our life was full of total insanity like this. There was also lots of fighting and drinking. Both my father and stepmother went out to the bar a lot, but often went to separate bars. My father liked to go do his own thing, which was having affairs. In my youngest years, I don't remember mention of my stepmother having affairs; however, as the years went by, there were a couple of them that came to light.

There were lots of fights over my father's affairs that he was always denying. One time my mother and one of our babysitters, who I think was only about 17 at the time, set my father up. They put a tape recorder in the room and the babysitter came on to my father. I remember being involved in the plot and being so excited by the thought of seeing him fall. He took the bait—hook line and sinker—and she had him red-handed. There was a horrible fight not only between my father and mother, but the babysitter as well.

My father's father was a preacher and every now and then my parents would go on a whim where they decided to be good Christians and we would go through a cycle of going to church three times a week and all the females in our family would wear dresses below the knee. It never lasted too long though and they would be back to their old ways. This was a back and forth pattern for many years. I tried to find comfort in God, but just couldn't find it. I would go to the altar weekly and sob on my knees, secretly praying that I would be delivered from the hellish household I was living in. I poured myself into the Bible looking for answers, but could never find any.

There were many women in my father's life. It's funny that after all this time I remember a couple of their names. One was Darlene and she was a barmaid at one of the bars where my father drank, and she lived in an apartment above the bar. My stepmother would load all of us kids up in the car and we would go ride past her apartment to see if my father's car was parked there. There were times when he didn't come home and we knew he was at Darlene's.

At one point, my father left us and went and lived with another woman. I think her name was Rose and she was also a barmaid from another bar he frequented. I remember the calmness, quietness and the ability to breathe without fear when he was gone, and I prayed he would never come back. I forget exactly how long it was, but he ended up coming back home and they reconciled. I remember the sinking feeling in my gut when he returned. Not only the fear of living with him again, but it meant I lost my relationship with my stepmother once again.

Sometimes I thought my stepmother loved me, but it wasn't reliable. She was very two-faced. One day she was my friend and the next day she was stabbing me in the back. I never knew what to expect from her. My relationship with her was completely dependent upon her feelings for my father on that particular day, and her feelings about my father were like a yo-yo. One day she hated him; the next day she loved him. One day she was my best friend; the next day she was my worst enemy. She was only my friend when she wanted someone on her side against my father.

When they were on the outs, she'd talk about him behind his back and tell me how horrible it was that he treated me so badly and she'd try to help me have some kind of life. In addition to beatings, my father grounded me constantly. I was almost never allowed to do anything my entire life. She would let me sneak out of the house when my father wasn't home and go do some normal things like visit a friend, go swimming or go to the park. Then the next week she'd turn on me completely and be on his side.

I was just a little girl, but she would talk about her relationship with him to me. She would cry to me and I would comfort her. During those times she would be incredibly loving, affectionate and kind to me. We would go places together, she would do nice things for me and we were like girlfriends. When she was angry with him, then we were partners in crime; but when they made up, she was the wicked witch from the west. She would waver back and forth like a seesaw between love, violence and betrayal. Most of the time, she didn't use the belt, although I remember her chasing me through the house with it a few times. Sometimes she would just hall off and belt me across the face with the back of her hand and she liked to use the fly swatter. The fly swatter really hurts on bare legs.

The most vivid and painful memory I have of my stepmother occurred one night when I had just finished doing the dishes. I left one pan that had something hard stuck to it on the stove to soak and went outside. It was a hot summer day and I was running through the sprinkler in the yard to cool off. I was soaking wet. She went on a rampage because I left that one pan on the stove not washed, brought me in and beat the hell out of me with the belt while I was wet. If you've ever been hit with a belt when you're wet, you would know that the water really intensifies the impact of the hit.

This was a very similar beating as the one my father gave me when I lost my eyeglasses. I thought I would pass out from the pain and she just wouldn't stop. The look in her eyes was that of a demented crazy person, totally out of control. I kept dropping to the floor and she kept picking me back up and swinging even harder. When it was over, I whimpered in the corner like an animal. This memory, too, has me quivering as I put down the words on this page. She often had that same demented look in her eyes when she came after me with the fly swatter.

The only time I ever received any recognition at all was when I did a good job cleaning the house, so I would try and clean the house immaculately. I would scrub till my knuckles bled. However, even this couldn't be trusted because sometimes no matter how sparkling clean it was, she still wasn't happy and would berate me.

The funny thing is that I don't remember ever having feelings of hatred for my stepmother. Even as a little girl, I, in many ways, saw her as a victim of the circumstance as well. I loved her and it was excruciatingly painful every time she betrayed and abandoned me; but each time she came back, I welcomed her with open arms. I found myself deeply dreading the times that she and my father made up, because I knew what that meant.

My father beat my stepmother too, quite frequently. My most vivid memory of domestic violence was my father holding my stepmother by her hair and tossing her out the door on the steps and beating the living shit out of her. Her blood curdling screams filled the house on a regular basis, particularly when he came home from the bar. I spent many nights with my head under the pillow trying to muffle the sounds and quivering in fear. He also beat my youngest brother from time to time, but for some reason he never touched the other three children. I later learned as an adult that he hated my younger brother because there was a rumor that he wasn't the real father of this child. I don't know if that's true or not.

Why he hated me, I never have found the answer to that. I know that my father was beat severely by his father with a razor strap. My father had terrible scars on his back to prove it. So that explains his violence, although I never understood why that violence didn't extend to the other children, which of course only made me feel like even more of an outcast and defective. As I grew older, I drew the conclusion that he despised my independent spirit. I defied him by being who I was and simply having a desire to live. I challenged his power and control by being an individual. He liked to keep me underneath his thumb and I didn't want to be under his thumb.

Other family members such as my stepmother's sister and her husband, my father's own sisters and brothers, friends of the family and all our neighbors recognized my father's cruelty and abuse, however, it was never spoken about publicly or to his face. Although I wish someone had intervened, I don't really blame them; it was a sign of the times. People just didn't go up against someone like my father. You just didn't tell on your neighbors or put your nose where it didn't belong back then. They would all talk about how horrible he treated me behind his back and tried in their own way to help me by getting me out of the house. Many of them enlisted me as their babysitter and invited me over to babysit even when they were home. They would create lies for my father and tell him that they needed me to come over and spend the night. Even our beloved family dog new the truth about my father and what he deserved. My father was also very cruel to our dog; he tortured and abused him as well. A couple of times after my father was cruel to him, the dog went upstairs and defecated on my father's pillow. My stepmother cleaned it up real quick so my father wouldn't kill the dog, but we all had a good snicker over it.

I truly have not one good memory from my childhood. Not a single one. I never experienced love, affection, acceptance or compassion in any sense. The only memory that even comes close to something good was that for some reason my father took me to work with him one day. Now this should have been a fun-filled day, but it was a terror-filled day for me. I truly believed my father was going to kill me. He was a truck driver and hauled coal. I thought for sure he was going to take me out into the coal yard, kill me and bury me under the coal. It was one of the worst days ever and I was so happy to make it home that night.

Back in those days, child abuse wasn't recognized as it is today. If the awareness and laws that exist today existed back then, my father would be in prison for being a child abuser. Unfortunately, I didn't have that option at that time. I hated my father. Deeply hated him. I felt so trapped and helpless that I actually used to lie awake at nights and fantasize about killing him, torturing him or how I could get him out of my life. However, on the other hand, I loved him and craved his love and affection, which I never got. So over time I developed a love/hate relationship with my father.

Initially I began drinking because that's what you did. Everyone around me was drinking and it was the thing to do. I was taking care of children, cooking and cleaning, and in many ways I felt like a grownup and so I mimicked the other grownups in my life. Since my stepmother allowed it the first time, it seemed acceptable and even encouraged. It also gave me an identity, which I was really lacking. I felt like a "somebody" when I drank and smoked. But shortly after the first drink, I discovered that it relaxed me. I was in a constant state of terror, anxiety and nervousness over trying to avoid the next inevitable beating and/or ridiculing. It also took the edge off from the stress of taking care of the children and all the responsibilities that I had.

I began to dip into the whiskey bottles when my parents weren't home, which was quite often. I would put the kids to bed and sip a little. To hide from my parents what I had drank, I would put water in the whiskey bottle to replace what was missing. My stepmother told me at one point that she knew I was doing this, but didn't even tell me to stop. Over time it became more frequent. I also started smoking cigarettes as well. My stepmother smoked, but my father didn't, so there were always cigarettes around. Cigarettes made me sick the first time I smoked them as well, but I continued anyways.

In every area of my life I felt like an outcast, a weirdo, inadequate, defective and no good. I didn't know how to fit in anywhere and learned that alcohol, cigarettes and eventually drugs would cover up those feelings temporarily. By the time I was a young adult, age 18, the only way I could feel normal was to be drunk or high. That big black hole inside yourself or that empty pit that you hear most alcoholics talk about—I carried it within myself for as long as I could remember.

During my teen years I found marijuana and that really took the edge off and relaxed me. I liked it more than drinking at that age and began smoking it as often as possible. Over the years I got into many different mind-altering substances and engaged in some very dangerous behaviors. There was cocaine, speed, huffing gasoline and lighter fluid, locker room, and eating diet pills like candy. I passed out once from the huffing of gasoline and that scared me so I stopped doing that and the lighter fluid, which was a real blessing because I was doing it quite frequently and we didn't know back then what we know today about the damage that this can do to the brain and the risk of death. Although there would often be periods when I experimented with different substances, and I may go on kick where I did a lot of one particular thing, such as cocaine or huffing, alcohol and marijuana became my true loves and constant companions.

When I became a teenager, my father didn't allow me to have a driver's license or to have boyfriends. I wasn't even allowed to ride in cars with my friends who had their license. I learned I wasn't allowed to have boyfriends when I already had my first one. He had given me his class ring and we were at the annual street fair. My stepmother came raging through the fair like a bull and ripped me away in front of everyone with a big scene that totally humiliated me. I was 13 and hadn't even considered the thought of having sex with my boyfriend yet, but my father was calling me a dirty slut, which became a name he called me quite frequently over the years. I was beaten and grounded to my room for the rest of the summer.

The more I wanted to live, the more my father tried to stifle and control me. I simply wanted to do the normal things that all other kids my age were doing. Go to football games and the pizza shop, get a driver's license and have boyfriends. So, of course, this began a cycle of lying and sneaking as I was aching to spread my wings and be a normal teenager. My father literally followed me around and spied on me, which resulted in me getting caught in many lies, endless beatings and being grounded to my room most of my teenage life. This began a love for books and writing. In spite of all the horror in my life, I excelled in school because it was a way to lose myself. I would become completely absorbed in reading, writing and studying. It was all I had.

Sometimes I'd be allowed to go to the football game, but I had to be home before it was even over. Sometimes I was allowed to go the football game, but not the pizza shop afterwards, which is where everyone went to hang out and have fun. So sometimes I would lie and say the game ran late so I could go to the pizza shop, and my father would be around the corner spying on me; which, of course, got me a good beating and grounded to my room again. "I give you an inch, you take a yard," he'd say to me, as if he had given me so much and I wanted something so abnormal.

At age 15 I had my first consensual sexual experience with a boyfriend and it turned into a real nightmare because I kept a diary. I look back on that now and say, "girl what were you thinking?" Why on earth I kept a diary around with the crazy parents I had is beyond me, because they read it several times in my life. I guess I thought that little lock and key was really going to keep them out. You'd think I would have learned the first time. When I wasn't allowed to hardly breathe in a life that consisted of constant violation, betrayal and abuse, they certainly weren't going to afford me respect and privacy, but I didn't understand that at the time. I had so many feelings and nowhere to express them, so I poured them onto the pages of my diary.

Naturally, as a young girl having her first sexual experience, I had written in explicit detail all the juicy events. Then, of all the unfortunate things to happen, I thought I was pregnant. Now, granted this is something every parent wants to avoid with their children and a very serious matter in deed, but there is a right way and a wrong way to handle such delicate situations. Instead of being a loving father and handling this situation with respect, integrity and sensitivity, he chose the lowest road possible. He called a meeting in our kitchen that included two family friends (the parents of my best friend), my stepmother and the now ex-boyfriend. As we all sat at the kitchen table, my father pulled out my diary and read all the juicy explicit details of my first heterosexual experience—out loud! After reading a sentence or two, he would turn to my boyfriend and say, "Is that what you did to her? Huh, huh?" He seemed to be jealous. His goal obviously was to punish me with humiliation, degradation and shame, and he succeeded quite well.

I was completely surprised to learn they even had the diary, because it hadn't been mentioned up until that point. They apparently had read it and put it back in my room and then got it back out for the meeting. My best friend's parents looked almost as shocked and humiliated as I did. They shared with me later that they were deeply sorry for his behavior and tried to offer me comfort. This truly was the most humiliating, degrading experience of my life. I remember feeling like I actually left my body and floated around the kitchen table. I so badly wanted to become invisible and disappear. The poor boyfriend was horrified as well. I could hardly stand to look at him, but gave a quick glance to his face that was white as a ghost. My father's cruelty never ceased to amaze me, but even this seemed out there for him. I was totally crushed once again by his inability to show love and compassion.

It turned out I wasn't pregnant, even though the first pregnancy test indicated I was. I found out I wasn't pregnant when I went for my appointment at the abortion clinic. I was grounded to my room for a good nine months or so. I didn't go anywhere. For the summer my father's solution was to ship me off to his brother's house in Pennsylvania. One would think that wasn't so bad, but it turns out the entire family is a bunch of abusers and perverts. I had to fight off my uncle's sexual advances the entire summer. He kept telling me he was an incredible lover and that he could give me much better sex than any other guy could. He would go on and on about all the things he would do to me to make me feel good. "You need a real man," he told me.

Now I was pretty messed up sexually, but even I knew this was sick and I didn't want anything to do with it. It made me sick at my stomach. I was really upset because I really liked him and he and his wife had always been good to me. They always talked about how horrible they thought my father was and gave me emotional support. So I was in great conflict on how to handle this.

His wife worked, but he didn't because he had a bad back, so we were home alone together all day, every day. He followed me around like a dog in heat, rubbing against me in the kitchen and touching me every chance he could. I would wake up in the morning and he would be standing at the doorway of my bedroom rubbing his crotch and staring at me. I just kept resisting in a loving way, because I was so confused and I cared about him. Fortunately, he had a younger daughter who was also home with us, so I was able to use her as a shield and somehow I made it through the summer without complete violation.

Eventually I was sent home and wasn't grounded anymore and continued on with the lying and sneaking.

I was very mixed up about sex in those days. I truly thought that if someone wanted to have sex with me, it meant that they liked me—and I desperately wanted to be liked. I wanted to be loved. I fell in love with the good feelings that accompanied touching, kissing, closeness and intercourse. I hadn't ever experienced any love in my life and I craved it. If someone paid a smidgeon of attention to me or showed any interest at all, I was putty in their hands.

Not only that, I also didn't know how to say no very well, even when I wanted to. Saying no or setting boundaries in my family wasn't allowed. When I did say no, it often wasn't respected. I had a couple of incidents that in this day and age would be considered date rape. With guys I really liked, I thought if I said no, they would go away and I wouldn't be liked. I thought if I didn't give them what they wanted, I was bad. I was willing to do about anything to get approval and affection. When someone wanted to have sex with me, it made me think maybe I wasn't so unacceptable or unlovable after all, but when they dumped me then I felt even more worthless than before.

Although I didn't understand it at the time, the problem was, of course, that I was always attracted to men who were just like my father—emotionally distant, unavailable emotionally and/or physically, unaffectionate except when they wanted sex, selfish, self-centered, only concerned with their own satisfaction, and/or abusive emotionally and/or physically. When I say men, I mean men. I never had intercourse with anyone my own age. The first time I had sex with a man I was 15 and he was 21. As most women who have abusive fathers are, I was naturally attracted to men who were older than me, sometimes much older.

So I ended up in a vicious cycle of having lots of sex with men who really didn't care about me, which hurt me deeply emotionally. Sometimes they stayed for weeks or months, but ultimately it always ended the same way—me consumed with the pain, grief and shame of being rejected, yet again. It was so incredibly hurtful at times that I thought I'd die from the pain. I simply couldn't understand it and I kept trying over and over again for years to figure it out. I didn't have a clue how to develop a relationship. I only knew how to allow myself to be used, because that's what every adult in my life had done to me.

Year after year I tried so hard to get it right. If I gave them sex immediately, they left; and if I withheld sex, they left as well. No matter what I did it was just never right. Each time they took what they wanted and left. I just couldn't understand how they could be so interested one day and then want nothing to do with me the next. Yeah, I know, it sounds pretty pathetic and hard to believe when I think about it now, but at the time I was really clueless. Each and every time I was rejected it was unexpected, shocking and confusing and left me consumed with shame. However, I craved the touch, the affection, the intimacy, the closeness and the attention so much and, even though it was only temporary, I simply couldn't resist it. I was used by many a men in my lifetime. It too became an addiction. I soaked up the attention and affection of intercourse like a dried up sponge in the desert.

Needless to say, this behavior presented a very distorted persona of myself to the world that was hugely misunderstood and resulted in a reputation of promiscuity in my small hometown, which only deepened the feelings of isolation, shame and pain I already endured, perpetuated the cycle of bringing unhealthy men into my life and fed into the cycle of alcohol and drug addiction.

No one could see the real me underneath my misguided intentions. I did not choose to be promiscuous because it's what I wanted in life. More than anything in the world I wanted to love and be loved by one man only, but the men I was attracted to did not want me for the long term. Each and every time I was rejected. Most of them had girlfriends or even a wife and I was the girl on the side. Even at the age of 15, I was always someone's mistress.

So naturally I kept moving on from man to man trying to find what I was looking for. I never did grasp that whole it's "just sex" concept. It was never just sex for me. I was looking for a relationship, love and connection, but didn't know how to get it, so I accepted the little crumbs they were willing to throw me. I didn't understand at the time that it was my choices in men that were the problem; I thought there was something wrong with me. Not only that, I didn't know how to make better choices. I just followed my attractions and every time they lead me astray.

I was also discovering that I was very alive sexually. I loved sex and had a very high sex drive from the get go. I was having sex with some of my girlfriends all through childhood and frequent masturbation was a regular part of my life even then. However, I really never understood how to have an orgasm until after I got sober. When boyfriends came into the picture it was a whole new ball game, since I didn't know how to get sex in the context of love and intimacy, this meant my experiences were also tainted with feeling dirty, shameful and empty afterwards. I learned later in my adult life, that part of my intense sex drive was due to physiological damage from the abuse in my life, but I was unaware of this at this time. My overactive sex drive perpetuated this problem with men for me for many years. I didn't know how to ignore or control my desires and often had unfulfilling sexual relationships just to satisfy the craving for physical and emotional pleasure, because I couldn't find one man to stay with me consistently.

Although I didn't realize it at the time, I had also discovered that sexual experiences were very spiritual. I was very in touch spiritually, even back then, but I didn't understand what it was, know what my spiritual yearnings were or how to fulfill them in a healthy manner. I know today that sex is one of the most powerful spiritual experiences you can have. It seems to put you in touch with the source of creation, whatever that may be, and results in feelings of intense connection and euphoria. However, I didn't understand at the time that sex with someone who's using you or doesn't have the ability to share true intimacy and connection is what leaves you with a feeling of deep emptiness when it's over. We'll talk in more depth about sex in Chapter 17, but for now I just want to call attention to the fact that it's very important to my life story because it perpetuated my cycle of addiction. The shame and pain of this cycle of having sex and relationships with dysfunctional men like my father all fed into the drinking and drugs; because in order to deal with the emotional pain and shame that these relationships created, I drank and used even more.

This was a pattern that took many years to gain understanding for and break, and didn't happen until long after sobriety. It took a very long time for me to understand that sex and love were not synonymous for the man and that my cravings for love, connection and affection could not be met by the men I was attracted to. Even after I finally learned to break the pattern of looking for love and affection in sex, it still took many, many years into sobriety to break my attraction to men who were like my father and stop having relationships with men who couldn't meet my emotional needs. I have 21 years sober and it has only been 7 years since I stopped being attracted to men like my father. I was trapped for a long time in the cycle of still trying to please my father through the men in my life. Trying to fix the past and prove I was worthy and lovable.

Even when I learned how to set boundaries, say no and develop a good relationship, I was still attracted to men who were alcoholics, addicts, abusers, users, womanizers, unavailable emotionally and/or literally, and not capable of real intimacy. I was still drawn to men who didn't want a committed relationship and the agony of not getting what I needed and wanted. Since all the men in my life were identical to my father, I always had the same experiences and outcome. I continually tried to please them and get it right and no matter what I did, I just never could get it right. I never could be good enough in their eyes, but I was addicted to trying.

I'm not saying that all these men were horrible people or blaming them. I believe we're all products of our environment and something in their environment created them into who they were. It's certainly not their fault that I continued a relationship with them. If I had known how to set boundaries, demand respect and not accept less than I wanted, I wouldn't have been in this position, but I didn't know how and this allowed me to be used over and over again.

Not all these relationships were bad in every way either. I had a lot of fun times and hold a lot of fond memories for many of the men in my past. The problem was that I wasn't looking for a good time. I wanted a relationship and when I accepted less than I desired, this created a great deal of emotional pain for me. I'll talk more about the process of relationships further on in this book, but for now we'll get back to the story.

The tension and conflict with my father intensified as I grew older and I began to challenge his authority more and more. Around the age of 16 or so I finally discovered that I could fight back both verbally and physically. I also started to hear things on television and in school about child abuse and ideas began to stir.

One night we were in the kitchen and my father was knocking me around the room, he pushed me against the sink and grabbed me by the throat and began choking me. I brought up my knee and rammed it into his groin, which of course resulted in him doubling over on the floor. I was terrified he would kill me and I ran to my bedroom, crawled out the window and ran across town to my aunt and uncle's house in my nightgown and socks. They, of course, had to let my parents know where I was and I was promptly returned. However, when my stepmother picked me up, I said to her, "if he ever touches me again, I'm reporting him for child abuse." I was shivering in my socks as I said the words, as I feared it may provoke another beating by both of them, but it didn't. My father and I never spoke about the incident, but to my amazement, he never touched me again physically.

For the last couple of years, tension and conflict had been brewing more and more between my father and stepmother. There was mention of divorce repeatedly. The more she distanced herself from my father, the closer she tried to get to me. She confided in me and talked to me about their relationship. The times that she went back over to his side and became my enemy grew further and further apart. She got a job at the local hardware store and began lying and sneaking too; however, I thought she was just trying to have a little freedom. My father was accusing my stepmother of having an affair with a coworker who was only two years older than me. She denied it to him and to me and I believed her.

She started shielding and protecting me from my father and allowing me to have a life. She would let me sneak out of the house all the time behind his back and covered for me so I could go to dances, football games, spend time with boyfriends and all the normal things a teenager should be allowed to do. We became very close—so I thought.

The day finally arrived when they actually did get a divorce and by some amazing chance my father let me go live with my stepmother. It was what I hoped and dreamed for, but I really didn't think he would allow it. I just couldn't believe it. I guess that shows his level of real love for me as well. It was a glorious day. I felt incredibly free to be out from under his iron thumb, but unfortunately it was short-lived happiness. Yes, there was a degree of relief to be out of his control, but what I didn't realize was that I carried all that had happened inside me. He was still with me wherever I went.

To my surprise, I also found that in spite of, or rather because of, the love/hate feelings I had for my father, I was not able to cut complete ties with him. Over the years I was drawn back to him over and over again, like a friggin magnet. They were inconsistent, infrequent and brief visits, but I couldn't stay away. I didn't realize it at the time, but I still kept trying to get him to love me. Every time it was so uncomfortable I could hardly stand it.

I was about 17 at this time and also around this period I started having severe anxiety attacks and shaking, which led into another vicious cycle with the mental health system. I was put on prescription medication to calm me down. Also around this time, I developed chronic headaches, which began a cycle of being completely dependent upon Tylenol. I ate Tylenol like candy all day long. I also started having suicidal feelings that were triggered by the emotional pain of the dysfunctional relationships I continued to engage in. I was involved and in love with someone who was having a relationship with someone else. She got pregnant and they were getting married. I was completely devastated. My best friend sat up with me through the entire night to keep me safe. I made it through and moved on to the next one.

Shortly after we moved out, I found my stepmother in bed with the young coworker she supposedly wasn't having an affair with. I got very upset because she had denied she was having an affair with him when I had asked her about it before the divorce. I felt betrayed and deceived again. I thought we had become so close and that I could trust her. This meant I still couldn't trust her and I thought we had turned over a new leaf. I wondered if she was lying about this, then what else was she lying about. I couldn't trust that her kindness and love towards me were real and would be stable. This meant she could still become my enemy again just like she always did before. I was also embarrassed, disgusted and repulsed by the fact that he was just a young guy, only two years older than me, and it just felt really sick.

We had a really big argument about it and I said I wasn't going to live with her and I stormed out of the house and walked a couple miles and called my best friend to pick me up. I never went back home except to get my clothes one day when she wasn't there, and she never came after me. I was only 17 and still in high school, but I had a part-time job because I was in the Cooperative

Office Education (COE) program where I worked a half day and went to school a half day, so I got an apartment on my own. It seemed my fears were totally accurate. She didn't make one attempt to bring me back home, talk to me or try and repair our relationship. It appeared she was relieved I was gone. We didn't speak again for a couple years. That certainly doesn't seem like the actions of someone who cared about me.

My drinking and drugging was now much more frequent and heavy. I didn't last too long in my own apartment, because I couldn't afford it; so I moved in with my best friend and her family. By this time I had graduated high school and a few months later I turned 18. At that time, this was the legal age for drinking beer. I could now go to the bars. Woo hoo, I had arrived! This was the greatest thing in the world at the time. There was nothing I loved more than that feeling of freedom and acceptance I felt walking in the door of a bar and all my drinking buddies glad to see me. It replaced the family feeling that I had missed all my life. I found a place where I belonged and fit in, so I pretty much lived in the bar. Miller Lite draft was my drink of choice and at the time was only 50 cents. With a few bucks I could get a good buzz on and then rely on friends or flirt with guys to buy me more.

Although I had great grades in school and had been trained well in the COE program to be a secretary, I was severely lacking in the self-confidence required to obtain a job in this area. I was also so severely depressed and overwhelmed with anxiety that I didn't feel capable of a job with responsibilities and interacting with people while sober. So I took a job at my best friend's pizza shop, owned and operated by her parents, that allowed me to be hungover and high while working and didn't have many demands.

For the next year and a half or so it was an extremely crazy time of consistent drunkenness and one painful dysfunctional relationship after another. I fell in love again with someone who was involved with another woman and this relationship was tearing me up emotionally. I kept waiting for him to choose me, but it didn't happen. My depression and anxiety were growing deeper and deeper and that empty hole inside me was growing bigger and bigger. I finally attempted to break it off with the hopes that he would come after me, but he didn't. However, when he didn't make any attempt to come after me, I actually went back and tried to reestablish the relationship, but he was no longer interested. I was deeply hurt, but quickly moved on and buried my feelings in alcohol, drugs and other men.

Moving quickly from man to man or having more than one man in my life at one time became a way of not having to feel the pain of the last rejection quite as fully, or worry about having to face being alone if one of them left. Now, don't get me wrong, not everything was horrible at this time. I was definitely having some fun and enjoying myself from time to time. The problem was that there was always this dark cloud hanging over my head. My heart ached consistently. I felt like I was just a raw bundle of pain, sadness and emptiness. It always blanketed and tainted everything.

My best friend's family truly took me in and treated me like a family member. I loved her and her family and I felt loved by them. They taught me to drive, took me to take my driver's test and her father co-signed for me so I could get a car. They bought me presents at Christmas and really treated me like I was one of their children. They didn't even make me pay any rent. You'll take note that it wasn't my family that did any of these things.

However, my best friend and her mother could not keep a secret to save their life. I would confide in them about things and they would tell a bunch of other people. I would share a secret with them and they were the only ones who knew about it except me and suddenly the whole town would know and I would have to face a great deal of embarrassment. Other people told me that they talked about me behind my back.

So although I loved them deeply and felt loved by them, I couldn't trust them and was hurt very much by their betrayal. There were lots of mixed messages that caused a great deal of internal conflict and confusion. It planted doubts and worry about the validity of our relationship and their love for me. I was pretty messed up, but if I loved you, I was extremely loyal, could be trusted with anything, was unwaveringly committed and would stand by your side no matter what. I felt I had no one in my life I could truly trust or who could show me the same loyalty.

Eventually I addressed this lack of trust with my best friend and she expressed regret and did work hard on changing this, but I was in constant worry that anything I shared with her would be broadcast to the world and doubt about her love for me or fear of betrayal was always hanging in the background.

During this time I developed another very close relationship with another girlfriend and her family that I loved as well. We were practically inseparable for about a year. The fondest memories that I hold in my heart to this day and the best times of my life at that time are from the moments and hours that I spent with these two girlfriends and their families. They were like sisters.

Although I often shared how depressed I was with my two best friends, I don't think anyone knew what was really going on inside me. No one was really aware of the depth of the sadness, loss, pain, emptiness and despair I was experiencing. I don't think it was possible to convey.

Within a very short amount of time of hitting the bar scene, I was already a full-blown alcoholic. I was having frequent blackouts, passing out and waking up with strangers. The only time I felt normal and functional was when I was drunk or high, so I stayed drunk or high all the time.

Being in the bar scene now connected me with men who were even more dysfunctional. Now not only were they unavailable emotionally or physically and rejecting me, my choices were now also becoming physically abusive. Oh yeah, I was moving up in the world. At some point I moved in with a new boyfriend who, of course, was even more of a chronic alcoholic than I was. Since he was older than me, he'd been at it a little longer than I had. Not too long into it, he beat the hell out of me. So I left and went back to my best friend and her family, but as abusive relationships typically go, he convinced me to come back.

My best friend's father tried to prevent me from going and he told me that if I went back to him that I wasn't allowed to come back to their house when he beat me up again. Well, I went back to the boyfriend anyhow, and naturally it wasn't very long before he beat the hell out of me again and, not only that, he poured sugar in the gas tank of my car, which screwed it up really bad. My car could be fixed, but I didn't have the money to pay for it. So now I had no car and nowhere to live. My best friend's father held firm on his ultimatum and didn't allow me to return to their home. I was totally distraught and had nowhere to turn.

Consumed with dread, I realized I had no choice but to go to my father. I shook inside and thought I'd throw up as I went to him in total humiliation to ask for help. He wouldn't give me any money to get my car back, even though he had more than enough money to do so; however, for some reason he said I could stay with him for a while. He was now living with a young woman who wasn't a lot older than I was and had a couple kids in a trailer and they had an extra bedroom. It was with great apprehension and trepidation that I moved in.

This was a disaster. I still carried deep hatred and fear of my father. Living in his home with him and his girlfriend was pure hell. Although I was now an adult, it was as if he once again had me under his thumb and control of my life. I also felt nauseas, dirty and ashamed when in the presence of my father. It triggered all my unresolved grief, pain and anger towards him and, at the time, I didn't know how to deal with it other than to keep drinking and drugging as heavily as possible. I felt exactly as I did as a child—full of terror and always looking over my shoulder.

Through a family member of my best friend, I got a nice paying job in a factory and thought I was going to be able to work my way out of my father's place, but then I got laid off shortly thereafter. Around this time my chronic headaches increased in severity and I started experiencing intense pain and pressure all through my body, but especially in my face, neck, jaw, teeth and head, that never stopped. I increased the frequency and dosage of Tylenol on top of all that alcohol.

I tried to stay away from my father's trailer as much as possible and didn't come home that often, which my father disapproved of as well. Once when we were fighting, my father's girlfriend shared with me that my father told her I had always been a slut. It was very painful to learn that this is the way my father talked about me to other people and the misery and depression of living with him grew deeper. The fear, shame, anxiety and nausea that were triggered from being around him became overwhelming. After a few months, I couldn't take it anymore.

Throughout the years after being taken from my mother, I had continued a relationship with my aunt (my mother's sister) and cousin from Pennsylvania. It had been quite some time since I'd seen them, but we still corresponded by phone now and then. I shared the struggle I was having in living with my father with my cousin and she invited me to come stay at her house. So she and my aunt came and got me and took me back to Pennsylvania.

Yes, a change of scenery and a fresh start was what I needed. That's what I thought would solve all my problems. But, you know that saying in AA about "wherever you go, there you are" turns out to be very, very true. A new town didn't change things at all. I, of course, found a job in a bar and during the year that I lived there I don't think I had one sober breath. I quickly became involved with a man who bartended down the street and, like all the other men I was attracted to, he naturally didn't want a committed relationship. So, I had another part-time uncommitted relationship with one of my regular customers.

As I mentioned earlier, I deeply wanted to be in love and have a steady relationship with one man. I didn't want several different relationships at one time. That was what they wanted and I didn't know how to get what I wanted. I was continually attracted to men who didn't want a commitment. I repeatedly accepted relationships that weren't what I wanted, because I couldn't find what I was looking for and this caused me immense emotional pain. I ached and longed for a normal committed relationship, but the relationships I had were with men who just wanted a good time and this left me feeling empty, unworthy, ashamed and deeply depressed.

Men who were married or already committed to someone else and men who were players were most attractive, but this wasn't a conscious choice I made. I didn't think in my head that I'd like to go find myself a married man, someone committed to someone else or someone looking for a good time. It was the last thing I wanted. I was looking for someone to be mine, but every man that came into my life that I was intensely attracted to was unavailable in one way or another. I didn't go looking for them, they just found me; but since my attraction to them was irresistible, I couldn't walk away. There was some kind of underlying force at work that was stronger than me and defied all rationale, logic and reason.

A lot of times when I would first meet someone, I wouldn't even know there was another woman involved. It appeared on the surface I had finally found someone that could be mine, but in a couple weeks or a month into the relationship I found out they had just broken up with their girlfriend and she came back into their life and they were still in love with her. Every time I just couldn't believe it had happened again.

I didn't want to be alone and none of my emotional needs were being met, so I compensated by having several relationships simultaneously. The idea of being alone for a while was a foreign concept to me at that time of my life. I didn't understand at the time, but each time I got rejected, I was reliving the pain, loss, grief and shame that I endured from the betrayal and abandonment of my mother, father and stepmother. It was like rubbing salt in those wounds. Every rejection just thrust me deeper and deeper into shame and pain, which provided more fuel for my addiction. Every rejection made me feel more worthless. I had to stay drunk and high to deal with this emotional pain and the physical pain from the continuing headaches and pain throughout my entire upper body that I was living with daily.

Somewhere in this mess, I went to visit my birth mother for the first time since my father had taken me away, 12 years ago. She only lived a half hour away from my cousin. I was looking for answers as to where she'd been all these years and why, but she didn't really have any that made sense or were acceptable to me. I don't really remember much about the visit, because much of that year is a complete blur, except that it was so extremely uncomfortable I could hardly bare it. Being in the presence of my mother also made me feel nauseas, dirty and ashamed. It brought up all the pain, hurt and loss of the little girl still inside me. It was unbearable and I never went back while I lived there. I developed a close friendship with a coworker and her boyfriend and they became like family.

I drank and drank and drank into oblivion. At some point, the bartender I was involved with broke off our relationship. By this time there had been so many rejections that the pain of this pattern was beginning to eat me alive. Each time it didn't work out, it reaffirmed what my father thought of me—that I wasn't good enough, that something was wrong with me, that I was worthless and unlovable. Every time I found a new man, I thought this would be the one, but it never was.

This man had actually told me up front that he didn't want a relationship and that he was just looking for a good time, and I still got involved with him. I guess I had some crazy idea that I could change his mind or something. I don't think I realized at the time that I actually had choices. I just always accepted whatever they were willing to give me rather than walk away or be alone.

My brain was so saturated with alcohol at this time that this rejection was overwhelming. My shame was smothering me, the hole inside me was starting to consume me, the depression was swallowing me and my anxiety was unbearable. I was feeling suicidal again, but didn't tell anyone. I went to a psychiatrist and got a prescription for some kind of sedative. This calmed me down some, but didn't relieve the agonizing emotional turmoil.

On Halloween we were having a party at the bar where I worked. It was one of those beautiful, warm fall days and I started out the day going to buy a Halloween costume. I was going to be a cat and tried really hard to get in the spirit, but I felt so dark inside and life looked so bleak. It felt like I was dragging my body along through the motions of life with a ball and chain around my ankles. I felt so alone and empty, it was like I was in a vacuum or a black hole in outer space. So, naturally I stopped in several bars on the way home.

I didn't make it home and the rest of the day is marked by intermittent blackouts. However, I do know that I got falling down drunk and went to where the ex-boyfriend worked. He was with another woman and I made a fool of myself by making a very big scene and getting thrown out. This, of course, only made me feel worse. I couldn't take it anymore. I went home that night and took the whole bottle of sedatives on top of all that alcohol.

It wasn't long before I collapsed on the kitchen floor and drifted in and out of consciousness. As I lay there and waited for death to happen, I started to feel very sick and the effects of the drugs in my head were scaring me. Then somewhere inside me a piece of me became very afraid and decided maybe they didn't want to die after all. I realized that I just wanted to escape. I just wanted the physical and emotional pain to stop. I crawled across the floor to the phone and called my coworker friend, and told her what I did. She came and got me and took me to the hospital.

It's all pretty fuzzy, but I faintly remember being taken in, having tubes shoved down my throat and having my stomach pumped. I wanted to sleep so badly, but nurses kept waking me up all night long and monitoring me. The next day a doctor came in to see me and admitted me into the psych ward. I spent a couple weeks there and I loved it and didn't ever want to leave. It felt so safe and comfortable. I didn't have to deal with anything in life. I was put on the antidepressant called Tofranil, the antianxiety medication called Ativan and maybe a couple other things. I felt high all the time.

Now, of course, you might have guessed by now, I also met a new man in the psych ward and we "fell in love." This was naturally a match made in heaven. He was there detoxing for alcoholism—how ironic. No one had mentioned to me that I might be an alcoholic and the thought had never crossed my mind. He was transferred to an alcohol treatment center before I left. When I got out of the hospital, I went to visit him at rehab; and when he got out of rehab, we moved into an apartment together. Once again I thought I had found my knight in shining armor.

For a while he faithfully went to AA and I went to Al-Anon, however, I wasn't really hearing anything they were saying. I was too medicated. I got a new job in another bar and, therefore, I was drinking on top of all the medication, even though the doctor told me that I should not drink on this medication. After a short time with me, the new boyfriend told me I was an addict and I didn't believe him. This was the first time that this concept had ever been presented. Our relationship didn't last long at all. He was drinking again in a very short amount of time and I found out later he was having all kinds of sex with women in our apartment when I was at work. We had a fight one night and he beat the hell out of me, stole a bunch of my money and took off. I never saw him again.

Shortly thereafter, I decided it was time for a change again. I loaded up my car, went back to Ohio and moved in with my old best friend. I reacquired my old job at the pizza shop and picked right up where I left off. One would think that surely things could not go on as they were, but they did. I returned to my old stomping grounds and continued all the same patterns. I also made an appointment at the county mental health center so I could keep my supply of Tofranil and Ativan on hand.

Drinking on top of these medications now made the effects of my drinking much more intense. My blackouts were even more frequent and severe and my behavior a lot less controlled. The funny thing was that the medication didn't really stop my anxiety or depression. As a matter of fact, my anxiety was getting worse all the time. This resulted in a heavier use of marijuana to control it and my endless shaking. Marijuana became a nonstop event. I smoked marijuana from the time I got up until the time I went to bed. It allowed me to function during the times I wasn't able to drink. It became my best friend and lover for many years to come.

At some point after returning home, I went to visit my stepmother. It had now been two years since we spoke, but I still yearned to see her and reconnect with my family. We had a long talk and I told her about the suicide attempt, which seemed to spark some concern. I don't remember all the particulars, but somehow we patched things up and decided to try and have a relationship again. I became a part of the family again with frequent visits and was invited to all the holiday events, etc.

I would also go see my father once in a great while even though it was an agonizing experience. Although it was against my better judgment, defied any common sense and always left me feeling even more worthless and empty, every now and then I longed to see him and felt drawn back. Our relationship had not changed in any way, except that he no longer had the ability to abuse me physically. However, he was still the cold, detached, unloving, emotionally distant, unaffectionate, selfish human being he had always been. The relationship was still very emotionally abusive, because I was still trying to get his love, approval and affection, but couldn't succeed.

After every visit, I left shaking my head and questioning my sanity as to why I kept trying. Our visits consisted of nothing but me trying to connect and him basically ignoring me. He would plop himself in front of the TV while his girlfriend tried to entertain me. I would try and engage in conversations with him, but he didn't listen or participate. Sometimes his girlfriend would try really hard to get him to join in, but he didn't respond. I could see in her face that she was embarrassed for him. Occasionally, she would even slap him on the arm and call out his name and he would just laugh, completely oblivious as to what she was trying to accomplish. There were times that she even apologized to me for his behavior.

He often fell asleep or went out to the garage to do something. His girlfriend would try and wake him up, but he wouldn't budge. I even followed him to the garage and tried to talk about something he was interested in, but again all I would get was an occasional, "uh huh" or "yeah." He showed no interest in me or my life at all. It was really rather pathetic. Many times I resolved that I would never go back only to find myself there over and over again.

It's also important to take note here that it wasn't my father or my stepmother who made any attempt to reconnect with me. I was the one who initiated all contact and made the effort. There would have been no visits if it were up to them.

However, a relationship with my stepmother did eventually evolve. She and my brothers and sisters became a regular part of my life, but the fact that I had been the one to initialize the reconnection hung like a gray cloud over my head. I naturally questioned how important I really was to her. Because of her past record with me in which her love could never be consistent or relied on, I could not trust her. I did not trust our relationship to be genuine. As a matter of fact, even though we were going through the motions, our relationship always felt fake and on shaky ground. I was always uncomfortable and waiting for her to put the knife in my back, but I loved her and I desperately wanted a family, so I hoped for the best.

Another painful aspect of this situation is that even though I was practically a mother to my brothers and sisters, I never felt like one of them. I'm not sure why that is. I think it may have been because their mother was not my birth mother, or perhaps it was because my father didn't treat them the same way he treated me, but I'm not sure. I always felt like I was on the outside looking in. I didn't fit in and my emotional connection to them was missing something, except for my connection with my oldest brother. I had and still have a deep and special connection with him. I loved and still love him deeply, even though I haven't seen him in years. My relationship with him was very important to me and I felt very close to him.

During this time, life was just a crazy frenzy of drinking, drugs and casual sex. I was a zombie going through the motions of life, while completely empty inside and consumed with emotional and physical pain. Then one night, when I was out at one of the local bars on a good bender, a new person came into my life, called Ron. I'm embarrassed to say that I woke up with this person and had not one recollection of the night before. I even had to ask him what his name was. Believe it or not, this man became my husband. It was a private joke between him and me over the years and we had many good laughs about it. Sometimes after we moved in together, after a good drunk I would roll over and say, "Hey, what's your name anyhow," and we would crack up. However, as I look back on it now, it really is rather sad.

Turns out he was as severe an alcoholic as I was; although neither one of us knew it at the time. He was eight years older than me and didn't have a driver's license at the time because of too many DUIs. He also had marijuana as his best friend and lover and our addictions became our instant bond. We became drinking and drugging buddies, and very shortly after meeting, we moved in together.

Our life consisted of nothing but drinking, drugs and hangovers. I had been having hangovers for a long time, but I remember this time of my life as when they became more severe. I continued to work at the pizza shop and he had a good job in a factory that he had been at for a long time. Fortunately, we both worked the afternoon shift and, with the help of marijuana and Ativan, we were able to recover enough to go to work most of the time.

We went through a phase where we got into cocaine use very heavily for a while. I don't remember how we got out of this addiction, because it had a really strong hold on both of us for a good while. We would snort our entire paychecks immediately after receiving them and almost lost our apartment several times because we couldn't pay the rent. Several times we borrowed money from his parents or he took out a loan at the bank to pay our bills. I believe this pattern continued until I became pregnant.

It was just total insanity for about six months or so. As I mentioned earlier, drinking should not occur when taking Ativan and Tofranil, and I was drinking extremely heavy. It is a miracle that I even made it to sobriety, because I surely should have been dead. We were so drunk we lost our car several times and didn't know where it was. I mean we were actually at home and didn't know how we got there or where the car was. We'd have to call around to find where we left it. Once we lost the keys and couldn't find them, so we had to junk the car. We lived and breathed to drink and be high and it was just one drunken fiasco after another.

Now you would think I'd be happy now that I found someone who wanted a relationship and wasn't rejecting me, but unfortunately that wasn't the case. Although I wasn't capable of figuring it out at the time, the problem was that this relationship was based purely on our love for alcohol and drugs. I kept him drunk and high and he kept me drunk and high. We had ended up together kind of by accident or default. I did not have, not even from day one, hot, passionate love with this man. I was not wildly in love like I had been in the past. We were like buddies who just kind of ended up together out of need. I didn't have the same kind of attraction to him as I did other men. I cared for him, but it wasn't that "sweep me off my feet" kind of love. It wasn't passionate and exciting and neither was our sex life. It was more a relationship of convenience.

Then another thing began to occur for me. Our way of life started to feel repulsive to me. Although I certainly was as much a drunk and druggie as he was, I began to see his drunken behavior as obnoxious. I started to feel tired of seeing him falling down drunk, slurring his words and passing out. It wasn't a fulfilling relationship. He wasn't attentive and I felt alone much of the time, even though he was in the room. I quickly began to grow discontent and I hadn't shared it with him yet, but I was contemplating a break up. Then, to my surprise I discovered I was pregnant and this changed my course of action. Although it wasn't planned, I was ecstatic about being pregnant. I wanted this child more than anything in the world.

Fortunately, I was having severe morning sickness that lasted all day long. This made it impossible for me to drink or smoke cigarettes. I got off the prescription drugs and tried to clean up my act. I did, however, continue to smoke marijuana like a fiend. It helped with the morning sickness and, as an addict, it compensated for giving up the alcohol and prescriptions.

We decided to get married so that the baby and I would be covered with health insurance. We had a very small ceremony by the justice of the peace, or maybe it was the mayor, at my husband's parents. My father, stepmother and best friend were there. My husband got shit faced, falling down drunk and passed out. I sat in the bathroom on the closed toilet seat and cried on my wedding night, because I knew I made a mistake.

It certainly wasn't the magical wedding every girl dreams of, but I decided to give this marriage thing a sincere try for the baby and threw myself completely into the planning of his or her arrival. I looked forward to it with great anticipation, however, I felt horrible physically and emotionally throughout the entire pregnancy. Actually, I was intensely miserable. I didn't understand it then, but I'm sure it was largely a result of suddenly not being sedated all the time and the change in hormones. The constant marijuana use allowed me to function and keep my addictions active, but under control.

My husband continued to drink heavily and this was the cause of many fights. Now that I wasn't drinking, I couldn't stand the smell of alcohol in the house and it smelled like a brewery. My morning sickness that lasted all day continued throughout most of my pregnancy and the alcohol made it worse.

The day finally came when my child arrived and he was the most beautiful and precious thing in the world. I was bursting with love. I loved him so much it hurt. I was overjoyed with being a mother and spent every second doting on him. I loved him as much as humanly possible. It was the best thing that had ever happened to me, and because nothing good had ever happened for me before, I was terrified that it would be taken away from me. For many months I lived in constant fear that my child was going to die. I was certain that he would. I checked on him constantly when he was sleeping. I often kept him in bed with me so I could check his breathing all night long.

I breast fed for the first few months and this cemented the incredible bond between us even more. I don't think there's anything that was ever more rewarding in my life than looking down at that beautiful little face while nursing and taking care of my child. He was the love of my life.

For about nine months I was so absorbed in being a mother that I was able to ignore my dissatisfaction with my marriage. However, things were becoming more magnified. I was still not drinking, but my husband continued to drink all the time. The house still smelled like a brewery and continued to make me nauseas. There wasn't really much of a relationship between us. I started avoiding him because I couldn't stand the smell of alcohol on him or his drunken behavior. I tried to fix it by talking to him and asking him to quit, but he wasn't willing to stop drinking. He would slow down for a few days and then start up full force again. He told me flat out, "You know I'll never stop drinking."

I began to grow discontent again and we didn't have enough money, so I went back to work. At first I got a job at the local restaurant/bar down the street where I started to have an occasional drink again. However, I wasn't allowed to drink while working and after a few weeks I got fired for not being friendly enough. Then my stepmother, who was now a boss at a pottery in my hometown, got me a job there. Not long after that I packed up my child and moved out. In spite of my unhappiness, it was really a difficult and painful decision and one that was full of conflict. We moved in with my stepmother for a short time and then I found a roommate through a friend of my best friend.

The ironic thing of this whole situation is that I left my husband because of his drinking; however, as soon as I left him, I began drinking again and the whole vicious circle started over. I immediately hit the bar scene again and picked up where I left off. I was also immediately back to one dysfunctional relationship after another. My stepmother was going through a difficult phase in her life and we were often going to the bar together. Although I hadn't drank in almost a couple years, I was right back to staying drunk constantly, severe hangovers and blackouts.

Needless to say, I was no longer being the good mother I had been up to this point. My child was with my brothers and sisters when my stepmother and I were out. If my stepmother was staying home, then he was with her. Putting all our differences aside, she was very good to my son. She apparently loved him and he loved her. She took good care of him and was there for him when I wasn't capable. She didn't treat him the way she had treated me as a child. I thought he was in good hands, although as we'll learn shortly, that was not the case.

I'm sorry to say that for the next four years my child probably spent more time with my family and other babysitters than he did me. I wanted to be in the bar as frequently as possible. My best friend's family now owned a bar, and I took a second part-time job with them, where I was allowed to drink while working. So I worked at the pottery all day and then nights at the bar on the weekends.

Life was immediately back to complete insanity. My hangovers were much more severe now and I was always late for work at the pottery or missing work completely. On the days I was there, I was in the bathroom puking my guts out for part of the morning. I don't know how I got through the days other than I was outside smoking marijuana on all my breaks and at lunchtime. If my stepmother hadn't been my boss, I would have been fired for sure.

My husband and I got into a cycle of getting back together and breaking up repeatedly over the next four years. I wanted so badly to just be a mother and a wife, but I just couldn't stay with him. When we were apart, I'd think I wanted to get back together. So we'd get back together. Every time we got back together, I would try and stop drinking. I continued all the drugs, but would stop drinking for a week or two. Then once I wasn't shit-faced drunk all the time and he still was, I'd be like, you have to quit drinking. He had no intention or desire to quit drinking so I couldn't stand to be around him when he was drunk and I was sober. So we'd break up again. As soon as we'd break up I'd be drunk again, then we'd make up and I'd think I'd want to be with him again, so we'd get back together and I'd quit drinking. Then I couldn't stand to be around him again. We did this over and over and over again right up until I got sober.

I discovered I didn't like him when he was drinking and I wasn't; however, all the other men in my life were drinking when we were broke up and I didn't have a problem with that. Although I couldn't understand it at the time, we had no relationship when I wasn't drinking. It's what our relationship was based on. However, we now had a child that bonded us as well. Since he was the father of my child and basically not a bad person besides the drinking, I wanted to make it work and I tried so hard, but just couldn't. I carried a great deal of shame and guilt over this at the time and it repeatedly thrust me in and out of this relationship.

It was just another vicious circle. When we were broke up, there were lots of other relationships. The funny thing was I never enjoyed casual sex. I found it very unfulfilling and basically despised it. If there weren't feelings involved, then there just wasn't any intensity to it. So although, in the midst of complete drunkenness, I did have occasional one-night stands and woke up with strangers, for the most part I had a very long string of short-term relationships. However, many of these relationships came about as a result of meeting in the bar and spending the night together, which I learned later, is not the best way to begin a relationship. I didn't understand at the time that relationships based on sex and drunkenness were doomed for failure.

The other big issue that continued to be a driving force in this pattern was my sex drive. I continued to have an intense physical desire for sex that I couldn't ignore. At the time I felt like I "had" to have sex. My preference was to have sex with someone who cared about me, but I couldn't find anyone who cared about me and I needed to have sex. My husband cared about me, but our sex life wasn't satisfying to me. There was no physical chemistry between my husband and me. That was also one of the issues that kept pushing me away from him. Sometimes the desire for sex was so intense I couldn't stand it and since I didn't have a steady relationship to fulfill these needs, I had many men I could turn to—friends with benefits—or sex buddies. However, this pattern always left me feeling empty and ashamed.

I also had a long string of relationships occurring simultaneously that involved no commitment and weren't exclusive. As you've heard, my husband and I were together off and on for a good six years and I had many other men that were in my life for many years at a time or who would come in and out or back and forth; however, none of them wanted a commitment. It was a very crazy period with boyfriends fighting with one another and me bouncing back and forth between them in utter confusion, because I didn't know who I wanted to be with.

At some point I became involved in a long-term affair with a married man. This certainly wasn't the first married man I'd been involved with and he wasn't the last either, but it was one of the most difficult relationships for me to walk away from and the emotional pain it caused me thrust me deeper and deeper into addiction very quickly. Since he was married, that meant my time with him was quite limited, so that meant I had a lot of other relationships to fill up my time when I was alone. I couldn't stand to be alone. However, the irony in this is that I was always alone. None of these men were really with me. No one took care of me financially or emotionally and they were only around some of the time. Most of the men I was attracted to needed me to take care of them. The emotional pain of this relationship was overwhelming and excruciating and intensified my drinking and drug use even more. I had so much anxiety I thought I'd have a heart attack. I literally ached every second of every day, but I simply couldn't stay away from him. I broke it off numerous times, only to find myself in his arms again.

After sobriety, and a couple years of counseling, I came to understand the reason he was so irresistible to me was that he was almost a clone of my father. He was quite a bit older than me, had physical features very much like my father, was completely unavailable to me and gave me absolutely nothing emotionally. Our relationship made me feel worthless and used. That was the pattern for me and the men I chose in my life over and over. The more a man rejected me, the harder he was to get, the less he had to offer, the more pain he caused me, then the more I wanted him. I had an unconscious need to be with men who reinforced all the worthless feelings that my father planted in me and try to win their love.

Thus, that is one of the other reasons I was not able to stay with my husband. My husband actually loved me and wanted me. I wasn't addicted to trying to make him love me. Over the years, from time to time, there were a couple other men who strayed into my life accidentally who had a true desire in being with me; but when that happened, I wasn't interested in them either. After a few dates, I wanted nothing to do with them. I was only intensely attracted to men who weren't available in some way and caused me deep emotional pain.

That old cliché "looking for love in all the wrong places" was certainly the motto I was unknowingly aspiring to. I was still searching desperately for that one special person that I would love and would love me back, but it just never worked out that way. If they wanted me, I didn't want them. If I wanted them, they didn't want me. So I was willing to settle for casual sex rather than be alone. Going home to an empty bed was excruciating and was avoided at all cost.

This "settling for what I didn't want" left me deeply unfulfilled and filled with shame and was a very strong catalyst in my addiction process. It thrust me into heavier and heavier drinking and using. I hated the life I was living, but didn't know how to stop it. That hole inside me was growing again. My depression and anxiety were intensifying and I was extremely miserable. I woke every day full of dread, darkness, loneliness, emptiness and despair.

There was no way to live with the emotional pain other than to be drunk and high. The more the pain grew, the more alcohol and drugs I needed. It took more and more to keep myself anesthetized. The headaches and physical pain throughout my entire body intensified as well. Any moments of sobriety were unbearable both physically and emotionally. My life was constant chaos and insanity. The drinking and drugs completely consumed my life. I drank every second I wasn't at the pottery and I stayed high on one thing or another during those hours to get me through. The weekends became almost complete blackouts as I started drinking at 3:30 on Friday afternoon when I got out of work and didn't stop until Monday morning when it was time to go back to work. I almost never made it to work on Mondays.

I could go on and on about all my drunken and sexual escapades, but I think it would only be redundant at this time. If you're reading this book, you're probably an alcoholic, and if you're an alcoholic and you lived in the bar scene, you know the drill. Drinking, drugging, blackouts, hangovers and casual sex are just part of the game.

During these years, I continued to be part of the family with my stepmother, brothers and sisters. My oldest brother that I was closest to was drinking heavy and getting into trouble as well. I was really worried about him and then one day he shocked us all by robbing a local grocery store. It was a devastating blow. It just came out of nowhere and we couldn't understand what prompted it. After an agonizing court ordeal, he was sentenced to prison for six years and I was heartbroken. We continued our relationship by phone and I went to visit him as often as possible.

I continued to have an on-again off-again relationship with my father, as he continued to show no interest in me when I visited him and he made no attempt to visit me. However, I still couldn't stop trying. Once I ran into him and his girlfriend in the bar and I was shit faced drunk. Somehow we ended up in an argument and my father and I actually had a physical brawl right there in the bar as adults. We didn't speak for a long time after that, and then after many months, I ran into him again at a bar and I attempted to repair things. I told him that I carried a lot of hurt feelings towards him because of the way he treated me as a child. He said, and I quote his exact words, "I didn't do anything wrong when you were a child, and if I had it to do over again, I'd do it the same." I was completely floored. I remember going home that night and feeling so crushed, dirty and shamed, and yet I tried to forgive him and still be connected.

One day in the midst of all this craziness the unthinkable happened. My son came to me, who was around the age of three or four, and said, "Mommy, I don't want to suck Brian's pee pee anymore." Brian was my other younger brother, he was around the age of 18, and he frequently babysat for me when my stepmother wasn't available. As a matter of fact, he took a great interest in and had been helping me with my child since he was a tiny baby. I was shocked and I went to my stepmother and told her what my son had said. She said, "Well, Brian is lonely. You know he's not like other people and hasn't had many girlfriends." Brian had epilepsy and was in special education as a child. He was pretty much a fully functioning adult; however, he was slow cognitively and couldn't hold a full-time job.

When I hear those words in my head today, I can hardly believe it. It's appalling. I am outraged and nauseas, but I am deeply ashamed and saddened to say that I was so screwed up and inebriated at the time that I really didn't understand the seriousness of this issue, nor did I have any idea how to handle this situation. I didn't know at the time that children don't make these things up. I was also not aware of the emotional damage that is done to victims of sexual abuse even though I was a living testament at the time. Sadly and deplorably I did not take the steps that I should have taken at that time to protect my child adequately.

I insisted we talk to my brother and so we did and naturally he denied it. My stepmother tried to convince me that my brother was telling the truth or if it did happen it was no big deal because he was lonely and didn't know what he was doing. I didn't want to believe it was true. We swept it under the rug and pretended it never happened. In the back of my head though there was a piece of me that wasn't sure. The next time my brother and sister came over to babysit, my son screamed, cried and threw a hysterical fit. He wouldn't settle down and there was no way he was going to stay with him. This is when I thought it must be true and I stopped having my brother babysit.

However, it was never spoke about in our family. I was not strong enough at the time to confront the family and I didn't have the necessary emotional skills to do what needed to be done. I was also in conflict about my brother's mental capacity. I wasn't sure how much he understood about his behavior or whether he truly understood right and wrong and I fell into my stepmother's dysfunctional way of excusing his behavior because of his brain damage. I tried to keep my brother from having any alone time with my son, but due to my drunkenness and dysfunction, my efforts were half-assed and I found out after I got sober that he was still getting access to him when my stepmother was babysitting. At the time I didn't understand how sexual abusers operate and I thought since we had confronted my brother, he knew we were on to him and surely he wouldn't do it again.

Yes, I know, it's totally insane. I should have never allowed my brother to be anywhere near him again. I was too wrapped up in the family dynamics and my brain and emotions were too saturated with alcohol and drugs. I was not aware that my stepmother was allowing my brother to be alone with my son when she babysat; but if I had not been a drunken mess, I would have done a more thorough job of making sure. There is nothing I have more sadness or regret over in my life than my atrocious lack of awareness, betrayal and inability to be there for my own son. It is the most difficult mistake I have to live with to this day. I wish more than anything that I could go back in time and take him in my arms and protect him the way I should have, but at the time, I simply wasn't capable.

I found many other babysitters and continued down my path of destruction. My prescription Ativan and marijuana were kept directly beside my bed. When I woke up in the mornings, I turned over, rolled a joint and smoked it, then took a couple Ativan before I ever even got out of bed. If it was the weekend, I then went directly to the kitchen for a beer and would drink nonstop. If it was a workday, I downed Ativan all day long, snorted cocaine in the bathroom, smoked marijuana on all my breaks and started drinking as soon as I got out of work.

Once again I was a zombie going through the motions of life. I was spiraling deeper and deeper into despair. I was growing very tired of the bar scene and was extremely disgusted with my life. I could hardly take it anymore. Things were completely out of hand. The hangovers were so severe I couldn't go to work and missing work grew more and more frequent. Getting through the days was more and more difficult.

In a state of desperation, I decided it was time for a change again. A little tiny voice was starting to talk inside my head and it was saying that perhaps I had a drinking problem. However, everyone in my life was drinking and drugging, so when I mentioned it, none of them agreed, and they encouraged me to keep drinking. Something inside me began to stir and I started to have a desire to clean up my act. By some miracle I had the ability to enroll in adult education classes at the Joint Vocational School. I quit my job at the pottery and tried to stop going to the bars.

I tried really hard to throw myself into school and return to being a good mother. I started staying out of the bars and was trying not to drink, but I could only go short periods of time and I would fall on my face. The marijuana and Ativan usage had to be increased to supplement the loss of the alcohol and I replaced the alcohol with Diet Coke. I drank Diet Coke like there was no tomorrow. I became addicted to it as well. I could only go a short while without drinking and then I'd go on a real good binge.

For about seven years I had been going to the county mental health center to get my prescriptions for Ativan and antidepressants. I would have to see the psychiatrist every so often and tell him how I felt and he'd keep writing the prescriptions. This man never questioned my drinking behavior or made any attempt to do any real psychoanalysis.

At some point, I finally started to think that maybe my drinking was a serious problem or something else was wrong with me, so I started seeing a different psychologist at the same mental health center because my depression and anxiety were getting worse. He recognized that I was addicted to my Ativan as I kept requesting higher and higher dosages and my anxiety continued to increase. This was the first time I began to realize that maybe I was an addict; however, I was only beginning to brush the surface. I asked this psychologist if he was going to take me off the drugs and he said no. He attempted to help my anxiety with biofeedback, but that didn't work.

For the next year I went to school and bounced back and forth between short periods of staying off the alcohol and intermittent binging. Every time I went on a binge I grew more and more disgusted by my drinking. It was getting to a point where I no longer wanted to drink. It was beginning to lose its appeal, but I couldn't stop.

Throughout all of this, I still continued to have one dysfunctional, painful relationship after another and still bounced back and forth with my ex-husband. I had finally extracted myself from the long-term relationship with the married man only to find myself involved with another married man I met at school. This time it happened without my consent. He neglected to tell me he was married until I was already hooked and then he told me that they were in the process of getting separated, but that was a lie and never happened.

So I started dating another man from school. At first this seemed like it was going to be a good relationship, and then after a couple months he broke it off because his ex-girlfriend came back into his life and wanted to get back together. He bounced back and forth between her and me for a while. I bounced back and forth between the two of them and my ex- husband. So you see what I mean? I wasn't looking for this kind of man—they just always ended up in my life, no matter where I went.

On one of my binges I got picked up for DUI. It was my first and fortunately my last. I really don't know how I managed to get only one in my lifetime, because the amount of times that I drove completely plastered in a blackout is quite frightening. I was out getting high with the married man from school and on my way home I stopped at the bar. That's the last thing I remember. Next thing I know, I'm at the police station and my best friend is there to pick me up and take me home and I'm being belligerent to the arresting police officer. My friend pulled me out of the building as I hollered obscenities.

I was supposed to spend a weekend in jail, and I reported to the jail to serve my time and they only made me stay for about two hours and then released me. I also went to AA; I think it was ordered by the court with my DUI. I didn't hear anything that was being said in AA. I was too interested in checking out all the good-looking men. Holy smokes, here was a whole population of men I had never seen before. It was a whole new pool of potential suspects for a possible relationship. Maybe my knight in shining armor was in here, I thought, but I wasn't ready to stay in AA yet. My attendance was brief; however, a few little seeds were planted in my head.

It was getting to the point where I couldn't drink anymore without blacking out. It was also getting to the point that my desire to drink was getting less and less, but I still couldn't stop. It was when I realized that I couldn't stop drinking that I began to understand I had a problem, but I wasn't ready to admit it yet.

By some miracle I was able to excel in my schoolwork. I had great grades and eventually finished as a certified Medical Transcriptionist. Now it was time to get a job, but I faced the same problems I faced when I graduated high school. I had no self-esteem and felt completely incompetent. I couldn't get through the days without being high, drunk or highly medicated every minute.

Even though I had the cognitive skills necessary to acquire a good job, I wasn't capable emotionally or physically. Instead, I took a job at a factory that had almost no responsibilities with very light bookkeeping skills and worked the 3–11 shift. It was only part-time and didn't require me to interact with too many people, other than a bunch of men, which of course led me into another new and depressing uncommitted relationship to add to the entourage of relationships I already had. However, even this menial job was too much for me to handle. I was immediately missing work because I was too hungover. I wasn't making enough money to live and I was really behind on the rent.

Now that school was over, I started drinking more often again. I was trying to stay out of the bar, but that wasn't stopping me. I was drinking everywhere I went. I tried and tried and tried not to drink, but I just couldn't do it. I wasn't able to take the birth control pill because it deepened my depression, and drunks never use condoms, so I got pregnant twice during these years and had an abortion each time. Although, I have no regrets over these decisions, it is not an event that leaves you without question or impact and it's not one you want to have to make again. After the second one, it was one of the issues that made me see my life was completely out of control.

I felt like a fragile piece of china that had been dropped on the floor and broken into a zillion little pieces. It was as if I had dropped into that black hole in outer space again. I grew deeper and deeper into despair. It felt like the deep hole inside me had actually become who I was. I truly felt completely empty, dead and hollow inside. Dread and darkness consumed every minute of the day. The anxiety, depression and physical pain were unbearable.

No matter how much I drank, smoked, snorted, or swallowed, I could no longer find any relief. I just couldn't get high enough and I didn't want to get out of bed anymore. I was a walking dead person.

Three
A Turn in the Road

"We know the truth, not only by the reason, but also by the heart."
~Blaise Pascal

I had just got off work and stopped in the bar where my best friend worked. I hadn't been there for a while so people were asking where I'd been. My friend, making her disapproval apparent, pointed out with a sarcastic snicker that I had been trying to stay on the wagon.

One of her regular customers, who was supposed to be staying sober as well and didn't let anyone know that he was still drinking, came in and sat down next to me. My friend secretly poured him a shot hidden in a coffee cup. He and I commiserated about all our failed attempts at staying on the wagon and concluded it was a lost cause. That's the last thing I remember. The rest of the night is a complete blackout except that I faintly remember doing back bends off the back of my barstool. Why? I couldn't tell you. I used to be in gymnastics when I was younger and I think I was trying to demonstrate that I was still limber and fit.

My friend tells me that I made a fool of myself all evening and stayed till closing when she and the man I was drinking with put me in her truck and she drove me to her house. My son was at her house with her husband and children. She left me in the truck to sleep it off. I woke up at some point and hit the gearshift and the truck drifted down the road and up on to the sidewalk. At some point she took me and my son home. I remember none of it.

I don't know what was different this time from any other time, but I woke that morning like every morning after a good drunk, and something happened inside me. I was severely hungover and I was supposed to go to work that afternoon. I rolled my morning joint and took my Ativans before getting out of bed, and then I checked to see if my child was in his bedroom. I called off work and then called my friend to find out what happened the night before and she told me the story I just described. I sat at my desk with my head in my hands full of shame, remorse and guilt for falling off the wagon, yet again, for a long time and was consumed with depression, pain and anxiety as I tried to figure out what to do. I couldn't go on. I was completely dead inside. I couldn't live one more minute like this. I was done.

It's all very fuzzy, but I faintly remember looking in the phone book and making phone calls to recovery centers. I had an appointment to be received that evening at an alcohol clinic about 40 minutes from where I lived. I called my stepmother, told her I needed to get help, and asked if she could take care of my son. She came over and got him and I packed my bags. I continued to get high all day up to the very last minute when I walked in the doors of the recovery center.

I saw my best friend when I went to get my car that I left downtown. I had a bag of marijuana and I kept just enough to smoke on my ride to the center and gave the rest of it to her. I remember the look on her face and she kind of snickered because she didn't believe for a minute that I was serious.

As I walked towards the building of the recovery center, I was terrified of the unknown, but determined. The parking lot seemed really long and I could hardly breathe as I approached the door. Once I stepped inside, my whole world changed. It was as if I entered a new galaxy. I immediately felt safe and accepted and knew I was in the right place. It's all pretty fuzzy too, but I know I was medicated for the first couple of days to get me through the initial withdrawal and I wasn't allowed to have any contact with anyone in the outside world for a period of time.

I was assigned a male counselor, we'll call him Hal to protect his identity, and he was the kindest, warmest, most sincere person I had ever met. I had an immediate connection with him and when I looked in his eyes I knew he wouldn't lead me astray. To this day, other than my son, he is the most significant and influential person who has ever came into my life. His impact on me was nothing short of profound. I was so broken and desperate that I completely let go and placed my life in his hands. I totally trusted him and was willing to do whatever he told me to do.

My withdrawal was excruciating, intense, severe and prolonged. I was told I had to give up the Ativan and antidepressants as well. I also learned from my counselor, Hal, that Ativan is only supposed to be prescribed for very short periods of time—30 days max. He and the staff were outraged by the fact that I had been on Ativan continuously for five years and another several years prior to that before my pregnancy.

It was the withdrawal from the Ativan that was responsible for the severity of my condition. I don't know how I got through it. I was up all night, every night pacing the floors, crying, unable to breathe with severe anxiety attacks. I was disoriented, shaking violently and uncontrollably and felt like I would lose consciousness. I had been self-medicating all these years partially due to the unbearable anxiety, depression and physical pain I lived with daily. I now had no medication at all and I had to feel these feelings full force. I thought I would lose my mind.

Hal, other staff members and other patients in the clinic sat by my side many times as I rode out the waves of agonizing anxiety and pain. I would go running through the halls in terror to Hal's office because I didn't think I was going to live. For many days, about the most I could do was to sit and rock back and forth or continuously pace. I was in detox for ten days and the anxiety and shaking just didn't improve. I started hyperventilating and this was really terrifying. Hal told me to go outside, walk briskly and swing my arms. So I was outside walking around that building like a mad woman every day. Round and round and round I went with my arms swinging back and forth as fast as they would go.

I couldn't sleep and sat up late every night in the cafeteria or in the courtyard that was in the center of the building talking with other patients. Now, being true to my colors, even in the midst of all this suffering and insanity I, of course, found a new man to latch onto. We'll call him Robert, to protect his anonymity. He was a drop-dead gorgeous Scottish man with an accent that made me melt. The experience of rehab is very intense and intimate and you share a powerful connection with your shipmates right away. We bonded very quickly and intensely, as he became my nightly companion when I couldn't sleep. We talked for hours on end and shared our life stories with each other. I felt like I had known him all my life within a few days.

His detox ended before mine did and when he left we were then talking to each other on the phone daily. He was also coming back to the center for AA meetings on the weekends and we would spend time together. If you've ever been through recovery, you know that they tell all patients not to have a relationship for at least a year. Now I was desperate for help, but "no relationship" for a year. You've got to be kidding! No men, no sex? I just couldn't see the reason for this, nor did I see how it would be humanly possible. So, Robert and I were hiding our relationship.

So, other than the relationship aspect, I was following Hal's instructions to the T. I was completely amazed to find that there was actually another way to live. All my life I had been surrounded by alcohol, drugs, violence, abuse and dysfunction. I didn't know any other way. I truly did not know there was a different way to live and once it was presented to me, I desperately wanted it. I wanted to stay sober more than anything in the world.

I gave 100 percent of myself to every aspect of the program. I hung onto the words of Hal and the AA meetings with a tight grip and waited for things to get better. They told us in one of our groups that in a year from now only three of us sitting in that room would still be sober. I was horrified by those statistics and I made a decision at that moment that somehow I was going to be one of those three.

It wasn't long and my ten-day detox was up. Because I was considered low income, I had been admitted to the recovery center on some kind of financial grant that paid for my stay. Hal tried to get me a grant so that I could stay as an inpatient for another 30 days, but there was no funding available. I was able to get funding for 30 days of outpatient care. This meant that I went home in the evenings and came back to the center during the day for the next 30 days for groups, meetings and counseling.

However, Hal and I were both acutely terrified that I wouldn't be able to maintain my sobriety with outpatient treatment. When the day arrived for me to leave, I was still as messed up as the day I first arrived. The anxiety, disorientation, depression, severe shaking and hyperventilation were still going strong. I could hardly function and didn't want to leave. I was terrified. Hal gave me a firm hug and I never wanted to let go. I could see the fear in his eyes as I walked down the hall towards the door trembling.

The world had never looked so big and menacing as it did the day I walked out those doors. I didn't have a clue what to do and I dreaded going home. Robert and I had made arrangements to meet down the street, so we went and spent the afternoon together making tender passionate love and talking. He was struggling to find a way to live in this world sober as much as I was. We took comfort and shelter in one another. I lay in his arms and delayed going home as long as possible.

When I finally made it back to my town later that afternoon, I felt like a foreigner. I didn't belong there anymore. It was as if I had been thrown into a war zone and was dodging bullets and land mines. Even though it had only been ten days, something drastic had happened to me. I was no longer the same person. I was immediately confronted with a barrage of temptations. As soon as I arrived in town, I ran into my best friend. I saw her coming and tried to hide from her behind an ice cream parlor. I don't remember my words to her, but I was able to escape safely.

I went to visit my son and although I was ecstatic to see him, I felt disconnected and lost. I didn't know how to be his mother at that moment and this made me deeply sad. He continued to stay with my stepmother since I would be returning to the recovery center every day. I wasn't in the door of my apartment five minutes and a man I was dating from work was calling. I told him where I had been, what I would be doing the next 30 days and that I couldn't see him right now. I kept the doors locked that night and waited impatiently for morning to arrive so I could return to the recovery center.

For several days I drove back and forth to the center. I was heartbroken and terribly distressed by the disconnection I felt with my son. In spite of all my dysfunction, my son meant the world to me and we had always been incredibly close. I ached to reconnect with him. I also had immense guilt because I had to leave him for so long. Hal told me not to worry about this right now; he said my focus needed to be on myself for a while. He assured me that I would be able to be his mother again someday and that my feelings would come alive again in time, so I trusted in him and kept doing what I was doing.

Robert and I continued to communicate and he was struggling to stay sober. It was only a couple days when he called from a bar and he was very drunk. I got directions to where he was and went after him. It's a miracle I didn't end up drunk, because I sat in the bar with him for hours. Talk about the blind leading the blind, but somehow I finally got him out of there and took him to the hotel where he was staying. We spent the night together and I took care of him. He had been drinking extremely heavy for a long time and was in very bad shape. I was afraid he was going to die on me and the next day he was admitted back into the recovery center for another round of detox.

I was beginning to unravel around the edges even more. My anxiety, disorientation, hyperventilating, and shaking continued to be unbearable and I was hanging by a very fine thread. I couldn't cope or think. I was completely overwhelmed and wasn't capable of anything except showing up for my treatment. I was having a very hard time making the 40-minute drive back and forth and it was a miracle I hadn't wrecked. My body and mind were screaming for some relief. The psychological, cognitive and physical misery was too much to bear.

A day or two later as I was driving to the center, I was struck with some very intense and overwhelming cravings. I pulled over to the side of the road and had a major fight with myself on whether I should go to the recovery center or go get drunk and high. There were actually two voices in my head fighting it out. The pull was incredibly strong and it was a brutal internal battle. I don't know how I managed it, but somehow I hurried up and put the car in gear and drove down the road as fast as I could into the parking lot of the recovery center, jumped out of the car and ran into the building. I felt like I was literally being chased by my addictions and I was running for my life. They were calling my name and trying to hold onto me.

I ran into Hal's office crying and told him what had just happened. "I don't want to drink, I don't want to drink," I told him, "but I'm afraid I'm going to." He comforted me, praised me for coming to him and being honest, and told me to sit tight. He left the room for a while and returned with one of the higher up staff members. They told me they were going to make an exception and allow me to be admitted into the inpatient program without paying. I was amazed and relieved beyond belief. No one had ever given me such an important and meaningful gift in my life as Hal did that day. I will be eternally grateful for his kindness and ability to see into my heart and know that I sincerely wanted and needed help. If I hadn't been able to receive the shelter and protection that inpatient treatment provides, I don't think I would have made it. They assigned another one of the patients to be my chaperone and we were sent together to my house to pick up my belongings for the month. I stopped to see my son and then I came back and stayed as an inpatient for the next 30 days.

Robert was getting through his detox again and I was finding it very hard to hide what was going on between us. I was so grateful to Hal for helping me and I felt incredibly guilty for being dishonest and sneaking. It started to eat me alive. I was trying to turn over a new leaf and lying and hiding just didn't seem the way to go. I didn't want to do anything that would mess up my recovery and I was afraid the dishonesty would get me drunk again. It was creating more anxiety for me and I was already overwhelmed with anxiety attacks. I couldn't hold it inside anymore so I spilled the beans to Hal.

He was very loving and understanding, but encouraged me to be honest with everyone in my group, so I did. Robert felt betrayed, was very angry with me for my disclosure, and pulled away from me completely. As a way to punish me, he then turned to another woman who just happened to be my roommate. They were two peas in a pod and flaunted their relationship in front of me every chance they could for the remainder of his stay, which fortunately wasn't too long. I was heartbroken and devastated again, but with the help of Hal and other patients, I stayed focused on remaining sober.

Since Robert wasn't low income and he was self-employed without any health insurance, he had to pay for his treatment and couldn't afford the outpatient or inpatient care. So once his detox was over, he left. Hal was unhappy with the way Robert was playing games with my roommate and me. He and the staff felt he wasn't serious about sobriety, so they kind of rushed him out of there, and Robert was resentful about that. I would see him from time to time at meetings and he came back for aftercare for a while too, but we didn't speak. However, as you'll learn later in this story, Robert came in and out of my life many times over the next few years.

For the next 30 days I ate, lived and breathed recovery for every second. Life consisted of constant groups, discussions, AA meetings and counseling. I continued to struggle with intense physical and psychological suffering. The anxiety, depression, disorientation and brutal shaking didn't let go. I was hyperventilating on a regular basis and had to carry a paper bag around with me. Sometimes when I was sitting in group it felt like my brain left my head and floated up in the air hanging above my head. I didn't feel conscious. I couldn't speak. I thought for sure they were going to put me in a straight jacket and lock me away. So many times I truly thought I wasn't going to live through it.

I just kept listening to and believing in Hal. He was my lifeline. I trusted him completely and followed his guidance blindly. For the first time in my life I felt loved and truly cared for and he wanted nothing in return. His only objective was my well-being and he had no other agenda. It was the first connection I'd ever had with a man that wasn't sexual. The black hole inside me wasn't so dark anymore. There was a small light in there and someone was showing me the way out. I hung onto those simple recovery clichés, "to thine own self be true," "fake it till you make it," "keep doing what you're doing" and "one day at a time," like they were gold. It was "one second at a time" for me for a long time.

As part of the recovery process, they encourage you to invite your family for groups and counseling. My stepmother actually gave me quite a bit of support through my recovery process and attended a couple of them when she brought my son to see me. I even invited my father for one and that was a big mistake; however, it did give me fuel to succeed. My stepmother said she had to work hard to convince him to come along; otherwise he would have never come.

He was his normal self-centered self and contributed nothing except sitting quietly in a chair without anything to say and giving me his glaring looks of disapproval and disgust. My stepmother told me the next time she came to visit that on their ride home my father said to her, "Who does she think she is? She'll never change. She's just like her mother." Well I was really crushed once again by father's opinion of me, but it triggered even more determination in me to stay sober. In my head I was thinking, "I'll show you, you dirty (bleep, bleep)," and I did.

I then shared most of my horrid family stories with Hal and he decided that I was better off not including my family in anymore of my recovery process except for my son. They had a special program for the children of the patients in treatment that would teach children about addiction and help them to begin to heal from the effects of living with an addict. It involved puppets and music and was a lot of fun for my son and me too. It was the only motherly activity I was capable of performing at that time and I really enjoyed those moments with him. My stepmother continued to bring my son for these visits.

Hal assigned me to an additional counselor who worked with women who had been abused as children and I began working on these issues as well. It soon became apparent that there were many areas of my life that would need work before I would even be close to being whole. However, even though life at that time was pure hell, it was better than it had ever been. I continued to be truly astonished that there was a whole other way to live.

Although I was suffering immensely, I was happy to have found a new way of life. I was now a sponge soaking up this newfound truth I had discovered. It was a miracle. It was a gift and this gave me fuel to go on in spite of how difficult it was. No matter how hard it was, the only choice was to go forward. I don't know how to explain it; something profound had happened inside me. It was as if a button had been switched in a different direction and couldn't be put back in its original place. For me, drinking again was just not an option. I could not go back to that emptiness, that black pit or that dead person I had become. Although it was difficult beyond belief, going back was no longer a choice. There was light, freedom and a sense of peace in the midst of the storm I was riding out. I loved the life I was building and felt good about the path I was following.

All of us patients in the clinic were taken out to a variety of different AA meetings across the city during the week and the recovery center had its own AA meeting in the cafeteria on Saturday nights, so I began to make friends with other AA people in the community. I was slowly building a new network of people.

My 30 days of inpatient was over way too fast and once again I was faced with the reality of having to go home and back into the world. I was still terrified, unstable and not ready. The anxiety, depression, hyperventilating, disorientation and shaking were still a daily event and completely disabling. I was not a fully functioning human being. It took everything in me to get through the days. There was no way I could maintain a job or be a mother.

Once again Hal intervened. He got me admitted to a halfway house for the next 90 days on the other side of town that also wouldn't cost me anything, because I had no income. It was pretty scary, because it was in a part of town that was high in crime, murder, drugs, etc., but I felt blessed to have somewhere to go. I was from a very little rural town; so being in the big city was a whole new experience. If you don't know what a halfway house is, it's a place to live where everyone living in the house is recovering from alcohol or drug addiction. It provides a sheltered environment as your body continues to heal and helps transition you back into life slowly. It was exactly what I needed.

Hal also sat down and prepared an aftercare plan for me. I would come back to the recovery center weekly for group meetings and individual counseling. He set me up with another counselor in the private sector to deal with my childhood abuse issues and got me involved in a recovery group for women only.

For the next 90 days I continued to live and breathe the 12 Step Program. I immediately got a sponsor and started working the 12 steps. My days consisted of nothing but AA and AA people. I loved recovery and the new life I had found. When you get out of recovery, they recommend that you attend 90 AA meetings in 90 days. I had at least 180 and probably closer to 270 meetings in 90 days. Fortunately, I was in a big city where there were several AA meetings in different places of the city every day of the week. I knew where all of them were and consistently made my rounds. I was in a meeting two or three times a day. I simply couldn't function in the outside world and the only place I felt safe was at a meeting or at the recovery center. I would go back to the recovery center every day and just hang out.

I faithfully attended my aftercare program, went to private counseling and attended many different groups. I gave 200 percent of myself to every aspect of my recovery and worked very hard on all of my issues. I very quickly had built an entirely new life and was surrounded by lots of new friends who were in recovery as well.

Through it all I continued to shake uncontrollably, have crippling anxiety attacks and hyperventilate daily. It was so unbearable I don't know how I lived through it. Sometimes it would scare me so bad I would go flying in the building of the recovery center, running through the halls to find Hal, hyperventilating so bad I thought I would die. He continued to sit by my side many times and help me ride through it. He just kept assuring me that eventually it would get better, and I kept believing in him and holding on to his words. Every time I saw him, he would hug me and say, "You're a miracle," and his face would glow with pride. It was the first time in my life that anyone had ever been proud of me and it made me feel so good about myself that it gave me the strength and determination to go on.

It truly was a miracle that I had made it this far, and I was acutely aware of what an amazing gift this miracle was and there was no way I was going to throw it away, no matter how painful or hard it was. As they say in AA, "keep doing what you're doing," and I did. I was literally on my knees several times a day in prayer, sometimes for an hour at a time, praying for relief and the strength to go on. Although praying felt good, it didn't really seem like anyone was there listening, but I continued to do it, because I was told it would keep me sober.

My shaking was so bad that I had a good, male friend in AA that gave me the nickname "shakes." Every time he saw me he would say, "Hey shakes, how you doin?" I would hold my hands out straight in the air, they would tremble like leaves on a tree blowing in the wind, and we would laugh. He would hug me and say, "You'll be all right some day."

When I went to the halfway house, my stepmother was no longer willing to keep my son, so my son went to live with his father. I was in great turmoil about this since his father was still an active alcoholic, but there was nothing else I could do. I so terribly wanted to be his mother, but I just wasn't capable. My ex-husband would bring my son to visit me or I would go to visit him. I would cry and cry and cry after our visits. The guilt was overwhelming. Hal assured me this was the best thing for both of us for the time being. He pointed out that this wasn't forever and my son would be okay for a short while and that I needed to take this time for myself to recover so that I could become a better mother and that eventually I would be able to be with my son again. It was really hard, but that's what had to be done.

There was only one aspect of the recovery process that I struggled to adhere to and that, of course, as you might have guessed, was the "no relationship for a year" aspect. I tried really hard to go that year, but just couldn't do it. I did manage to go six months without any actual intercourse; however, I had two relationships during my first six months, not simultaneously though and I had several other men I spent time with.

I was making progress. I was no longer having one-night stands or waking up with strangers and I was sticking to one relationship at a time. I wasn't trying to meet my emotional needs through sex. I was also making a little better choices. Now although these men fit the criteria of being like my father, in that they were emotionally unavailable, they weren't bad men. They were men struggling to stay sober and understand themselves. Each of them had a couple years of sobriety already and other AA members were on their back for being a 13 stepper, so they eventually pulled away from me to allow me time to grow.

Because I wanted so badly to follow the rules and be successful, I didn't want to admit I was having a relationship, and the men I was involved with were also trying to do the right thing, but we couldn't fight our attraction. We simply didn't admit to having a relationship even though we were clearly having one. We kept saying we weren't having a relationship because we weren't having actual intercourse. We were sleeping together, engaging in heavy petting, going to meetings together and spending as much time together as possible, but since we weren't having intercourse, we weren't having a relationship.

We had the Bill Clinton syndrome going on, "no sexual relations." No disrespect meant to Bill. I really love him and understand completely where he was coming from. He was a prime example of how confused our society is in relation to sex and relationships. Even the President has sexual conflict and this sheds light on the depth of this issue for all of us. Unfortunately, he had to go through his process and learn his lessons in front of the entire country. Fortunately, my process was a little more private.

I'll talk more about the process of relationships later on in chapter 16, but for now I'll just say my relationships posed no threat to my sobriety because my life was so full of other recovering people and activities. My life did not revolve around the relationship and I had a very strong support system in place. I talked openly about my feelings whenever these relationships caused conflict or emotional pain and worked through it.

I had been at the halfway house a couple months when my ex-husband threw a wrench in the plan. He was having a very difficult time being a full-time father and taking care of our son appropriately. It was interfering with his drinking time and he really wasn't capable of doing the job. He started pressuring me to come and get my son, but I kept telling him I wasn't ready yet, so he used master manipulation. He told me that if I didn't take my son right now that he would sue me for full custody and never let me have my son again. As I looked back on it later, that probably wouldn't have been possible, but I didn't know that then and it scared the hell out of me. I could also see that he was clearly not meeting my son's needs adequately and I was worried. Although I really didn't feel that I was anymore capable of taking care of my son than he was, I felt I had no choice but to try. In spite of the continued anxiety attacks, shaking, disorientation and hyperventilating, I went out and by another miracle found a job as a secretary in the town I was now living in.

Going back to my hometown would have set me up for failure for sure and frankly I just had no desire at all to be there. The thought of it made me shudder. There was nothing but emotional pain, addiction and dysfunction for me there. In four months I had become a new person and there was no way I could go back there to live. I needed to be near the new network of people I had in my life at this time. So a group of AA people came with me and we packed up my stuff and moved me to the big city. I never looked back.

I would visit once in a great while, but I no longer fit in there. My best friend cried every time she saw me or talked to me, but for me, it was a clean break without any regrets and doubts. I still loved her, but couldn't be a part of her life. That part of my life was over, just like that. I was excited about my newfound life and relieved to be out of there, even though it was extremely difficult.

A friend of the family gave me enough money to get set up in a duplex apartment and my son and I moved in and began a new life together. I wish I could say that this life was great from here on out, but it continued to be extremely challenging. My son was deeply damaged from all that he had been through—the sexual abuse, a drunken mother and father and the separation from me over the last four months. He was suffering from separation anxiety and this resulted in a lot of clinginess and fears. He was afraid every time I left the house that I wouldn't return to him and was attached to my side like glue when we were together. There were lots of fights and crying to get out the door when I went to work or places without him. He never wanted to be away from me. If I was a few minutes late picking him up from somewhere, he would be hysterical. He was also extremely hyperactive and his behavior was completely uncontrollable and unbearable to live with at times. He was literally bouncing off the walls and hanging from the chandeliers. His schoolwork was suffering and he couldn't keep up with the rest of class. He simply couldn't sit still or concentrate.

Once again, I thought I would lose my mind. I could hardly take care of myself, how was I supposed to deal with this, I kept asking those around me. My sponsor kept telling me, "He won't be a child forever." I was so overwhelmed with my own anxiety attacks, agitation, shaking and inability to cope that I didn't know how to deal with his issues. I struggled with feelings of resentment towards him and then guilt over feeling resentful. Being a mother under these circumstances was beyond difficult to say the least.

The issues that each of us were struggling with triggered off one another. My anxiety fed into his anxiety, his anxiety fed into my anxiety. His fears created clinginess; I was already feeling smothered by all that I was dealing with and his clinginess made me feel more smothered. I pushed, he pulled. He pulled, I pushed.

However, our love for one another and our bond to each other was indestructible, tenacious and unyielding. In spite of ourselves and all that we had to overcome, the invisible force of love worked miracles behind the scenes. It was much more powerful than we were and picked us up and carried us through. I recognized that I was responsible for the mess that he was and we were and I had to find a way to help him and us heal.

My job as a secretary was another overwhelming source of stress and burden. My anxiety, shaking, disorientation, etc., were excruciating and made it nearly impossible to work, and yet I had to do it. I really don't know how I pulled it off for a year. I was in the bathroom praying, crying and pulling myself together many times throughout each day.

To say that the next year was very hard is a vast understatement. My son and I went to counseling together and I continued to go to private counseling. This counselor was another very significant person in my life. Her name was Stephanie and she was the most beautiful and spiritual woman I'd ever seen. She had long flowing hair like a goddess and was full of wisdom and insight. We worked together for several years and she taught me many things about life, parenting, spirituality, love, sex and relationships. She helped me immensely on my journey to know who I was and become who I wanted to be.

I attended parenting groups, seminars and educational workshops. I went to groups for alcoholic women to work on women's issues, Adult Children of Alcoholic groups, Adult Children of Abuse groups, Adult Children of Sexual Abuse groups, self-esteem groups and assertiveness training. There was a group for everything under the sun and I needed them all. I read every book I could get my fingers on about recovery and worked diligently on all my issues.

Additionally, I was still very active in AA and attended four or five AA meetings a week. I chaired meetings, set up meetings and tore down meetings. I also volunteered my time at the alcohol clinic to help new patients. I consistently went to AA functions, dances, picnics, conferences, banquets and campouts. I worked the 12 steps forwards and backwards more times than I could count. I continued to be on my knees many times a day and literally prayed every minute for the next year for my misery to improve and have the strength to go on.

When I had been sober for about seven or eight months, I gave my first lead. If you don't know what a lead is, it's when you get up in front of the AA meeting and you tell your alcoholism story. It was one of the scariest things in the world for me. I'm terrified to speak in front of a group of people. My counselor, Hal, and all my best AA friends attended. I just looked out into his eyes and was filled with courage. After the first few minutes of forcing the words out of my mouth, my story flowed out like a river. It was an exhilarating experience. I felt higher than a kite and after that I started leading all over the tri-county area.

During this time, I continued relationships with my family, but as I continued to grow and learn, I started to see their dysfunction more clearly and the relationships started to feel more uncomfortable and unfulfilling. I kept trying to build healthier relationships with them, but they weren't capable. I continued to try and connect with my father, but he was still exactly the same. Our visits still consisted of me trying to interact and him ignoring me. He still had no interest in me or my life at all and never expressed any kind of affection or love. I still felt dirty, nauseas and ashamed in the presence of my father and visits with him left me deeply depressed and conflicted. The healthier I got emotionally, the more difficult it was for me to be around him, so the visits grew less frequent and briefer, but I still couldn't stop trying.

The same applied to my stepmother and brothers and sisters. The longer I stayed sober, the clearer my head got, and the more I had to face reality. The feelings of distrust and fear about my stepmother and her feelings for me grew stronger as I worked through my childhood issues. I loved her, but I had a lot of unresolved hurt and anger. I mentioned earlier that her feelings for me always seemed fake, forced or unreal and now that I wasn't inebriated all the time this was a constant issue for me. As I examined our relationship as a sober person, I began to feel that her love for me and our relationship was based on guilt over all the things that had occurred to me as a child that were never talked about. I wasn't sure she truly loved me and I was still in constant fear of when she would stab me in the back again.

She was an important person in my son's life and she did give me some emotional support, so I was trying to hold on to this relationship, but my awareness and improved emotional health began to drive a deeper wedge between us. At some point early in this process, I instructed my stepmother that my brother who had abused my son was not to have any contact with my son. All my recovery classes, groups, counseling and books talked about and encouraged confronting your parents about your childhood abuse. I was not ready to do that yet, but I was beginning to pull away slowly and I was struggling to find a way to still fit in this family.

My other brother, who I was closest to, was still in prison and I went to see him one more time after sobriety. I was now a different person and my life was focused on staying sober, so our relationship had changed as well. I didn't realize at the time that this would be the last time I saw him, unless he finds it in his heart some day in the future to reconnect with me. So many things unfolded over the next few years and life got in the way of making visits and he got angry with me, so we rarely talked.

Somewhere around seven months of sobriety or so, Robert came back into my life. I had a lot of unresolved feelings around what had occurred between us in rehab and the truth was he had never left my heart. I thought of him often and wondered how he was doing. When you go through something as life altering and intense as being in rehab together, you have a bond that lasts forever.

I called him and we talked for hours. Our connection was still very much alive and we immediately forgave one another for what had transpired in rehab and began a new relationship. However, it was short lived. I was doing some major changing as a result of my counseling. Although, I didn't know how to stop being attracted to men who didn't want a relationship, I now knew what I wanted. I knew I wanted more than sex; I wanted an actual relationship with commitment and intimacy. Robert, however, was still married and in the process of a divorce. Although, he wouldn't admit it to me, he was still in love with his wife. I was once again caught in the vicious circle of trying to make someone love me who wasn't capable. I broke it off with him after a couple months, because we didn't want the same things.

However, in the midst of my heartache and vulnerability, I fell into my old pattern of relationships and quickly found myself involved with a married man, getting caught in that vicious circle of not getting my needs met even deeper. There are a few sharks floating around in AA, just as there are anywhere else, that find a way to use spiritual principles to justify using and taking advantage of other people. This didn't last too long either, as it wasn't really what I wanted and violated everything I stood for at this time of my life. It brought back the deep emotional pain and conflict I was so familiar with in relationships, but I now no longer had the same tolerance for it.

I was now at a point in my life where I could recognize that I chose men who weren't good for me to have a relationship with and the truth was I didn't want them, but I was still not able to stop being attracted to them. Men like my father, who were aloof, detached, emotionally cut off, unaffectionate, incapable of true intimacy, unavailable and/or not interested in a relationship were still simply irresistible to me. Sometimes they were users and abusers. It was like I was wearing a magnet that just pulled me towards them even though it wasn't what I truly wanted.

Robert and I decided to be "just friends" and he continued to be in and out of my life periodically for the next few years. We often commiserated together and gave each other comfort as each of us went through a string of short-lived relationships. We often teetered back and forth between friends and lovers.

The good thing was that growth was happening. I didn't used to be aware that I even had any needs and I never attempted to get them fulfilled. I was simply willing to accept whatever little crumbs the man was willing to toss me. That was no longer the case. I was aware of my needs and I was at least attempting to have them fulfilled, the problem now was that the men I was picking were still not capable.

Many things had changed and improved. Life was definitely better than it had been. In spite of the suffering and struggles I faced every day, I continued to grow emotionally and spiritually in leaps and bounds. The deep black pit inside me was completely gone. I was no longer a walking dead person. I was no longer empty inside. I was no longer disgusted with who I was and the life I was living. I had peace in my heart, mind and soul and my life was full and satisfying on some level. I had never felt this way my entire life, so it in itself was something I was incredibly grateful for.

However, the daily anxiety attacks were so unbearable that they overshadowed everything. My physical pain from the waist up and headaches were a constant in my life and I was also still struggling with mood swings, agitation, depression and an inability to think clearly. My depression had improved drastically in comparison to what it had been most of my life, but I still had frequent bouts that had no apparent cause. It had been almost a year and it was still an immense struggle to get through the days. I had finally stopped shaking violently on a regular basis, although it would still return intermittently.

My son was still bouncing off the walls with hyperactivity and falling behind in school. We had to hold him back for a year and he repeated first grade so that he could catch up. I was slowly learning how to be a sober mother and day-by-day he was beginning to trust that I wouldn't leave him, although it really took about six years before this completely stopped being an issue for him. We were definitely making some progress and a great deal of healing had occurred, but we still had a long way to go.

His hyperactivity, my anxiety attacks and physical pain together were still just too much to handle and had been going on for so long it was beginning to wear me away. I had been doing everything I was told to do in recovery and then some. I was doing all the right things and this area just wasn't improving. I was miserable, frustrated and overwhelmed. I was at my wits end and ready to pull out my hair. Although I wasn't actually experiencing cravings to drink or drug, I was feeling frightened by a tug to get some relief from the physical and psychological suffering. I didn't know how I could keep on like this. I had been white-knuckling it for a year now and I was beginning to lose my grip.

Then a woman who ran one of my women's groups from AA gave me a book to read called *The Missing Diagnosis* by Dr. Orion C. Truss and once again I was presented with information that blew my view of the world apart and took me on a whole new journey. It was another one of those profound "aha" moments, when the lightbulb came on and life was never the same again, just like I experienced when I found recovery.

The information in this book was life altering. It was as if it was written specifically for me and I found myself on all the pages. It was the life raft I desperately needed at that time and saved my life and my sanity. What I learned in this book was that I had a health condition called Candida and so did my son. It was this issue that was at the root of my anxiety attacks, agitation, disorientation, mood swings, irritability, depression, etc., and my son's hyperactivity.

I found a doctor in Pennsylvania who was a specialist in environmental medicine. I told him I was an alcoholic and he said, "Yes, many people with Candida become alcoholics." Further research into the subject revealed to me that it was actually one of the root causes or perpetuators of alcoholism and that there were many other factors involved as well that led me to a variety of other books and down a new path.

Through this doctor, I also learned that I had food allergies, nutritional deficiencies, hypoglycemia, multiple chemicals sensitivities and hypothyroidism, which further research revealed are also leading contributors to alcoholism. When I addressed these issues, my recovery made a complete turnaround and I was no longer white-knuckling it. I began a new journey that led me to the real truth about alcoholism and here is what I learned.

Four

Addiction and the Reward Pathway

"All truth passes through three stages. First, it is ridiculed. Second, it is violently opposed. Third, it is accepted as being self-evident."

~Arthur Schopenhauer

B efore we go any further, we need to talk about the science of addiction and what is called the reward pathway to understand the importance of the material that is about to be presented in the next chapters. Everything we are about to explore will link back to this crucial point.

There are four important criteria that define an addiction:

1. Psychological – The addicted person uses the substance or activity compulsively regardless of the negative impact it has on their health or life.

2. Physiological – The substance or activity stimulates the reward pathway in the brain. The intense euphoric feelings that are experienced cause the person to repeat the behavior over and over again to keep experiencing the feelings.

3. Tolerance – As the brain adapts to excess stimulation of the reward pathway, it needs more and more of the substance or activity to achieve the same results.

4. Dependence – Over time the addicted person's brain and reward pathway can't function normally without the substance.

The reward pathway, also known as the mesolimbic pathway or the pleasure pathway, resides in the center of the brain and is what drives our feelings of motivation, reward and behavior. Its primary job is to make us feel good or "reward" us when we engage in behavior that is necessary for survival, such as eating, drinking water, being nurtured and procreating.

It's also responsible for making sure that we repeat these behaviors over and over to ensure survival of the species. It achieves this goal by giving us feelings of pleasure when we engage in these behaviors. In other words, it reinforces behavior by giving us pleasurable rewards.

This pleasure is given by releasing neurotransmitters. Neurotransmitters are chemical messengers in the brain that make communication between nerve cells possible. The critical neurotransmitter involved in the reward pathway is dopamine. However, there are two other crucial brain pathways that make use of dopamine—the nigrostriatal pathway and the tuberoinfundibular pathway. It is these two pathways together with the reward pathway that make up the dopamine pathway. Therefore, any drug that impacts the reward pathway also impacts these other dopamine pathways as well.

All drugs, and remember alcohol is a drug, stimulate the dopamine pathway—reward pathway. Some drugs work by stimulating the release of excess dopamine, while others block receptor sites; however, the end result is that the brain is flooded with high levels of dopamine.[1] They also impact the serotonin pathway and other crucial neurotransmitters like GABA, glutamate and acetylcholine, but we'll be focusing mostly on dopamine.

GABA is our main inhibitory neurotransmitter. It works as a natural tranquilizer, stops us from being impulsive and prevents over stimulation. Glutamate is important because it's needed for most of the neurotransmission that takes place. People with imbalanced levels of GABA have problems with impulse control, anxiety, nervousness, restlessness and irritability to name only a few, while glutamate is associated with obsessive tendencies.

Dopamine gives us pleasurable feelings. It makes us feel good, confident, euphoric and relaxed, and instills a heightened sense of overall well-being. It improves mood, alertness and libido. Serotonin plays a major role in mood, sleep, appetite, pain and regulating body temperature. It also contributes to good feelings of well-being and makes us feel euphoric. People with anxiety disorders, obsessive-compulsive disorder, and depression often have a problem in their serotonin and dopamine pathways. Both dopamine and serotonin are sometimes referred to as our "happy hormones."[2] Without them we feel empty and depressed, flat and lifeless.

Here's an example of how the reward pathway works: You're hungry and you see a big plate of spaghetti in front you. Your five senses gather information about what you see and send a signal to your brain. Your area of the brain that controls memory tells you that if you eat this plate of spaghetti, it will make you feel good, so it tells you to pick up the fork and eat it.

When you eat it, your five senses tell the brain you're eating something good and that your stomach is getting full. At this point the brain releases the neurotransmitter dopamine from the reward pathway, which gives you a little surge of pleasure. This is your reward for eating the spaghetti.

The reward pathway then connects with other areas of your brain that control memory and behavior and tells it to remember that eating spaghetti makes you feel good. This reinforces that you will repeat this behavior again, to receive the reward and feel the good feelings.

Here's what happens in the reward pathway when you ingest alcohol or drugs: They bypass the five senses and within seconds go directly to the brain's reward pathway. Instead of just a little surge of pleasure, they stimulate the release of excessively high levels of neurotransmitters, which results in an immediate surge of extremely intense pleasure. The amount of dopamine released by drugs of abuse can be two to ten times higher than the amount released by natural means, such as food, and the effects usually last much longer.[3]

This is what is commonly called the "high." The reward pathway connects with other parts of the brain and tells it to remember that drugs and alcohol create this incredibly good feeling and this is an extremely powerful reinforcement that you'll repeat it again so you'll continue to have the pleasurable experience. Now every time you see or think about drugs or alcohol, the brain remembers that it will feel pleasurable and you desire to take them again.

The impact of the excessively high levels of dopamine on the brain is so powerful that the brain must find a way to adapt to these powerful surges. One of the ways that it does so is by desensitizing itself or reducing the number of dopamine receptors at the synapse and reducing the amount of dopamine it releases. This results in what we call "tolerance." Once the feelings of pleasure have dissipated, it will now require more of the drug to achieve the same results. The more often you use the drug, the more sensitized your receptors become and the more drugs you require to get high.

With repeated use of a drug, the neurons, which are where the neurotransmitters like dopamine reside, in the brain become dependent upon the drug—they can no longer function normally without it. The brain no longer produces or releases the essential neurotransmitters that allow us to feel pleasure on its own. When this happens, the user feels depressed and unable to experience pleasure in activities that used to be enjoyable to them and they experience withdrawal symptoms when the drug is not in their system and, thus, they will use again in order to feel better. They now need and crave the drug of abuse to simply bring their dopamine levels back to normal.

Over time, as the brain is forced to continue to adapt to alcohol or drugs, the other areas of the brain outside the reward pathway become affected. The circuitry of the brain that is responsible for memory, learning and judgment becomes hardwired to perform addictive behavior almost innately. It disrupts crucial brain structures that are critical for controlling behavior, especially behaviors related specifically to alcohol or drugs. It erodes one's ability to display self-control and make good decisions. Thus, the drug user is now a drug addict.

The faster a substance reaches the brain's reward pathway, the more addiction potential it holds. The quickest route to deliver a drug to the brain is through smoking it and, thus, why substances like crack cocaine and cigarettes are so highly addictive. The second fastest route is through injection, while the third quickest is snorting or sniffing and the least quick is ingestion.[4]

This is why many people advance from one addiction to another. They start out with sugar, caffeine or cigarettes. As the brain adapts and needs more and more to get the same feeling, sugar no longer does the trick, so they move on to cigarettes, after a while cigarettes no longer provides the same relief, so they move on to alcohol. After a while alcohol no longer does the trick and they move on to cocaine and so on and so on.

The most crucial step in recovering from any addiction is to stop stimulating the reward pathway in the brain with artificial sources that cause it to release excessive levels of neurotransmitters so that the brain can recover and restore natural order. As long as the reward pathway is excessively stimulated, then cravings for drugs and alcohol will occur and relapse is pretty much imminent.

This is the physiological process that is at the base of all addictions. Addiction, regardless of the substance or activity, is all about neurotransmitters. This is a crucial point to understand, as it will be weaved through all of the issues we'll be discussing throughout this book. We'll go into more detail about neurotransmitters in chapter 13, but for now, you just need to understand the basics of how they are involved in the addiction process and keep this in mind as we examine the next chapters.

What I'm about to illustrate is that there a variety of different factors that interfere in the goal of balancing the neurotransmitters that the alcoholic is unaware of that undermine their recovery process. When these issues are addressed, the chances of maintaining long-term sobriety increase drastically.

Five

Candida Albicans

"Truth is more of a stranger than fiction."
~Mark Twain

In chapter three, I shared with you that I had just stumbled upon a doctor of environmental medicine and had learned I had what is called Candida overgrowth and that it is an underlying factor in alcoholism. As I learned more, I discovered that it plays a crucial role in maintaining sobriety, because it has a detrimental impact on those critical neurotransmitters involved in the reward pathway and serotonin pathway, and results in many debilitating physiological and emotional symptoms that often push the alcoholic to relapse.

Candida Albicans is the formal name for the fungus or yeast that is responsible for yeast infections. Normally it lives in symbiosis in the human body along with a variety of other healthy bacteria. It actually has the important job of helping to detect and destroy other pathogenic bacteria that may enter the body, but sometimes something happens in the body that allows it to grow out of control and it outnumbers the healthy bacteria and creates infections accompanied by a variety of unpleasant symptoms and debilitating health problems. One of its other functions is to decompose a dead body; and when it proliferates in a living body, it still tries to do its job.

It has a variety of names and is also known as thrush, athlete's foot, vaginal yeast infection, Candida, Candida yeast, yeast syndrome or yeast infection. When it enters the blood stream it is then called Systemic Candida or Candidiasis.

Candida yeast is the yeast that's responsible for the common "yeast infection" that many women endure from time to time, and is the term that most people are familiar with. However, "yeast infections" are not limited to just women. It inflicts men and children as well and it can affect almost any part of the body. In fact, uncontrolled Candida yeast overgrowth can cause just about any mental or physical symptom you can think of.

It flourishes in environments that are dark, moist and warm; and thus why it tends to proliferate in some areas more than others, like the mouth, feet and genitals. One of the other most common areas to be infected with Candida is the gastrointestinal tract.

Once Candida Albicans sets up house in the gastrointestinal tract, it can change forms, penetrate the intestinal wall and enter the blood stream, which allows it to travel all through the body. It may then take up residence anywhere it likes such as the lungs, joints, muscles, sinuses, brain, spine, gallbladder, liver, nervous system, etc. When it permeates the intestinal wall, it leaves microscopic holes, which may lead to the development of leaky gut syndrome and food allergies or sensitivities as undigested food particles and other toxins enter the body.

Candida releases over 70 different toxins like ethanol and acetaldehyde into your blood stream that not only cause a host of problems in the human body, but also weaken the immune system. Ethanol is an alcohol and acetaldehyde is related to formaldehyde. These toxins disrupt normal functioning of the body's systems. It can also interfere with and mimic estrogen, thyroxin and other hormones in the body, therefore, creating hormonal imbalances and problems with the thyroid or other major glands. These toxins can also overload the liver and impede normal liver functions. It is also responsible for major disruption of important neurotransmitters in the brain like dopamine and serotonin.

Candida Albicans and its toxins can infiltrate and affect any organ or system in the body and can be responsible for a large variety of physical and mental health conditions that we see so commonly in people today. Most people are unaware that it may be the cause of their arthritis, headaches, migraines, anxiety, depression, aggression, mood swings, fatigue, sore throats, gas, bloating, persistent cough, irritable bowel syndrome, hyperactivity, memory problems, attention deficit, cold sores, eczema, hormonal fluctuations, menstrual difficulties, inability to lose weight and much more. It can even be a factor in serious conditions like Crohn's disease, autism, prostatitis and many other health issues, conditions and problems.

A lot of mental health problems such as depression, anxiety, mood swings, anger management issues, obsessive compulsive disorders, schizophrenia, rage and hyperactivity can be a result of Candida overgrowth. Cognitive functioning such as memory and learning can also be greatly impaired as well.

Symptoms of Candida

Once Candida yeast proliferates in the body, it wreaks havoc in many ways and is the instigator of many common maladies, conditions, syndromes and illnesses we see so frequently in our population. The symptoms of Candida are vast and all encompassing and can even incapacitate the individual. Here is a list of some of the most frequent:

- cravings for alcohol
- cravings for sweets
- abdominal gas
- headaches
- migraines
- excessive fatigue
- anxiety
- vaginitis
- rectal itching
- inability to think clearly or concentrate
- hyperactivity
- mood swings
- diarrhea
- constipation
- hyperactivity
- itching
- acne
- eczema

- depression

- sinus inflammation

- pre-menstrual syndrome

- dizziness

- poor memory

- persistent cough

- earaches

- low sex drive

- muscle weakness

- irritability

- learning difficulties

- sensitivity to fragrances and/or other chemicals

- cognitive impairment

- thrush

- athlete's foot

- sore throat

- indigestion

- acid reflux

- generalized itchiness

Yeast overgrowth is considered to be a leading contributor in alcoholism, multiple chemical sensitivity (MCS), chronic fatigue syndrome (CFS), fibromyalgia syndrome (FMS), autism, Crohn's disease, irritable bowel, prostatitis, attention deficit disorder, multiple sclerosis, leaky gut syndrome, asthma, food allergies, muscle and joint pain, arthritis, clinical depression, anxiety disorders, obsessive compulsive disorders, schizophrenia, asthma, repeated urinary tract infections, hormonal imbalances, endometriosis, PMS, digestive disturbances, psoriasis, lupus, rheumatoid arthritis, Addison's disease and many more.

The organ most frequently affected by yeast overgrowth is the brain, but it also affects these systems:

- digestive

- nervous

- cardiovascular

- respiratory

- reproductive

- urinary

- endocrine

- lymphatic

- musculoskeletal

Candida symptoms can vary from one person to another and often move back and forth between systems within the same individual. One day you may experience symptoms in the musculoskeletal system and the next day it could be the digestive system, etc. Some people may even become allergic to the yeast itself. Candida is believed to occur more often in women than men, but the truth is that it occurs in high numbers for men as well, but it is reported and diagnosed less frequently.

Men are less likely to be diagnosed with Candida for two reasons:

1. They don't seek help for their symptoms, because symptoms of Candida in males are often dismissed or denied by the man. He will just live with them because he thinks it's unmanly to talk about them or get help. Men are socialized to just live with pain and discomfort rather than address it.

2. Candida in males gets mislabeled as all kinds of other disorders because there is a lack of education about Candida in the mainstream medical society.

Males with Candida tend to get these labels:

- chronic prostatitis

- hyperactivity

- learning disabled

- attention deficit disorder

- conduct disorder

- anger or rage disorders

- alcoholic

- drug addict

- anti-social disorder

- autism

The instigator in all these conditions can be Candida. A variety of other factors like food allergies, hypoglycemia, nutritional deficiencies, chemical sensitivities, etc., may be the culprit as well, but these too are all part of the Candida syndrome. Where you find one, you usually find the others and we'll talk more about those issues later on.

Some of the most common Candida symptoms in males may consist of irritability, cognitive difficulties, depression, inability to concentrate, fatigue, restlessness, anxiety, forgetfulness, diarrhea, constipation, headaches, frequent stomachaches, indigestion, heartburn, excessive shyness or feelings of being self-conscious, rashes and many more.

As children, males with Candida typically experienced a lot of earaches, which resulted in antibiotics that only aggravated the Candida. As children and as men they may get in fights a lot and have difficulty excelling in school. They may be underachievers, due to Candida inhibiting their brain function. They were likely to be diagnosed with hyperactivity and/or attention deficit disorder. Two more very common Candida symptoms for males are jock itch and athlete's foot. In these cases, the Candida has localized in the feet or the genitals.

Since one of the most common organs to be affected by Candida is the brain and the nervous system, it results in a variety of symptoms that exhibit themselves as psychological or cognitive problems.

Candida and Alcoholism

So why is all this stuff so pertinent to alcoholism? Research has found that 55 percent of women alcoholics and 35 percent of men alcoholics have Candida overgrowth.[1] However, it is my opinion that it is much more common than this. A person with Candida doesn't always become an alcoholic, but an alcoholic almost always has Candida. It is unclear in some cases, which came first, the chicken or the egg; however, they go hand in hand. Where you find one, you usually find the other. They perpetuate one another. It is almost always an underlying factor in not only alcoholism, but addiction in general, and if not addressed, puts you at high risk of relapse.

If we look over the list of symptoms of Candida overgrowth, we see the top symptom is a craving for alcohol itself and we also see a vast list of many very common symptoms that recovering alcoholics struggle with on a daily basis.

One of the most common reasons relapse occurs is from the need to self-medicate these uncomfortable symptoms. Additionally, we see that Candida releases toxins into the body. Two of the most abundant toxins are ethanol and acetaldehyde.

First let's talk about ethanol. Ethanol is alcohol. It is the ingredient in beer, wine, liquor, etc., that gets us drunk. So when the alcoholic puts down the drink, but continues to have a Candida problem, they are still getting small amounts of alcohol in their body. This often results in strong cravings for alcoholic beverages that can seriously sabotage your recovery program.

Candida Albicans survives by fermenting sugars to generate energy it needs to live. Candida's diet consists almost exclusively of sugar. Alcohol is a sugar that doesn't have to be digested to get into the blood stream. It is absorbed very quickly through the stomach wall. When an alcoholic craves a drink, it really isn't alcohol they are craving at all. It is the sugar. The alcohol just works as a catalyst to provide a quick fix. Candida is craving the alcohol because it wants the sugar. Thus, this plus a few other issues in relation to sugar that we'll discuss further ahead is why all alcoholics are addicted to sugar in recovery.

Candida creates alcohol as it processes the sugar in your body. If you're eating a diet high in sugar and refined carbohydrates, which most people are, you are giving the Candida an endless source of food that it continuously breaks down and produces more alcohol in the process. So even though you're not drinking, you can still experience many of the same physiological and psychological effects as if you were. There are some reports that people with severe Candida can actually feel and appear intoxicated and have levels of alcohol so high in the body that they can be detected in the blood stream, even though they have not touched an alcoholic beverage.

Next let's look at the issue of acetaldehyde. Acetaldehyde is an insidious neurotoxin that makes its way into our body through four main sources. They are alcohol, Candida overgrowth, car and truck exhaust, and cigarette smoking.[2] Thus, one of the reasons we'll talk about later as to why alcoholics must stop smoking as well. It is believed that acetaldehyde is the chief cause of tissue damage found in alcoholics.

Another one of the byproducts in Candida's fermentation process of sugar is acetaldehyde. As with any of the toxins that Candida creates, acetaldehyde can enter the blood stream and travel to other parts of the body. One of the areas where it collects most frequently is the brain, where it causes damage to brain function and structure.

Acetaldehyde alters red blood cell structure and reduces their ability to perform their essential functions, resulting in less oxygen to our brains. It also interferes in the ability of protein tubulin to form into microtubules that are essential for a variety of functions in the brain cell and disrupts prostaglandin metabolism. It causes deficiencies in vitamin B1, niacin, NAD, acetyl coenzyme A, and pyridoxal-t-phosphate (P5P), and destroys essential enzymes. Acetyl coenzyme A is crucial for vitamin B5, one of the most critical vitamins for normal brain function and cellular energy production.[3]

We'd have to get pretty technical to go into an in-depth explanation of why this is all so important, so we'll just sum it up in an easy way by saying that all the damage caused by acetaldehyde mentioned above interferes in normal brain functioning and is often exhibited in a variety of symptoms that are experienced by alcoholics in recovery.

Acetaldehyde poisoning in the brain causes the following symptoms:

- impaired memory
- inability to concentrate (aka brain fog)
- depression
- slower reflexes
- lethargy and apathy
- irritability
- mental fatigue
- anxiety and panic attacks
- impaired sensory acuity
- loss of sex drive
- increased tendency towards alcohol, sugar and cigarette addiction
- PMS and breast swelling/tenderness in women
- chronic pain in the body

Take note that these are a lot of the same symptoms that most recovering alcoholics struggle with on a daily basis. The damage to the brain from acetaldehyde is extensive, but it also poisons the spinal cord, joints, muscles and tissues. It is particularly toxic for the central nervous system, kidneys and liver as it overloads them with poison. It inhibits proper functioning of the thyroid, pituitary, and adrenal glands and impedes normal hormone functioning. It also impacts the neurological, metabolic, endocrine and immune systems.[4]

One of the most important consequences of acetaldehyde in regard to addiction is the following:

Acetaldehyde promotes addiction to toxic substances. Perhaps one of the most surprising ways acetaldehyde may alter normal brain function is due to its tendency to combine in the brain with two key neurotransmitters, dopamine and serotonin. When AH and dopamine combine, they form a condensation product called salsolinol. When AH combines with serotonin, another product called beta-carboline is formed. Salsolinol and beta-carboline are two of a group of inter-related and interconvertible compounds called tetrahydro-isoquinolines. The various tetrahydro-isoquinolines which both animal and human research have shown to occur at high levels in the brains, spinal fluids, and urine of chronic alcoholics are closely related in structure, function, and addictive power to opiates! Successfully detoxifying alcoholics have been shown to excrete especially high levels of these opiate-like chemicals in their urine. Thus, these AH-generated, opiate-like biochemicals may at least partly explain why alcoholics are so addicted to alcohol, cigarette smokers to cigarettes, and Candida-sufferers to sugar, since all three of these conditions promote chronic excessive body AH levels. And, like opiates, these tetrahydroisoquinoline biochemicals would tend to promote lethargy, mental cloudiness and fogginess, depression, apathy, inability to concentrate, etc. These, of course, are symptoms common to both alcoholism and Candidiasis, the two conditions which would tend to generate the highest chronic AH levels in the body.[5]

So in summary of the connection of Candida to alcoholism, we find that as drinkers of alcohol we have already been exposing ourselves to high levels of acetaldehyde and suffering the damages that naturally ensue; but even when we quit drinking we are still being exposed to alcohol and acetaldehyde through Candida and this sets us up for a vicious cycle with a vast amount of psychological and physical symptoms that, if not understood, has a high probability of leading to relapse in order to get relief from the suffering.

In addition to that, Candida's byproduct acetaldehyde is stimulating the crucial neurotransmitters, dopamine and serotonin to create opiate like substances; thus keeping the brain and body in a physiological state of addiction. Remember in our discussion about the reward pathway and addiction, it is these neurotransmitters that are at the root of addiction. Candida toxins simulate the experience of drugs and alcohol in the reward pathway. When the recovering alcoholic continues to have a reward pathway that is excessively stimulated by other sources, they will most likely experience cravings for alcohol and/or drugs.

Two Main Causes of Candida

We all have millions of bacteria living in our body at all times. Some are considered good bacteria while others are considered bad and can cause a wide variety of health conditions. In a healthy body, the good bacteria keep the bad bacteria in check so there is a nice even balance. When someone develops Candida overgrowth, the balance has become upset and the bad bacteria have taken control. Something has gone awry and allowed the Candida to flourish and grow rampant.

The overgrowth of Candida Albicans is rampant in our society due to two main factors. Those factors are the overuse of prescription antibiotics and a diet that is low in nutritional value and high in refined sugars and simple carbohydrates.

1. Antibiotics – One of the biggest causes of Candida is the overuse of broad-spectrum antibiotics. When you take an antibiotic, it kills all the bacteria in your body, the bad and the good. The problem is that your body needs the good bacteria to maintain health and keep opportunistic invaders like Candida from taking over. Antibiotics don't affect Candida, therefore, when all the good bacteria are eliminated by antibiotics, the Candida is free to grow rampant and take over.

Prescription antibiotics are overused in our society. They are prescribed too frequently for conditions that don't even require them. This has resulted in making bacteria become completely immune to them. If you're a woman, you may have noticed that anytime you take an antibiotic you develop a vaginal yeast infection and your children develop oral thrush and recurring ear infections. This is the result of antibiotics encouraging Candida to flourish.

Even if you don't take antibiotics, most people are exposed to them unknowingly. Farm animals are routinely fed antibiotics, our meat supply is injected with hormones and antibiotics, and the feed that our farm animals eat is laced with antibiotics, all under the false pretense that it makes our food safer, when in fact what it really does is contribute to this problem of making bacteria immune to antibiotics and the overgrowth of Candida. When you eat these animals or drink their milk, you absorb the antibiotic into your body. The average person is ingesting antibiotics in one form or another on a daily basis.

2. Poor Diet and Nutrition – Poor diet and nutrition is the second largest cause of Candida. The standard American diet that is high in sugar and refined carbohydrates creates a fertile breeding ground for Candida to proliferate freely. Candida thrives on sugar and carbohydrates. Sugar is its primary food source. A diet high in sugar and refined carbohydrates is also deficient in vitamins and minerals; thus doesn't nourish a healthy body that can resist Candida overgrowth.

The present day American diet has almost no nutritional value at all. It's packed with a bunch of fast food and junk food like candy, doughnuts, cookies, soda and chips. Even the foods you think would be healthier such as breakfast bars and cereals are loaded with sugar and lacking in nutrients. As a matter of fact, almost everything you buy at the grocery store contains sugar of some sort.

In spite of the fact that we have a society that is growing rampantly with grossly overweight and obese individuals, we are actually malnourished because the foods we're eating do not contain nourishment. It is all this excess sugar and starches that is responsible not only for Candida yeast overgrowth but many other health conditions like obesity, malnutrition and diabetes.

Since the primary food source for Candida yeast is sugar, anything in the diet with excess sugar, starch or simple carbohydrates will help feed the Candida yeast and allow them to grow and multiply within your body faster. The higher your level of Candida overgrowth, the more symptomatic you will be.

Starchy foods or simple carbohydrates break down in the body into sugar very quickly so they too are a primary source of food. The more refined these foods are, the quicker they are converted to sugar. When you eat sugar, starchy food and simple carbohydrates it gives the yeast a delicious feast. The more food it has, the more it proliferates.

Other Causes of Candida

Other contributing factors to the overgrowth of Candida Albicans include the use of cortisone, birth control pills, or other steroid type drugs, immune suppressing drugs, and synthetic estrogen. All these create a hormonal imbalance in the body and allow the Candida to thrive and take over.

Antacids, ulcer medication, a weak immune system, heavy metals, mercury leaching from mercury dental fillings, environmental toxins, chlorinated drinking water, insufficient levels of hydrochloric acid and other essential digestive enzymes, excessive ongoing stress, a pH level in the body that is too acidic or too alkaline, and a toxic malfunctioning bowel that develops when we eat a diet high in sugar and refined foods also contribute to Candida overgrowth.

Individuals with diseases that weaken the immune system such as diabetes, cancer and HIV are also more vulnerable to Candida yeast.

Candida Treatment

The overgrowth of Candida yeast is an extremely complex and difficult condition to overcome once it infiltrates the body. It is one of the most insidious, obstinate, clever and highly adaptive organisms you will ever encounter. It has the ability to mutate and develop stronger forms of itself. There are approximately 30–40 different strains of Candida and many of them can be extremely resistant to treatment.

It is beyond the scope of this book to address Candida treatment completely, because we would spend the entire book, and then some, to cover all that it entails. However, I will give you a brief overview of the basics and guide you to the best resources you can find on the topic.

Many people have written about Candida extensively and you should read everything you can get your hands on regarding the subject matter. The most crucial key for individuals who have a Candida problem is to educate themselves as much as humanly possible. Consult with a variety of practitioners and educators in different fields of thought. The more you know, the more effective your Candida treatment approach will be.

The three most popular and informative books include *The Missing Diagnosis* by Dr. Orion C. Truss, *The Yeast Syndrome* by Dr. John Trowbridge and *The Yeast Connection* by Dr. Crook. I recommend that you read all three, because each one contains material that the other does not. These are the three most well recognized books on Candida, however, you can find many other books out there as well and the more you educate yourself the better. You must be very proactive in the battle against Candida.

I also publish a little electronic Candida booklet of my own called *Candida Secrets* that I encourage you to pick up, because I highlight all the crucial points that you won't find covered in the other books. It's a quick, easy read that will get you on the right track from the beginning. I give a copy of it for free to clients who come to me for sobriety coaching. You can find out more about it by visiting my website which is listed at the end of this book.

The best Candida treatment involves a combination of self-care approaches mixed with the knowledge of a competent holistic or alternative health care provider.

Treatment Basics

1. Antibiotics must be avoided unless absolutely necessary to save your life.

    A good alternative health doctor can offer you alternatives for antibiotics for many problems.

2. Follow a Candida diet.

    • No Sugar

    The first and most important item to be removed from the diet is sugar. Especially white refined sugar, however, sugar comes in many different forms, and Candida will feed on all of them. So, all forms of sugar must be removed from the diet, including maple syrup, fructose, corn syrup, honey, molasses etc.

- No Alcohol

- No Caffeine

- No Refined and Processed Foods

Eliminate refined and processed foods. Eat only whole foods. Since carbohydrates are broken down in the body into sugars, even complex carbohydrates must be reduced.

A basic Candida diet is one that consists mostly of meat protein and low carbohydrate vegetables. It should also be organic to avoid antibiotics, hormones and pesticides.

Snacking should be limited. If you do partake, it should be in the form of veggies, yogurt or nuts, if these are tolerable.

- No Yeast

- No Wheat

- Low in Fruit

- High in Protein and Low Carbohydrate Vegetables

- No Preservatives and Additives

- No Moldy Foods

- No Dairy except yogurt and butter

  (Cheese and milk contain lactose—milk sugar—that the Candida will feed on. Some people can do small amounts of cheese and cottage cheese.)

- Low in Complex Carbohydrates

- Tomatoes are high in acid and aggravate Candida, so they should be minimized.

- Vinegar also encourages Candida for some people, so it should be minimized as well. However, raw and unrefined apple cider vinegar has been found to be helpful in eliminating Candida for some people.

3. Replenish Healthy Bacteria in your Gastrointestinal Tract by Taking a Probiotic Supplement

4. No Smoking

5. Identify and Address Nutritional Deficiencies

6. Boost the Immune System – Exercise and take immune boosting supplements.

7. Antifungals

An antifungal is a product that actually kills the Candida yeast. There are prescription drug antifungals and natural antifungals. They may be oral or topical. Oral is taken to address Candida in the gut and systemic Candida. Topical is used on a particular area of the body, such as the feet or vagina.

Natural antifungals usually consist of a combination of herbs and/or nutrients and other natural sources that have antifungal properties. Natural antifungals can be just as effective, if not more so than drug therapy, but you may have to try several of them to find what works best for you.

Since there are different strains of Candida, and it mutates over time, what is effective one week, may not be effective the next week.

Some of the most common natural Candida treatments are garlic, grapefruit seed extract, oregano oil, colloidal silver, caprylic acid, tea tree oil, taheebo tea, olive leaf extract, coconut oil, barberry, food grade hydrogen peroxide and other oxygen-based products.

Some of the most common prescription antifungals are as follows:

- Diflucan

- Amphoetericin B

- Nystatin

- Nizoral

- Lamisil

- Sporanox

The problem with drugs is that they usually come with a variety of side effects. Some of which can be quite serious. The most dangerous side effect is their impact on the liver. Liver enzymes need to be monitored while taking any antifungal drugs. However, I don't believe there's anything wrong with getting a little help now and then with a prescription if you're very careful.

In my opinion, it is best to only do a short course of prescription antifungals perhaps when one is just starting out a treatment plan to help get a good boost or if there are severe Candida symptoms that need immediate attention or as an addition to a natural treatment to help progress move along faster.

Prescription drug antifungals can only be acquired with a prescription. Your doctor should monitor your liver very closely while taking any prescription antifungals. This is done by ordering a simple blood test.

8. Remove Environmental Toxins From Your Living Space

   Environmental toxins weaken the body and encourage Candida to proliferate more, in addition to that, you'll learn later on in this book that they also damage neurotransmitters and alter the reward pathway.

9. Cleanse the Colon

   Most Candida resides in the colon, therefore, it is essential to cleanse the colon in one way or another. This may be achieved through some of the popular colon cleansing products on the market or with the use of enemas or colonics.

Four Key Points when Treating Candida

When you read the most popular books on the market for Candida, there are a couple of key points that you won't hear about that you must be aware of.

1. Even many of the doctors who are treating Candida do not have a thorough understanding of the deep complexities and full extent that Candida encompasses.

   Unfortunately, there are very few Candida physicians or experts manufacturing treatment products that have a thorough understanding of all the facets of Candida. There are a lot of practitioners and treatment manufacturers out there, but they come with varying levels of expertise and knowledge. Not everyone grasps the profound ramifications of Candida and is capable of addressing the many different issues involved.

   For example, even in the excellent books that are considered to be the leading authorities on Candida, they are missing some of the pieces of the puzzle. In the *Missing Diagnosis, Yeast Connection* and *Yeast Syndrome*, they all present a scenario where if you just follow the diet and take Nystatin, you will eliminate yeast overgrowth. That is not the case with most people. I talk with hundreds of people every year who struggle with this protocol and, personally, I have not seen success like this myself. There are a variety of problems with Nystatin and the other popular antifungals. As soon as you stop taking the product, Candida comes back full force. Candida gets resistant to Nystatin, and for some people, the die off with Nystatin is so severe that taking the product is not possible.

   Some practitioners or manufacturers get very knowledgeable in one particular aspect, while another practitioner is more skilled in a different aspect. So it's necessary to read everything out there and consult with a variety of different practitioners in different fields of thought about Candida, so you can piece it all together. It's very hard to find everything you need to know in one place, since very few health care providers, educators, etc., have mastered the complete picture.

2. Candida is not easy to treat or overcome.

You will see a variety of products and information across the Internet and throughout natural health publications claiming you can cure your Candida in 12 hours, or cure your Candida without following the diet and a variety of other outrageous claims that make it sound very easy and simple to achieve by taking their product. Your Candida physician may even think they have the magic potion and believe it's no big deal if they aren't fully educated. However, these claims are simply not true.

There is no one miracle drug, natural cure or treatment by itself. Yes, their product or products may definitely be effective and help reduce symptoms, but successful treatment of Candida requires that many steps be taken in conjunction with the other. The truth is that it takes a lot of time, patience and persistence. Candida is extremely resilient and difficult to treat. There is no magic bullet.

Even when incorporating the most effective holistic approach, lifelong adherence to the Candida diet, continued use of probiotics and periodic administration of antifungals will likely be necessary to remain symptom free. If you return to eating the standard American diet, take antibiotics or engage in any of the high risk factors believed to contribute to Candida, your symptoms are likely to return.

Additionally, regardless of what others tell you, there is not a reliable test you can take to see if you have Candida. None of them are reliable. They often fail to find Candida when it is indeed an issue. The most reliable way to know if you have Candida is through a written questionnaire that you can find in Dr. Crook's book, *The Yeast Connection*; additionally there is a test called the spit test that is pretty reliable as well. When you get up in the morning, get a clear glass and fill it with water, spit in the glass of water and let it sit for 15 minutes. If your saliva stays at the top and you see thin strands that look like strings or spider legs extending downward, or your saliva floats to the bottom and looks cloudy, or your saliva is suspended in mid-air and looks like little specs are floating, then these are indications that Candida is probably present.

3. Candida mutates.

All the books on Candida make it sound so easy to overcome, however, the majority of people I work with, including myself, have not had an easy path like they describe in the books or you may see in products promoting for treatment.

The most important piece of information I will share with you about Candida is that <u>Candida Mutates</u> and <u>Candida becomes Resistant</u>. It changes form, it becomes resistant and/or immune to whatever antifungal you take. This is one of the main reasons Candida is so difficult to treat and why treatment fails so often.

This is exceptionally crucial to your Candida treatment protocol. You rarely hear about this issue from anyone treating or selling products that kill Candida. Most people, including physicians treating Candida, are unaware of this characteristic. If it is mentioned, it is brief and doesn't cover the severe consequences one can face as a result or offer an explanation of how to address it effectively. Everyone says, "Oh, just take my product and you'll get better." But it isn't that easy. Yes, the product may work great for a period of time, but if you take only one product for several weeks, the Candida becomes resistant to that product and you stop achieving results.

In order to prevent Candida from mutating and becoming resistant to a particular herb, nutrient, drug, etc., you must rotate or alternate your antifungals. This means that on week one of your treatment plan you take Antifungal A, then on week two you take Antifungal B, then on week three you take Antifungal C and on week four you take Antifungal D. Then start all over again with the Antifungal A. You should pick four antifungals and take a different one each week. This way the Candida doesn't have a chance to become resistant.

I learned this information firsthand the hard way. When I first began treating my Candida 19 years ago, absolutely no one was aware that Candida mutates and becomes resistant. I would take a particular herb, nutrient or prescription and it would work fantastic for a couple weeks. I would think I was on my way to a complete cure, then "Wham" it would just stop working completely, and all my symptoms would return. I witnessed it in my life over and over again. At first I wasn't sure what was happening; my doctor didn't have any explanation. He would just tell me to use a different product. Eventually I had made my way through every alternative and traditional treatment product out there and none of them gave me any relief anymore.

Then one day I stumbled upon an article in something like *Discover* magazine, I think it was, that talked about how Candida mutates and the lightbulb came on. I then knew exactly what was happening to me. Through some more extensive and thorough research I found that it's necessary to rotate antifungals to keep it from mutating. I then started over by rotating my antifungals.

However, it was now too late, because my Candida was now resistant to every antifungal out there. The best I can do is keep my Candida level at bay by doing enemas, taking acidophilus and following a strict Candida diet. I have to keep my eyes open for new products on the market that I have never taken before. So be sure you don't let this happen to you. Alternate your antifungals!

Unfortunately, Candida treatment is not always a straight and narrow path. It often takes a lot of trial and error. It definitely takes a lot of persistence, education and patience, because Candida is astonishingly persistent, resilient and hardy. You may make progress for a while and then experience a setback.

Candida is very cunning, enigmatic and complicated, and involves many different factors. It requires a comprehensive and long-term approach. Be prepared for a battle.

4. Die off can be excruciating and interfere in the recovery process.

When you take antifungals and kill off the Candida, it releases toxins into the body. If you kill off the Candida too quickly, you will experience what is called "die off" or the "Herxheimer response." This is exhibited by an intensification of symptoms as the body struggles to eliminate the toxins.

If you have a liver that isn't functioning adequately, which most alcoholics do, the liver has a hard time handling all the toxins as you kill off the Candida and you feel sicker.

Die off can be so severe that you can't function. For some people this can be a serious roadblock to eliminating Candida completely as it is too unbearable to endure. Die off can be reduced to some degree by taking high doses of vitamin C, bentonite clay, activated charcoal, exercise or enemas.

Why Haven't You Heard of Candida?

At this point you may be wondering, "Hey Cynthia, why haven't I heard about this Candida thing?" Candida yeast overgrowth has grown to epidemic proportions in our society and most people are not even aware of the profound role it plays in our mental and physical health. This lack of awareness is due mainly to the fact that mainstream medicine is not educated about Candida yeast and is resistant to learning. Therefore, knowledge of this condition is not readily accessible, unless you're turning to alternative medicine, but as I mentioned, even those treating Candida have a limited understanding of how complex it really is. People suffering from Candida often go from doctor to doctor for years and are usually told they are a hypochondriac or that it is stress or that it's a psychiatric problem before ever discovering the real culprit.

If we look over the list of symptoms, illnesses and conditions that are a result of Candida overgrowth, we will see that we have found the culprit of many health problems that plaque millions of people. If all of society were to become aware and make the changes needed to eliminate Candida, they would also eliminate all these health problems. Quite frankly this means the pharmaceutical companies would lose billions of dollars. Our medical universities and communities are funded and controlled by the pharmaceutical companies.[6]

For the most part, the cure for Candida requires a drastic change in diet, environment and a variety of natural or alternative health treatments that cut the pharmaceutical companies out of the picture. There are a few prescriptions that are effective against Candida for short-term relief, but they are not the answer in the long run and won't be effective in and of themselves.

Contrary to what they'd like you to believe, many of us in the natural health field believe that our pharmaceutical companies have no interest in finding true cures for anything, because it does not benefit them financially. We feel their goal is to deceive us and keep all of us stuck in the vicious cycle of being dependent upon them so we keep putting more money in their pockets.

Not only that, as we see in the list of causes for Candida overgrowth, the leading cause of this condition is created by the pharmaceutical companies and mainstream medicine itself. To acknowledge the far-reaching extent of this problem would require them to change their entire protocol and stop prescribing their own products, which again would cause them to lose billions of more dollars. So it seems to me that not only does most of mainstream medicine refuse to acknowledge the seriousness of the debilitating condition of Candida, but they vehemently try to discredit it and deny its existence, all in the name of money, to protect their own interests.

Now, I'm certainly not criticizing anyone for not wanting to lose billions of dollars, we'd all be billionaires if we could; however, in the process of making money, we are obligated to do it in an honest and ethical manner. We must tell the truth, provide products and services that are truly helpful and beneficial and empower individuals, not keep them dependent.

There are medical doctors that are not part of this conspiracy to hide the truth, who truly care about your well-being and improving your health, however, you need to know where to find them. You need a medical doctor who only uses pharmaceuticals and surgery when absolutely necessary to save your life and incorporates a variety of alternative health treatment approaches into their practice.

They usually go by titles such as a Doctor of Environmental Medicine, a Doctor of Orthomolecular Medicine or a Naturopathic Doctor and can be found by contacting the American Holistic Medical Association, the American Academy of Environmental Medicine, the American Association of Naturopathic Physicians, American Holistic Health Association or www.orthomolecular.org. Each of these organizations has a database of physicians where you can get a referral for your state.

Six

Hypoglycemia

"Man prefers to believe what he prefers to be true."
~Francis Bacon

R esearch also tells us that most, if not all, alcoholics have hypoglycemia. It, too, interferes in neurotransmitter functioning and is responsible for many of the debilitating symptoms that alcoholics suffer with. I have found in my life that it is another one of the most crucial keys for maintaining sobriety.

Hypoglycemia, also known as low blood sugar, can be the culprit of many physical and psychological symptoms. It's a very common occurrence in our society and often goes undiagnosed. It can mimic most every medical condition and is often misdiagnosed or labeled as hypochondriasis.

In lay terms, hypoglycemia is when your blood glucose levels drop too low and your body and brain can't function properly. The brain is very sensitive to the levels of blood sugar and needs glucose to function adequately. It is fuel for the brain. The brain doesn't have the ability to store glucose so it needs a continuous supply from the blood. It extracts it from the blood as it does oxygen. If the brain does not have enough oxygen or glucose, it can go into a coma.

Symptoms of hypoglycemia can be mild, moderate or severe and may consist of any of the following:

- sweating
- shaking between meals
- crankiness
- weakness
- anxiety
- irritability
- confusion
- inability to concentrate
- nervousness
- tingling
- pounding/racing heart
- speech difficulties
- fuzzy head
- mood swings
- feeling faint
- nausea
- fatigue
- melancholy
- depression
- obsessive/compulsive behavior
- slurred speech
- poor coordination
- glassy eyes
- headaches
- migraines

Severe symptoms, which require immediate medical attention would include:

- unresponsiveness

- highly agitated

- unconsciousness

- convulsions

You may feel a little confused by the fact that we're talking about the body needing sugar to keep the blood sugar stable, since we already said that sugar is bad for you, but the difference is we're not talking about refined white sugar. We're talking about "natural sugars." The body needs healthy sugar that comes from whole food sources like bananas, apples, oranges, nuts, vegetables and other complex carbohydrates, but not refined white sugar or simple carbohydrates.

White refined sugar contains no nutritional value for the body and is not really a food. It's a chemical that damages the body in many ways. However, natural sugar from "whole food" sources is essential for the body in limited amounts. It provides the brain and body with nutrients it needs to function adequately.

Hypoglycemia occurs when the body does not metabolize blood glucose properly. Abnormal metabolism can be caused by a variety of factors such as:

- excess refined sugar and white flour in your diet

- pancreatic or adrenal under activity or over activity

- excessive use of alcohol, tobacco, and coffee or other products with caffeine

- overeating of refined carbohydrates

- allergies

- severe emotional stress that doesn't go away

Probably the biggest contributor to hypoglycemia is the consumption of excess refined white sugar, white flour and other refined carbohydrates. Our bodies were not designed genetically or physiologically equipped to metabolize the mass amount of refined food, which is stripped of any nutritional value, found in the typical diet of this day and age. This creates a continuous strain and abuse on the body's organs, such as the pancreas, the liver, the adrenals and other endocrine glands. The continuous ingestion of empty refined foods leads to malfunctioning of the glandular and metabolic systems.

What happens when we eat sugar and other refined foods? They are absorbed into the bloodstream very quickly and raise the blood glucose level to abnormally high levels at a very fast pace, which gives us that boost in neurotransmitters we often feel when eating sweets. These are those critical neurotransmitters that are involved in the reward pathway and at the root of addiction. This causes the pancreas to overreact with an emergency response and releases an excessive amount of insulin into the bloodstream to try and bring the blood sugar back to normal. The excessive amount of insulin brings the blood sugar down, but it brings it down too low and it brings it down too fast. This is when hypoglycemia symptoms occur.

The body then calls on the adrenal glands to release cortisol to bring the blood sugar levels back up because it works in conjunction with insulin to keep blood sugar in balance. Every time you eat sugar and refined foods, the pancreas and the adrenals go through this cycle and this puts too much demand on them. In time as the adrenal glands are called on over and over to regulate this vicious pattern, the adrenal glands become depleted and they no longer release the amount of cortisol that is necessary for adequate functioning; thus blood sugar levels stay in a consistently lower state and this perpetuates the problem of hypoglycemia even more.

When we provide our body with the natural sugar it needs from whole food sources rather than refined white sugar or other simple carbohydrates and eat adequate protein, then this cycle does not ensue. Everything functions as it should in the body, the blood sugar stays balanced and hypoglycemia symptoms don't occur.

To keep blood sugar stable and avoid hypoglycemia symptoms it's necessary to avoid eating refined sugars or any food that easily converts to sugar. Your diet should consist of foods that take a while to digest so there won't be a rapid rise in blood sugar and then the plummet that causes hypoglycemia symptoms. Foods that digest slowly consist of meat, fish, eggs, yogurt, cheese, beans, nuts and seeds, and complex carbohydrates, which are whole grains, fresh vegetables, and fresh whole fruits—not juice. Although beans, whole grains and cheese are on this list, there is great debate in the health field, whether these foods are really good for us at all. It's best to at least keep these foods to a minimum.

No alcohol, tobacco or caffeine, because as we'll learn in the following chapters, all three of these perpetuate the cycle of hypoglycemia by dumping excess sugar in the bloodstream. Reduce emotional stress as much as possible. Stress releases sugar into the bloodstream; so if you have excessive stress, your body will repeatedly be putting out too much sugar. For stress that can't be eliminated, find ways to cope effectively with the use of exercise, meditation, massage, counseling, etc.

Meals must be eaten consistently at regular intervals. If you go too long without food, then your blood sugar levels drop. Many people with hypoglycemia find that it is easier to maintain their blood sugar levels if they have four or five small meals a day instead of just three. Alternatively, you can have a healthy snack such as fresh vegetables, a serving of yogurt or a handful of nuts or seeds in between meals. This keeps a steady stream of sugar flowing in the body. This is especially helpful for people who are just beginning to address their hypoglycemia issues. Over time, as your body begins to repair, you may then be able to go back to three meals daily.

Once metabolic damage has developed and you have difficulty metabolizing sugars and carbohydrates, it can then spread to not only refined white sugar and simple carbohydrates, but the body can have difficulty with any carbohydrate whether it is a whole food or not. So initially you may have to limit even wholesome carbohydrates. Some people never do well with complex carbohydrates and must limit them forever. It's also important for women to know that hormonal fluctuations that occur with the menstrual period can also cause the blood sugar levels to drop, so you may have to be extra careful with your hypoglycemia diet during these days.

When I first started working on my hypoglycemia I had to eat every couple hours to keep my blood sugar stable, but after a couple years I was able to shift to three meals daily with an occasional snack in between. Now I eat every five hours. However, I must eat every five hours like clockwork, or I will have hypoglycemia symptoms.

There are a variety of different approaches and diets for hypoglycemia, different ones work for different people. You'll have to experiment and find the one that works for you. Most alcoholics do best on a diet that is high in meat protein and low in carbohydrates because we don't metabolize sugar properly. Even complex carbohydrates break down into sugar in the body, so they need to be minimized.

For example, in my own life I have found that I must eat a balanced meal that consists of a large portion of meat and vegetables, and a small amount of complex carbohydrates. I tried being a vegetarian once, but I couldn't function. It must be meat protein; any other form of protein will not balance my blood sugar. If I don't eat meat, and it must be at least six ounces of meat for each meal, as well as an equal amount of vegetables, I will have severe hypoglycemia. My head will spin, I'll be dizzy, shake uncontrollably, won't be able to concentrate, irritable, want to cry and fuzzy headed. I'll be so weak I can't stand up, feel like I'll pass out and I get a migraine. It must be actual meat—eggs, cheese, yogurt, etc., will not balance my blood sugar.

Additionally, supplementing the diet with a variety of vitamins and minerals like B vitamins, magnesium, chromium, amino acids, pantothenic acid (vitamin B5) and especially vitamin B3 also known as niacin, and Vitamin C will aid in the maintenance of blood sugar stability.

If we look over the list of symptoms created with hypoglycemia, we once again see many common symptoms that recovering alcoholics struggle with every day. That's because even though they've given up the alcohol, they are still eating sugar and other refined carbohydrates and caught in the vicious cycle of hypoglycemia. The so-called "dry drunk" syndrome is really nothing more than low blood sugar.

This is important because it is these uncomfortable and sometimes unbearable symptoms that are a frequent cause of relapse. When blood sugar drops, the alcoholic will have a continuous desire to self-medicate, which often leads to a drink or a drug. Additionally, hypoglycemia makes you crave sweets to bring your blood sugar up again. The alcoholic's body is accustomed to receiving its sugar in an ultra fast and concentrated dose— through alcohol—so sugar alone often doesn't do the trick and instead of craving sugar when the blood sugar drops, we crave alcohol.

Those extremely important neurotransmitters involved in the addiction process, dopamine, serotonin, etc., are haywire in hypoglycemia. They go up and down like a yo-yo in response to the blood sugar level. As we learned earlier, the main goal in maintaining long-term sobriety is to keep those neurotransmitters in balance and that is not possible without keeping the blood sugar balanced.

Seven

The Three Imitators – Sugar, Nicotine and Caffeine

"Three things cannot long be hidden: the sun, the moon, and the truth."

~Confucious

I call sugar, nicotine and caffeine the three imitators, because as you're about to learn, each one of them simulates the physiological process of addiction in the same way as alcohol and drugs. Their impact on the brain and the critical neurotransmitter involved in the reward pathway, dopamine, as well as serotonin, is so profound that if they are not removed from the alcoholic's life, almost guarantee that relapse will occur. First we'll take a look at what I call sweet poison or the sugar connection.

Sugar

The sugar connection for alcoholics is complex and multi-faceted. If there is nothing else the alcoholic does in regard to addressing the biochemical issues mentioned in this book, the most important step you can take is removing sugar from the diet. Even if you follow none of the other steps in this book, you can make drastic improvements and greatly increase your chances of success with sobriety with the removal of sugar alone.

First of all, we learned in the Candida chapter that sugar is its favorite food. Therefore, any food that contains sugar will feed your Candida and keep the whole Candida cycle going strong. Additionally, we learned that it plays a crucial role in the development and perpetuating of hypoglycemia. So for those reasons alone it must be avoided, but it is much deeper than that.

Sugar addiction is the most common addiction in our society today. The average American consumes 32 teaspoons of sugar a day or more than 150 pounds a year.[1] Not only is it addictive, but this very common everyday product that is falsely believed to be harmless is responsible for many health problems we find in our society.

Many people will deny, rationalize and justify their addiction to sugar in the same way as alcoholism. As a matter of fact, if we examine our behavior as a society in relationship to sugar, we will see that we respond to sugar in a very similar way as lab rats pressing a lever to get their reward.[2]

There's a very significant difference between white refined sugar and naturally occurring complex sugars that are found in whole foods. At this moment we are speaking specifically of refined white sugar, or its cousins, the other refined sugars, such as brown sugar, powdered sugar or raw sugar.

As I see it, white refined sugar is not a food. It is a chemical. It is an addictive drug. Yes, that's right, an addictive drug, and when you remove it from your diet you can experience withdrawal symptoms as excruciating and serious as alcohol withdrawal, including tremors, flu like symptoms, headaches, and mood swings so intense you would damn near kill for a chocolate bar. Some say it is as addictive as heroin.

Recent research suggests that it is more addictive than cocaine, one of the most addictive substances on the planet. When lab rats were given the choice of sugar water over cocaine, 94 percent of them chose sugar water over cocaine. Even rats that were previously addicted to cocaine would switch over to sugar water when they were given the choice.[3]

White sugar is a natural substance that has been refined to intentionally maximize its chemical surface area and biological activity, just like cocaine and opium. Cocaine is refined from coca leaves, opium is refined from poppy seeds and white sugar is refined from cane sugar.[4]

Refined white sugar is stripped of any nutritional value and is an empty calorie food. In addition to that, in order to be metabolized in the body it has to draw from your vitamin and mineral reserves and, therefore, is responsible for depleting mineral and vitamin levels in the body, which in itself creates numerous health problems.

What is very sad and devastating is that sugar addiction is an acceptable addiction. It is basically a legalized recreational drug that most of society takes part in. It's not uncommon for people to know they have a sugar addiction and to make a joke of it. It's not seen as a serious matter, when in reality it is very serious indeed. We use it to self-medicate and to boost our energy and mood.

The list of health problems associated with sugar is enormous and too large to go into at this time, but some of the most common symptoms created are: depression, mood swings, irritability, depletion of mineral levels, hyperactivity, anxiety, panic attacks, chromium deficiency, depletion of the adrenal glands, type 2 diabetes, hypoglycemia, Candida overgrowth, obesity, high cholesterol, and it even creates anti-social behavior such as that found in crime and delinquency.

Most people who are alcoholics were addicted to sugar before becoming alcoholic. We become addicted to sugar in childhood and then because of the process of tolerance that we discussed in chapter four, it progresses onto other things like alcohol, caffeine, huffing, nicotine, marijuana, cocaine and so on and so on. However, the true addiction is to sugar, and once the alcoholic becomes sober, they return to the original source and once again crave sugar.

The molecular structure of refined white sugar is almost identical to alcohol and dramatically alters brain chemistry in the same way as harder addictive substances.[5] Alcohol and sugar have a very similar impact on the neurotransmitters of the brain. As we saw in the Candida section, alcohol is a sugar. Therefore, alcohol = sugar. Sugar in the form of alcohol gives the body what it craves instantly in a much more potent format and, thus, incites the cycle of addiction to the alcohol. Alcoholics as well as people with type 2 diabetes, Candida, obesity and hypoglycemia have a biological inability to metabolize refined sugar effectively.

Since sugar and alcohol are essentially sisters biochemically, when you continue to eat sugar in recovery, it can make you crave alcohol. When your body and mind are screaming for an alcoholic beverage, what it's really craving is sugar. The body of an alcoholic has grown accustomed to receiving its sugar in a much more intense and faster route—through the alcohol. When you drink alcohol, it is very quickly absorbed through the intestinal wall. When you take the alcohol out of the picture, you crave sugar. When you eat sugar in cookies, candy bars, doughnuts, etc., it relieves some of your symptoms, but it doesn't give you the same intensity or bring you as high as it does with alcohol, therefore, the consumption of sugar leads to cravings for an alcoholic drink.

How Does Addiction to Sugar Develop?

Sugar addiction is rampant in our society because of the standard American diet that consists mostly of highly refined and processed sugar and foods that contain little, if any, nutritional value.

Each organ in the human body needs a particular mineral to function properly. If the organ doesn't receive what it needs, it has built-in mechanisms for protection. The pancreas is the organ that is largely responsible for controlling the sugar levels in the body and it needs the mineral chromium to perform its duties properly.

When the pancreas is in need of more chromium, it tells the brain to find some and this makes us crave something sweet, because natural sweets contain chromium. Now, the way nature originally intended it was that when the pancreas sent out this message that it needs more sweets, we were supposed to eat natural sweets in the form of berries, bananas, apples, oranges, nuts, vegetables etc. It was supposed to be derived from whole and natural food sources. When you eat whole and healthy sweets that contain vitamins and minerals, then the pancreas gets the chromium it needs and the craving for sweets disappears.

The problem developed when the modernization of the food industry introduced refined white sugar to our diet. As I mentioned above, white sugar has no nutritional value. The chromium, as well as all the other vitamins and minerals, have been stripped out of it. So when your pancreas tells you that you need to eat something sweet and you eat a candy bar or a box of cookies that is made of refined white sugar and flour, your pancreas does not receive the chromium it needs to perform its job. Therefore, it will make you crave more sweets, in hopes that you will give it what it needs. This is how the vicious cycle is created. The pancreas never receives what it needs and you never stop craving sweets.[6] This often leads to a chromium deficiency, which perpetuates the problem even further.

Additionally, when your body doesn't receive the sweets it needs, it calls on the adrenal glands to release cortisol. This sets up the whole adrenal system for exhaustion and deterioration as this vicious cycle puts a never-ending burden on the adrenal organs that we discussed in the hypoglycemia section. Over time the adrenal glands stop releasing adequate amounts of cortisol. The adrenal glands are responsible for the production of hormones that are critical to many body functions and systems like maintaining blood sugar and managing stress. Malfunctioning adrenal glands lead to excessive fatigue, exhaustion, cravings for sweets and caffeine, inability to handle stress, unstable blood sugar, and a variety of other debilitating symptoms that may result in cravings for alcohol to get relief. This vicious cycle with the pancreas and the adrenal glands also leads to the development of hypoglycemia, and we already discussed the importance of hypoglycemia in the previous chapter.

In addition to that, none of the other body organs or systems are receiving the nutrients they need to function adequately, which leads to a variety of debilitating health conditions. Sugar also suppresses the immune system. It depletes levels of phagocytes (the white blood cells that are needed for strong immune function and that eat up harmful bacteria) and this reduces the body's ability to fight infection and disease.

The second contributing factor to sugar addiction is that when we eat sugar it gives us a temporary boost in the neurotransmitters in our brain. Remember these neurotransmitters are our "happy hormones." They make us feel good. The two most important involved with sugar are dopamine and serotonin, which are also the two most important neurotransmitters involved in the reward pathway and addiction to drugs and alcohol. Remember, dopamine is the neurotransmitter responsible for releasing endorphins that give us feelings of pleasure. Serotonin is responsible for that all over good feeling of well-being.

When you eat refined white sugar and simple carbohydrates, it triggers a very intense and large supply of dopamine and serotonin into the body all at once and we feel great, kind of "high." Unlike whole and natural sweets, which give us a slow and steady supply of natural sugar that keeps our neurotransmitters in balance. The problem is that since refined white sugar isn't a whole food, the "high" doesn't last very long and not only that, once it's processed, our neurotransmitters crash to very low levels, which makes us feel bad, lethargic, depressed or very "low." We then crave more sugar to bring us back up or to feel high. This is also true of other highly refined and processed foods found in the average diet today such as white flour. With natural sugar found in whole foods, there aren't any extreme highs or lows.

The more often you engage in this vicious cycle, the more sugar you will need to achieve the same high because, as we discussed in the section on the reward pathway, the dopamine and serotonin receptors will become desensitized when they are forced to deal with excessive stimulation. Tolerance develops and eventually you'll no longer be able to feel normal, happy and enjoy pleasure unless you eat sugar.

This is very important because this is the exact same thing that happens to the brain in the addiction process to alcohol or drugs. Just like drugs and alcohol, sugar stimulates the reward pathway in the brain excessively. An excessively stimulated reward pathway is what gives you the incredible euphoric feeling that keeps you coming back for more. When the reward pathway is excessively stimulated by sugar, it keeps the physiological process of addiction in the brain and body active. This leads to cravings for alcohol and/or drugs and most often results in relapse.

I remember very clearly being a sugar addict as a child. I used to hide hoards of candy, cookies, etc., in my bedroom to savor all by myself. One of my favorites was Blackjacks and when I would run across the street to pick up some bread and milk for the family, I would sneak a bag of Blackjacks in the mix and hide it in my room. I had four brothers and sisters and it was often hard to get the amount of sugar I wanted because they would eat it, so I would stash mine away.

We had a little store downtown that had a whole isle of penny candy. I used to collect all the change I could find in the cushions of the couch, sneak down to the store, and get as much candy as I possibly could and hide it in my room to eat when I was alone. I was in pure heaven with a bag of Fireballs to suck on. I would also make batches of no bake oatmeal cookies when my parents weren't home and then hide the whole batch in my room and wash the dishes up very quickly, so no one would know I made them.

I was sneaking around like an alcoholic hiding my cookies and candy. If you look back on your life, you'll probably remember some similar incidents; and if you look around any AA meeting, you can clearly see addiction to sugar, caffeine and nicotine going strong.

Some people are born with a deficiency in serotonin and/or dopamine or circumstances in their childhood like child abuse or neglect may result in deficiencies, and cravings for sweets is often the bodies way of trying to get more serotonin and dopamine. However, since most people are unaware of the dangers of sugar, they eat white refined sugar instead of whole and natural foods and set off the process of addiction.

Although, not part of the true addiction process to sugar, other factors that cause cravings for sugar and can perpetuate the addiction to sugar are Candida overgrowth, sugar allergy and hypoglycemia. Candida makes you crave sugar because it wants to eat it. Food allergies, as you'll learn in that chapter, often result in cravings for the allergenic food in the advanced stage of allergy and many people are unknowingly allergic to sugar. As we saw in the previous chapter, hypoglycemia creates cravings for sugar as well because of fluctuating blood sugar levels. So in order to overcome sugar addiction, these issues must be addressed as well.

In order to stop cravings for alcohol and allow the neurotransmitters to normalize, the alcoholic must remove refined sugar from their diet completely and keep it out.

Kicking the Sugar Habit

Removing sugar from your diet is not as easy as you think, because sugar is used as an additive for preservation and to make things more palatable. So it is basically found in most commercial foods. Unless you are living a health-conscious lifestyle and picking your food very wisely, sugar is in your catsup, morning cereal, spaghetti sauce, soup, salad dressing, peanut butter, pancake syrup, bread, yogurt, you name it and it probably has sugar in it. They even put sugar in your salt. You must learn to read labels very carefully to eliminate sugar from your diet.

Other steps to take to help you kick the sugar habit are as follows:

- Keep sugar and all sugar products out of the house, so you won't be tempted and give in during times of stress and hunger.

- Eat more protein.

- When you go to a social event, take your own food, or eat before going.

- Use alternative whole foods snacks such as bananas, pears, berries, dates, nuts and seeds in place of sweets.

- Exercising will reduce cravings.

- Glutamine is very effective for reducing cravings of all sorts, but should be balanced with other amino acids and nutrients.

- Get emotional support.

- Keep healthy snacks on hand at all times for when cravings come on.

- A chromium supplement may be helpful.

- When cravings for sweets arise, eat protein instead.

- Don't skip meals.

Be patient and forgiving of yourself. It will take time to be successful. More than likely you will fall off the wagon repeatedly. Get back on and start again.

Once sugar addiction is set in motion, honey, molasses, fructose, maple syrup, date sugar, maple sugar, brown rice syrup and all other forms of sugar will also set off cravings for more sweets and may be addictive as well. For some alcoholics, they also trigger cravings for a drink. These foods, although not as detrimental to our health as white refined sugar, still contribute to hypoglycemia, type 2 diabetes, obesity, Candida overgrowth, etc. as well, if they are eaten frequently, because they impact the adrenal glands, insulin and blood sugar in a similar way. This is also true for organic sugar, which is falsely believed to be healthy by many.

For alcoholics who have a biological inability to metabolize sugar properly, all forms of sugar need to be removed from the diet, especially in the early stages of recovery. Many people find that they must also remove or restrict even whole fruits that have high sugar content, such as bananas, grapes, dates, raisins and figs. Once neurotransmitters have balanced and the endocrine system has repaired to some degree, then some natural sweets may be brought back into the diet, as long as they are small servings on an infrequent basis.

Nicotine

Most of us are aware of the vast amount of health risks associated with cigarette smoking that should be motivation to quit, such as heart disease and cancer, so we won't even go into those obvious points. However, for the alcoholic, it is a much deeper issue. We're talking about addiction here. The bold and blatant truth is that if you are still smoking cigarettes, then you are still a drug addict.

Almost all alcoholics are smokers. It's pretty rare to find an alcoholic that doesn't smoke. As a matter of fact, as we mentioned in the opening chapter, even the founding father of Alcoholics Anonymous, Bill Wilson, died of a disease directly related to smoking, emphysema, and so did the co-founder, Dr. Bob Smith; he died from cancer, which was likely linked to his heavy smoking as well. They go hand in hand and perpetuate one another and there are a variety of physiological reasons for this.

For one, when you smoke it constricts your blood vessels, but when you drink alcohol it dilates them. Therefore, smoking and drinking is an antidote to one another and create a vicious cycle in your body for needing each one to counteract the other.[7] If you continue to smoke after getting sober, you set yourself up for possible relapse as your body will still desire alcohol to self-medicate this cycle.

Next, let's take a look at nicotine. Nicotine is an addictive drug. It is a powerful neurotoxin. It is a poison so powerful that it is sometimes used commercially as a pesticide and it affects the body in a similar way as pesticides do. We'll be discussing the impact of pesticides and their relationship to addiction in further detail in chapter ten. Not only that, nicotine also contains high amounts of actual pesticides, herbicides, fungicides and fertilizers that are applied to it while it is growing. One cigarette contains approximately 10 mg of nicotine. Only about 1 to 2 mgs of nicotine are inhaled while smoking one cigarette. If an adult were to ingest one drop of pure nicotine, it would kill them.[8]

Addiction to nicotine is one of the hardest addictions to overcome. It causes changes in the brain that are similar to the brain changes created by heroin and cocaine addiction. It is often considered the gateway drug or the drug of entry, meaning that this is where addiction originates for some people and then leads on to alcohol and/or other heavier drug usage. New research indicates that nicotine actually incites a biological urge to drink more. Yes, it actually creates cravings for alcohol.[9]

This is largely the result of the tremendous impact nicotine has on our neurotransmitters. Nicotine stimulates the release of excessive amounts of acetylcholine, norepinephrine, epinephrine, vasopressin, arginine, and the all-important dopamine. Remember, dopamine is the neurotransmitter involved in the reward pathway that gives us feelings of well-being and pleasure when we drink alcohol. It stimulates the brain to produce more endorphins. Endorphins are the body's natural painkillers and produce a feeling of euphoria.[10]

Another crucial aspect is that cigarettes contain over 4,000 toxic chemicals of which at least 43 of them are carcinogenic. Some of them include, but are not limited to, arsenic (also known as rat poison), benzene, tar, carbon monoxide, nitrogen oxides, cadmium, formaldehyde, ammonia, hydrogen cyanide (also known as gas chamber gas), acetone (also known as nail polish remover), and here's the big one—acetaldehyde.[11] Remember our lengthy discussion about acetaldehyde, its detrimental effects on the body and its relationship to alcoholism in our Candida chapter? If not, you may want to go back there and read it over again. When the alcoholic continues to smoke, you keep yourself stuck in that whole acetaldehyde addiction process. It will feed your body with higher amounts of acetaldehyde and this will trigger the opiate-like substances that can make you crave alcohol. Ammonia and acetaldehyde are intentionally added to cigarettes to increase the addictive potential of nicotine while other ingredients are intentionally added to alter your brain chemistry so you're more receptive to nicotine.[12]

The last critical factor related to smoking is that nicotine causes the liver to release high levels of sugar, which gives you a nice relaxing high, but as we've learned, high levels of sugar in the blood alert the pancreas to release insulin to bring the sugar levels down. This results in a plunging of the blood sugar level and hypoglycemia symptoms like fatigue, irritability, intense hunger, cravings for sweets, alcohol or caffeine occur. Thus, you crave another cigarette to get relief from the hypoglycemia symptoms. It's impossible to keep blood sugar levels stable if you're a smoker. Not only that, one of the ingredients added to cigarettes is sugar. So you're filling your body with sugar even if you're not eating it, and giving the neurotransmitters in the reward pathway and serotonin pathway a double whammy when you light up. Both the sugar in the cigarettes and the liver releasing it in the bloodstream will also feed Candida yeast and make it impossible to make improvements in that area as well.

This is also why smoking works as an appetite suppressant. When you eat, it takes about 20 minutes for your food to bring your sugar levels up, but when you smoke it happens in a only a matter of seconds. It provides you with an instant sense of false satiation and why people usually gain weight when they quit smoking. Once you stop giving your body nicotine, it takes time for the body to learn how to adjust its blood sugar levels on its own. Additionally, this roller-coaster ride with blood sugar takes the adrenal glands on a vicious ride and also contributes to depleting the adrenal glands in the same way as sugar.

To illustrate this more clearly, let's look at what happens in the brain when you smoke. You light up the cigarette and inhale. Within seconds the nicotine is in your brain. Once in the brain, it stimulates the release of high levels of dopamine, acetylcholine and other neurotransmitters. This results in the relaxing high you feel. A few seconds later nicotine enters the liver and stimulates the liver to dump sugar into the blood stream. You now get another emotional boost from the sugar high and feel energized and confident. However, now the pancreas recognizes there's too much sugar in the blood stream and releases insulin to bring it down. Your blood sugar level crashes to levels lower than you started out with and at the same time your neurotransmitters have stopped releasing in excess. You now feel tired, cranky, depressed, irritable, nervous, and hungry and need another cigarette. Over time, as this pattern continues, the brain becomes desensitized to the high levels of neurotransmitters and requires more and more nicotine to achieve the same feelings of pleasure. In time, the only way to function normally or feel relaxed, pleasure, etc., is to have a cigarette.[13]

What we see here is that nicotine affects the brain in the exact same way that alcohol does. Once again we find a substance that stimulates the reward pathway in the brain in the same manner that drugs and alcohol do. Remember the reward pathway is what gives you the incredible euphoric feeling that leads to addiction of drugs and alcohol. If the recovering alcoholic continues to smoke in sobriety, the nicotine is keeping the body and brain in a physiological state of addiction. The process of addiction has never stopped and this leads to cravings for alcohol and or drugs. Since the reward pathway is still in a state of hyper-stimulation, it never has a chance to normalize; thus putting the alcoholic at high risk of relapse. One addiction leads to another.

Caffeine

Caffeine is a stimulant drug that has serious negative effects on our central nervous system, adrenal system and cardiovascular system. It is found in a variety of plants and in nature it acts as a natural pesticide by paralyzing insects that feed upon the plant.[14] As well as sugar and cigarettes, it is one of the most widely used and socially acceptable mind-altering substances in society. Its effects on the body and brain are similar to many major drugs like amphetamines, cocaine and heroin.

In the brain there is a chemical that acts as a neurotransmitter, called adenosine. It is responsible for making you sleepy. The caffeine molecule looks very similar to adenosine, so when you drink caffeine, it tricks the brain into taking the caffeine molecule instead of the adenosine molecule and this prevents you from getting tired.

Just like any other addictive drug, after chronic consumption of caffeine, tolerance develops. The brain adapts by modifying its adenosine receptors and over a short period of time more and more caffeine is needed to achieve the same results. The more you consume caffeine, the more you need. Pretty soon you can't function or feel normal unless you drink caffeine.

Consumption of caffeine also results in an increase in the release of a variety of neurotransmitters like norepinephrine, acetylcholine, glutamate and, yes, the all important dopamine, which results in the improved mood and clarity in thinking often experienced by caffeine drinkers. Its impact on dopamine is similar to that of amphetamines and it decreases production of serotonin. Caffeine also interferes with GABA, another important neurotransmitter involved in addiction, by preventing it from performing its functions, like stress management, impulse control and mood control.

Caffeine elevates our stress hormones. It triggers the body to release adrenalin, norepinephrine and epinephrine, the hormones involved in our stress response system, also known as the fight or flight response. Stress hormones are needed when we are facing a dangerous, threatening or emergency situation; they provide us with extra strength, energy and alertness to deal effectively with the situation at hand. However, in the case of caffeine, there is no emergency to deal with and your body is put into the stressful fight or flight response on an ongoing basis for no reason at all. Your body is in a chronic state of stress.[15]

An hour or so after you ingest caffeine the stress hormones dissipate and then you feel tired, hungry and cranky, so you reach for more caffeine. This cycle puts excessive wear and tear on the adrenal glands and over time leads to adrenal exhaustion.[16] As we discussed in the sugar section, this means the adrenal glands no longer function adequately and leads to a variety of problems like hypoglycemia, fatigue, irritability and inability to handle stress that often lead the alcoholic to relapse as they attempt to relieve these symptoms.

Another crucial factor is the effect caffeine has on our blood sugar. It is a major contributing factor to hypoglycemia as it makes it impossible to stabilize blood sugar. As we learned previously, keeping the blood sugar stable is a priority for the alcoholic. When you drink caffeine, your liver dumps large doses of sugar into your blood stream. This results in the sugar high that we already discussed, and then insulin is released to control the blood sugar levels and the blood sugar drops very rapidly to below normal levels. When blood sugar levels are too low, then hypoglycemia symptoms such as irritability, fatigue, depression, and cravings for sugar and alcohol may occur. Additionally, this releasing of sugar will also feed Candida yeast and interfere in your efforts to eradicate its overgrowth.

What we want to pay special attention to here is that once again we have a substance that affects the important neurotransmitter, dopamine, involved in the reward pathway in the same manner as drugs and alcohol. When the alcoholic trying to stay sober drinks caffeine, the physiological process of addiction is still in play on a lower scale; but because caffeine doesn't give the same intensity of a boost to the neurotransmitters as alcohol or drugs, it often leads to cravings for alcohol or drugs and results in relapse.

In my work as a sobriety coach, I have found that the caffeine connection is a major downfall for many people and a frequent cause of relapse. They will make great progress in staying sober by following the hypoglycemic diet, giving up sugar, taking their nutrients and not smoking, but then they have a cup of coffee and they are off and running. It is one of the most difficult hurdles for people to overcome because of society's acceptance of caffeine. Most people fail to see how harmful it is and encourage the caffeine addict to continue drinking it. As there is with sugar, a great deal of reprogramming the mind is required.

Sugar, Nicotine and Caffeine Conclusion

It's very important to note here that all three of these substances fulfill the criteria of being an addictive substance that we discussed earlier. On the psychological level the user uses them compulsively, on the physiological level they each stimulate the reward pathway in the same manner as harder drugs and alcohol, and they each result in building tolerance and dependence. All three of them stimulate the reward pathway in the same manner as alcohol and drugs.

The bottom line is that the most essential factor for long-term recovery from alcoholism or drug addiction is to keep caffeine, sugar and nicotine out of your body or cravings to drink or drug will continue. In order to quit one, you must quit the others. They are all interconnected and perpetuate the addiction to one another.

When you continue to engage in any substance that simulates the physiological process of alcohol or drug addiction in the brain, then your brain and body are still addicted. You have not stopped the physiological cycle of addiction. It has only been replaced with something else. They all work as substitutes and you are still an active addict as far as your brain is concerned.

This is one of the main reasons that traditional treatment has such a low success rate for recovery. All alcoholics and drug addicts continue to use sugar, caffeine and/or nicotine. The boost in neurotransmitters from sugar, caffeine and nicotine isn't as intense and quick as alcohol or drugs and it eventually leads you back to the drink or the drug to experience that intensity again. It is responsible for the constant battle of cravings for alcohol and/or drugs. We can very clearly see that this is true by taking a look around any AA meeting. Most everyone in there is still an addict of some kind. They are eating donuts laced with sugar, pounding down the coffee and smoking cigarettes.

Additionally, sugar, nicotine and caffeine are major instigators and perpetuators of Candida overgrowth and hypoglycemia, so it is impossible to make significant improvement in either one of these crucial areas if one continues to eat sugar, smoke and drink caffeine.

To break these addictions, you must be willing to be honest with yourself and accept the truth. You must change your mindset and view these substances for what they truly are—addictive drugs. You must not allow yourself to participate in society's delusion and denial. You must give up all addictive substances in order to achieve successful sobriety without cravings.

Eight

Food Allergies

"As scarce as truth is, the supply has always been in excess of the demand."
~Josh Billings

Dr. Theron Randolph, who is the leading pioneer in environmental medicine, contends that alcoholism is a symptom of advanced food allergy. In his practice he has found that it is not the alcohol that one is addicted to, it is the food source of which the alcoholic beverage is made. Alcoholic beverages are made from food such as malted grains like barley, wheat, corn or rice or fermented grapes. Alcoholics have a food allergy to these substances. In advanced food allergy, the individual craves the allergenic food.[1]

When you're allergic to a particular food, they are not metabolized correctly in the body and result in psychoactive chemicals that give you a temporary high similar to alcohol.[2] Yes, here it is again, these substances interfere in neurotransmitter functioning and simulate the physiological process of addiction in the brain like addictive substances and lead to cravings for alcohol and/or drugs. Randolph proposes that the alcoholic is craving what the beverage is made from, not the alcohol itself. The alcohol serves as a catalyst to help the food be absorbed more quickly, because alcohol doesn't have to be digested so it is absorbed rapidly throughout the gastrointestinal tract.

This is another one of the reasons why most alcoholics struggle to stay sober and relapse is so common. Because, when alcoholics put the alcohol down, they are continuing to eat wheat, sugar, corn, etc., and when they eat these foods it triggers cravings. The food itself cannot provide the quick fix that the alcohol can provide because of its rapid absorption and this results in cravings to drink or drug.

Food allergies, food sensitivity or food intolerance is very prevalent in our society but often goes unacknowledged or undetected. There's very little awareness in the mainstream medical society about the deep impact it can have on physical and mental health.

Sensitivity to food occurs when the naturally occurring chemical composition of the food eaten has a direct effect on the brain or body. They exist without IgE antibodies and, therefore, can be hard to detect. It is believed that about 80 percent of the population has undiagnosed food sensitivities, while true food allergy occurs in only about 5 percent of the population.

Although the terms are often used interchangeably, a true food allergy is not the same as a food sensitivity, which is also known as food intolerance. Food allergy creates an immediate and pronounced effect like breathing difficulties or anaphylactic shock and is IgE mediated, while reactions from food sensitivity or food intolerance are usually delayed or hidden and the symptoms are not as recognizable. They are IgG mediated. A good book to read on this subject is called *Your Hidden Food Allergies are Making you Fat* by Roger Deutsch and Rudy Rivera, M.D.

Food sensitivities or intolerance are often associated with poor digestion and, therefore, with the assimilation of partly undigested proteins can also directly disrupt neurotransmitter function. Another excellent book that provides extensive information on this topic is called *Brain Allergies* by William Philpott, MD, if you'd like to learn more.

Sensitivities or allergies to food can be caused by a variety of factors such as a weak immune system, heredity, repeated exposure to the same foods over and over, Candida overgrowth and leaky gut syndrome. The individual living with food allergies or sensitivities often faces a lack of support from friends, family and the uneducated medical community, because they refuse to believe or acknowledge that food can cause such debilitating symptoms.

The effects of food allergies or food sensitivities on the brain can be exhibited in numerous ways. Here are some of the most common symptoms:

- ADHD

- irritability

- mood swings

- depression (mild to severe—can even create feelings of suicide)

- anxiety (mild or that seen in anxiety attacks)

- aggression

- violence

- euphoria

- anger or rage

- hyperactivity

- headaches (mild to migraine)

- extreme fatigue and sleepiness (even narcolepsy)

- inability to remember and concentrate

- listlessness

It is not only our mental state that is affected by food allergies or sensitivities, but our physical health as well. If you have an allergy, sensitivity or an intolerance to a particular food, it can cause a host of physical symptoms that may include some of the following and many more:

- muscle pain

- weight gain

- edema

- asthma

- itchy eyes

- aching legs

- arthritis pain

- myalgias

- palpitations

- irregular heartbeat

- indigestion

- heartburn

- irritable bowel syndrome

- diarrhea

- constipation

- coughing

- breathing difficulties

- rashes

- itching

- indigestion

- stomachaches

- earaches

- sinus infections/irritations/congestion

- shaking

- restlessness

- restless leg syndrome

Two very common symptoms of food sensitivity or allergy are recurring earaches seen in children and arthritis. Eliminating the offending food, which is likely to be dairy or soy, can often clear chronic childhood ear infections. Sufferers of arthritis can often find relief by eliminating foods in the nightshade family, such as potatoes, onions or tomatoes.

While it is possible for any food under the sun to create symptoms, these are some of the most common culprits:

- chocolate

- wheat

- dairy

- eggs

- corn

- soy

- cane sugar

- beef

- pork

- chicken

- apples

- grapes

- yeast

- peanuts

- coffee

Sometimes it is not the actual food causing the sensitivity, but the additives and preservatives in the food that is detrimental to our physical and emotional health such as:

- preservatives

- nitrates

- pesticides

- food colorings or dyes

- fungicides

Some of the most common symptoms from additives and preservatives are anxiety, hyperactivity, learning disabilities and disturbances in mood and thought to name a few. Considerable scientific data is emerging that links food additive intolerance to various mental and physical disorders, especially hyperactivity.[3]

Dr. Schuitemaker cites a study that found a dramatic effect on antisocial behavior of criminal children by changing the diet to whole healthy foods and eliminating foods that contained coloring, preservatives, additives and sugar. Antisocial acts were diminished in 80 percent of the subjects. In a follow-up study they used the same diet and reduced antisocial acts by 50 percent. What was most interesting about this study was that the offenders who had been convicted of the worst crimes were the ones who benefited the most. The institutions that cooperated in this study were so impressed with the improvements they did not return to their old diet menu.[4]

How Do You Know if You Have Food Allergies or Sensitivities?

Foods that you crave are a good indication that this food is an offending substance for you. This may be confusing because initially you feel good after eating a food you crave, but then after the initial positive response, the negative symptoms occur and then your craving for the food may return. Foods that you have a strong aversion to may also be a clue that this is one of your food allergies.

Do you crave specific foods in the same way you crave alcohol? If so, then you probably have food allergies. When I first learned I had Candida and a cane sugar allergy and I was trying to give up sweets, I literally wrestled a friend to the floor in the aisle of a grocery store for a Twinkie. I had asked her to help me kick my sugar habit so she was intervening by taking the Twinkie away from me, but I wouldn't have it. After fighting to the death for it, I ran to the checkout line, out the door and shoved it in my mouth. Now this is clearly the behavior of a sugar addict.

The biochemical process that occurs with a food allergy can trigger loss of control such as my behavior described above and binging. I struggled with bouts of food binging for a couple years when I first gave up cigarettes and began to work on my food allergies. When you try and give up the foods you are allergic or sensitive to, you may even have withdrawal symptoms similar to that of alcohol withdrawal.

To discover if food allergies or sensitivities are creating your symptoms, you can begin by keeping a journal of what you eat and how you feel. Jot down notes of your mood state, energy levels and physical symptoms. Keep in mind that some symptoms are delayed. Meaning they occur a good period of time after the food is eaten. For example, pain in the joints may occur the following day after eating an offending food rather than immediately after eating the food. The book I mentioned a little earlier called *Your Hidden Food Allergies are Making You Fat* can help you understand this aspect in more depth as well.

Sometimes your reaction to a food may be dependent upon other factors such as how much of the food you consume, or did you consume it on an empty stomach, what other foods have you eaten in conjunction with it or how frequently have you consumed it. It is possible, for example, that you only have a reaction to a particular food if you eat it on an empty stomach, or you only have a reaction if you eat it in conjunction with some other particular food or only when you have eaten it three times in one week.

To help you isolate your food villains, it is best to seek out the care of a qualified medical professional who is knowledgeable about food allergies and sensitivity. It is unlikely that your local General Practitioner will be able to help you with this. Once again, like I mentioned in the Candida section, your best choice for a competent doctor knowledgeable in these areas is a Doctor of Environmental Medicine, a Doctor of Osteopathic Medicine, a Doctor of Orthomolecular Medicine or a Naturopathic Doctor and can be found by contacting the American Holistic Medical Association, the American Academy of Environmental Medicine, the American Holistic Health Association or the American Association of Naturopathic Physicians.

Once you find the appropriate health care professional, they can help guide you in this process with perhaps food allergy testing or elimination diets (meaning you eliminate suspected foods to see if there is improvement in your symptoms). It is very important to be under the care of a physician during elimination diets because once you remove an offending food from your diet and reintroduce it, severe life-threatening symptoms can possibly occur. This is rare, but possible. Standard food allergy testing will not identify food sensitivities. This requires a different kind of test. I recommend the ALCAT test.

After your offending foods are identified, you can improve your mental and physical health by removing these foods from your diet or following what is called a rotation diet. Some people may continue eating the foods they are allergic to by receiving allergy injections, but this doesn't work for sensitivities. A health care professional can help you determine which of these paths is best for you and will also help you identify any other nutritional imbalances you may have such as deficiencies that may also contribute to your symptoms.

10 Tips for Sticking to Your Dietary Restrictions

Giving up some of your favorite foods will be difficult, but don't despair; it may not be a life sentence. A lot of times tolerance can be built back up for a particular food by keeping it out of the diet for a period of time. This time period can be 6 to 48 months. If your symptoms are mild, then perhaps the time period will be closer to 6 months. If your symptoms are more severe, then it will probably be closer to the 48 months. Although, some very strong sensitivities may never be overcome.

There are a variety of alternatives you can find to replace the foods you remove. For instance, if you are an ice cream lover and you must give up dairy, there are several delicious ice cream alternatives, or if you are a chocolate lover, you can learn to savor the delicious flavor of carob. Both of these can be found in health food stores.

The following tips will be helpful not only for staying away from allergenic foods, but also in kicking the sugar and caffeine habit.

1. If you are going to a social event, take your own appropriate food with you. It is very tempting to throw your restrictions aside to be part of the crowd and fit in. Pack up your own little meal and take it with you. Yes, you may feel embarrassed at first, but over time you will become more comfortable. You could also try eating a healthy meal at home

before going to the event so that you won't be hungry and then you can just skip the eating aspect of the event and enjoy other aspects.

2. When you are going to be away from home during meal times or snack times, pack up a little lunch in a small cooler and keep it with you. If hunger hits you when you are out and about, it is very easy to give in to unhealthy temptations that you will pay for later. Take your own water as well, so you have something pure and healthy to drink.

3. Find alternatives to replace your restrictions. If you can't eat wheat, then get products made with alternative grains. If you can't eat chocolate, then try some tasty carob. Use sugar alternatives like agave and brown rice syrup. If you can't have dairy, there are numerous delicious dairy alternatives that can satisfy your craving for ice cream or cheese. It is essential to find alternatives, so that you will not feel deprived. If you are feeling deprived, you will be more likely to cheat.

4. Once a week, reward yourself with something you aren't usually allowed to have. For instance, once a week allow yourself to have a healthy sweet. Something made with a healthy sweetener, not sugar. Replace sugar with things such as dates, bananas, pears, nuts, raisins, agave, brown rice syrup or stevia. These sweets are whole foods and will not damage the body like sugar. They will help wean you off sugar.

5. Exercise regularly, at least three times a week for 25-30 minutes. It not only burns off calories, but it improves immune function, and boosts self-esteem by stimulating our happy hormones. Exercise is essential, but it should be mild exercise, not anything excessive or intensive, or this will over stimulate neurotransmitters.

6. Call a friend. If you can get a buddy system going, this can be very helpful. Call your friend during times of weakness and talk it out. Make arrangements with your friend ahead of time and have a plan of action. Have your friend remind you of your goals or how badly you will feel after you eat them. Have specific phrases for your friend to repeat back to you.

7. When cravings come, remind yourself that a craving usually only lasts a few minutes and it will be gone. Remind yourself that you will be able to have your reward on your specified day. Ride it out. After you ride it out a few times, it will become easier.

8. Reframe your thinking. For me it is simple to avoid unhealthy foods, because I simply do not desire to eat poison. I don't want to do that to myself. So try to reframe your thinking about the foods that you desire. Try to think of them as poisons instead of delicious forbidden treats.

9. Don't let emotions build up. Express yourself regularly. Keeping emotions pent up can cause you to eat unconsciously. Unexpressed feelings can also decrease self-esteem; and if self-esteem is low, you will be more likely to give in to cravings.

10. Forgive yourself. When you fall down and give in to your temptations, don't beat yourself up for it. Forgive yourself and let it go immediately. Just start over again. No harm done. To criticize will only be self-defeating. Don't let the weak moment become a reason to stay off the restrictions for a longer period of time or to give up completely. Just pick yourself up and begin again. Don't think of it as failure, but rather as a minor setback. Change happens slowly and usually involves many setbacks.

Change is always difficult and changing your diet can prove to be one of the most difficult to achieve. If you are eliminating just one food, this may not be as big a challenge as someone who has found that they have 10 or 12 offending foods. You may be looking at profound life alterations such as no eating out, taking your own food to social gatherings, etc. You will probably have many setbacks and struggles on your new path. You may even grieve the loss of your beloved food. Be patient and forgiving of yourself, but also be persistent and self-disciplined. If you fall off the food allergies, sugar or caffeine wagon and give in to temptation, don't beat yourself up. Just brush yourself off and get back on. Understand that it is a process and seek emotional support if necessary.

Nine

Nutritional Deficiencies

"You shall know the truth, and the truth shall make you mad."
~Aldous Huxley

Alcoholics are deficient in a variety of extremely important nutrients, which leads to malfunctioning or depleted neurotransmitters and a sea of psychological and physiological symptoms that often result in relapse. Thus, identifying and correcting these deficiencies is another essential step in maintaining long-term sobriety.

The lack of nutrients in the diet is falsely believed to be rare in industrialized societies while, in reality, nutritional deficiencies in our society are practically epidemic. Up to 50 percent of our population may fail to ingest even the recommended daily allowance for various vitamins and minerals.[1] The leading cause for this issue is the standard American diet that is high in sugar, starches, refined foods, processed foods and simple carbohydrates. It is estimated that at least 75 percent of the western diet consists of processed foods, and on the average each person consumes 8–10 pounds of food additives each year.[2] Processed foods with food additives are stripped of their nutritional value and, therefore, are extremely lacking in the proper nutrients needed for the mind and body to function properly.

Recent research indicates that the average American diet has less than 80 percent of the recommended daily allowance (RDA) of one or more of the following nutrients: calcium, magnesium, iron, zinc, copper and manganese. The average American diet provides only 40 percent of the RDA of magnesium, and leading authorities estimate 80 percent of the population is deficient in magnesium, 68 percent of the population receives less than two-thirds RDA of zinc, and 80 percent of the population is deficient in chromium.

Diets that are high in sugar, white flour, refined foods, pesticides, and additives and low in nutrients lead to many health conditions including a malfunctioning endocrine system and depleted adrenal glands. Our diets are not healthy because we eat food that is grown in overworked soil, sprayed with numerous toxic chemicals and fertilizers, then refined and processed with mass amounts of food colorings, preservatives and dyes. When we ingest these foods, we become toxic and malnourished.[3]

One of the first indications of a nutritional deficiency is psychological disturbance.[4] The brain is a very delicate, sensitive organ and controls our mood, thoughts, perceptions, emotions and behavior. It has a protective barrier called the blood/brain barrier that selectively transports nutrients and other substances that are needed for brain function.

The production of proper neurotransmitters is highly dependent upon this uptake from the blood, so if the nutrients are inadequate, then imbalances of the neurochemicals of the brain can occur and result in disturbance of thought, mood, emotion, perceptions or behavior.

Disorders such as depression, addiction, hyperactivity and learning disorders, anxiety, alcoholism, schizophrenia, and even behavioral problems such as crime and violence or conduct disorder and anti-social personality respond very well to dietary changes and nutritional supplementation. Dr. Linus Pauling, the winner of two Nobel Prizes in Medicine, believes that every sickness, every disease and every ailment can be traced to a mineral deficiency.

Most people are living on a diet that consists of nothing but sugar and highly refined foods. Remember these foods contain little, if any, nutritional value. Not only that, as we mentioned in the sugar chapter, in order for your body to metabolize sugar, it depletes your vitamin and mineral levels.

We should absorb balanced levels of minerals and vitamins from our food, but this does not occur because our food is stripped of its nutrients in processing and our food is grown in soil that is depleted of minerals and vitamins. Soil is destroyed with chemical fertilizers, insecticides, overuse of soil, etc., which makes our society more deficient every day.

Minerals work as building blocks for our bones, muscles, teeth, nerves, connective tissue and body fluids. They are cofactors to enzymes that speed up the biochemical reactions required by the body to function effectively and are also cofactors with vitamins. Each vitamin needs a specific one to make it work. Vitamins can't be utilized if minerals are not present. Therefore, if you're taking vitamin supplementation without the proper mineral balance in your body, it is useless.

Minerals are necessary for every biochemical process and activity of the body. They are responsible for maintaining the (pH) balance of the body, proper cellular metabolism, nerve conduction, muscle function, organ function, hormonal secretion of glands and digestive competence. They are also necessary for activation and utilization of amino acids, carbohydrates, enzymes, fats, oils, phytochemicals, proteins, sugars and vitamins, providing nutrients into our cells, and removing wastes from all cells, tissues, fluids, glands and organs. They provide structure and function for the hair, skin, nails and five senses. They are essential to the anti-oxidation process and protect us from toxic heavy metals, such as mercury, cadmium, aluminum, arsenic and lead.

If minerals are not present in the body in adequate amounts, the body will find alternative pathways to use, which are less efficient, and this will lead to chemistry imbalances, which leads to deterioration in the organs, glands and body systems. The result will be poor health and degenerative health conditions.

Most of us know that osteoporosis is linked to a deficiency in calcium, but most are not aware that diabetes and hypoglycemia are connected to chromium and vanadium, and that cancer and heart disease are connected to selenium and copper. Anxiety and depression are linked to selenium, magnesium and many others. Muscle pain and spasms are connected to magnesium.

The list of symptoms that can develop as a result of a deficiency is vast, but some of the most common include: depression, thyroid disorders, compromised immune function, liver dysfunction, anxiety, hypertension, headaches, migraines, insomnia, stroke, arthritis, hypoglycemia, diabetes, cancer, osteoporosis, arteriosclerosis, high cholesterol, fatigue, PMS, food cravings and binging, obsessions, muscle pain and spasms, asthma, heart disease, irregular heartbeat, Candida, and even cancer. In more serious cases, even an unexpected sudden onset of death, which is often unexplained.

There are two types of minerals—macro and trace. The body needs larger amounts of macro and a small amount of trace. Macro may consist of calcium, magnesium, phosphorus, sodium, potassium, chloride and sulphur, while trace may include manganese, iron, copper, iodine, zinc, cobalt, selenium, boron, chromium and molybdenum.

Minerals are the cornerstones to good health. They are essential for all prevention and treatment programs. It is important to work with a physician knowledgeable in this area and not treat yourself, because supplements should be highly absorbable, balanced and individualized. The symptoms of mineral deficiency overlap with many other illness symptoms and it will be necessary to rule out or in other factors that may need addressed.

The other leading contributor for nutritional deficiencies is Candida overgrowth. As we discussed in the Candida section, acetaldehyde, which is a byproduct of Candida released into the body, is responsible for deficiencies in B1 or thiamin, vitamin B3/niacin, vitamin B5, NAD, and pyridoxal-5-phosphate (P5P).

Vitamin B1 or thiamin is crucial for proper functioning of the brain and nerves, essential for the production of adenosine triphosphate (ATP) bioenergy in all body cells and the production of acetylcholine, the brains major neurotransmitter. A lack of adequate acetylcholine is found in disorders such as Alzheimer's. A deficiency in vitamin B1 leads to the syndrome often found in chronic alcoholics called Wernicke-Korsakoff syndrome and is distinguished by poor memory, impaired neuromuscular coordination, visual disturbances and mental confusion. Even a mild deficiency in this vitamin can result in impaired brain function and be exhibited in symptoms such as fatigue, emotional instability, confusion, indifference or lack of interest, headaches, depression, irritability, feelings of impending doom and insomnia.

NAD is critical for burning sugar and fat into energy for the cells, and it functions as a catalyst in the production of many of the major brain neurotransmitters like serotonin. It's also crucial in the production of enzymes that break down alcohol and acetaldehyde. In addition to being our happy hormones, neurotransmitters are what the body uses for nerve cells to communicate with one another.

The most severe form of niacin (also known as B3) deficiency results in the disease known as pellagra, however, even a mild deficiency will produce a host of psychological symptoms including an inability to concentrate, excessive worry, headaches, irrational or unfounded fear and suspicion, apprehension, gloomy angry or depressed perception, agitation and disruption of sleep patterns.

Acetyl coenzyme A is probably the most crucial biochemical involved in cellular biochemistry, because it's needed to power the Krebs cycle, which is what produces 90 percent of all energy needed for every cell in the brain and the body. It's also needed to produce acetylcholine, the brain's major neurotransmitter that is critical for memory, learning and concentration.

A deficiency in P5P is significant because it is the primary coenzyme essential to produce all the chief brain neurotransmitters. It's crucial to many different conversion processes in amino acids, essential fatty acids and other important vitamins like B3 or niacin and helps regulate the entry of magnesium into our cells.[5]

Alcoholics are also deficient in the all important group of B vitamins, essential fatty acids and digestive enzymes, which also have a profound impact on brain chemistry and mood. To make matters worse, once alcoholism is set into motion, then the consumption of alcohol on a regular basis itself leads to more deficiencies from an even less nutritious diet and poor absorption. Alcoholics often drink in place of a meal or eat very little, and alcohol damages the body's ability to absorb the nutrients it needs from the food you do eat.

Unfortunately, the body will run on alcohol alone because it gives a temporary boost to the system; however, this only deprives the body of even more nutrients and sets up another vicious cycle. Deficiencies create a variety of emotional and physical symptoms that make the alcoholic crave a drink in order to relieve the symptoms. The drink perpetuates the problem of deficiencies.

One of the most common deficiencies in alcoholics and the most crucial to address is amino acids. Amino acids are the building blocks for neurotransmitters. You can't have balanced neurotransmitters if you aren't getting adequate amino acids and, remember, if you don't have balanced neurotransmitters, then cravings for alcohol and/or drugs occur. Amino acids come mostly from protein and most people aren't getting enough protein. This is another reason you should eat a diet rich in protein and balanced with healthy fats when recovering from alcoholism. We'll talk in more depth about amino acids in chapter 13, so that is something you'll want to pay special attention to when we get there.

All this biochemistry talk can get a little technical and difficult to understand, but the bottom line is this: Nutritional deficiencies result in a malfunctioning brain and body that gets exhibited in a variety of undesirable and even dangerous psychological and physical symptoms. Once again, when we look over the list of symptoms that are the result of nutritional deficiencies, we see the typical profile of an alcoholic. When the recovering alcoholic addresses their nutritional deficiencies, they can alleviate the psychological symptoms that so often lead to relapse.

Since most people are eating a diet that is toxic and lacking in nutrients, nutritional deficiencies are usually present in the alcoholic or addict prior to addiction. It is one of the things that lead to addiction. We don't have enough dopamine, serotonin, GABA or glutamate and our reward pathway doesn't work properly. Drinking or drugs, as we've learned, gives that temporary boost to those neurotransmitters, so it is actually giving us something we're missing. However, in the long run, the artificial stimulation of neurotransmitters only depletes them even further and leads to the much bigger problem of addiction.

Here again is this very important issue of neurotransmitters. When your diet is deficient in the proper nutrients it needs, then your brain is deficient or out of balance in neurotransmitters. Those crucial chemicals that are responsible for feeling happy, relaxed and normal are not present or working efficiently. Your sense of well-being is in disaccord. You feel depressed, sad, anxious, tired, compulsive, confused, hyperactive and can't think clearly. When neurotransmitters are not balanced or deficient, then we crave things like alcohol, drugs, cigarettes, sugar and caffeine to give us the feelings we should have naturally.

To address deficiencies, you'll want to eat a healthy diet that will provide you with as many of these nutrients as possible and probably take a nutritional supplement. Treating yourself with random supplementation can cause problems, because too much of a particular mineral, amino acid or vitamin can create illness or disease as well. They need to be balanced and individualized to meet your specific needs. Some need to be taken in conjunction with others to work properly or taking one without another can cause a deficiency in another area.

Blood tests or urine tests can be taken to determine which minerals and vitamins you need and how much. These are not the basic tests the average MD would use. The average MD or even Nutritionist is not educated in the facts about soil depletion and the epidemic of nutritional deficiencies in our society. Once again, an alternative health doctor with a biochemical or nutritional approach like an orthomolecular doctor, doctor of environmental medicine or clinical ecologist would be educated about which tests are necessary and guide you in the proper direction. They too can be found at places like the American Holistic Medical Association, the American Academy of Environmental Medicine or www.orthomolecular.org. There are a variety of simple, yet accurate and reliable, test kits that can be purchased online as well, where you can collect your sample at home, mail the kit to the lab and receive your results in the mail.

Ten

Environmental Toxins

"Truth stood on one side and ease on the other; it has often been so."
~Theodore Parker

Scientific studies tell us that pretty much every modern day health condition, illness, syndrome, disease, problem or symptom can be linked either directly or indirectly to environmental toxins, nutrition and lifestyle choices and in no other place is this more apparent than in the case of alcoholism and addiction. However, most alcoholics are completely unaware that environmental toxins wreak havoc on crucial neurotransmitters and the reward pathway and contribute to a wide variety of physical and emotional symptoms that are often at the root of relapse.

We are all subjected to an enormous amount of environmental hazards on a daily basis. Toxins are found in your soil, water, air, construction of your home and place of employment, schools, colleges, furniture, carpeting, air fresheners, cleaning supplies, laundry soap, fabric softener, dryer sheets, shampoo, body soap, makeup, food, cooking utensils, prescriptions, over-the-counter medications and even your toothpaste.

Our soil is contaminated with pesticides, herbicides, lead, industrial pollutants, fertilizers and heavy metals to name a few. Food grown in this soil absorbs these toxins, and when we eat them, it's absorbed into our bodies. Food that is less nutritious and poisoned leads to many chronic mental and physical disorders, conditions and diseases. Our water is also contaminated with pesticides, herbicides, lead, leaching of wastes from landfills, direct discharge of industrial pollutants, fertilizers, pharmaceuticals, arsenic and heavy metals to name a few. The addition of chlorine to the drinking supply exposes all of us to a variety of risks associated with the toxic impact of chlorine on the human body.

Most people are living and working in a toxic time bomb and are totally unaware of the crucial impact it has on their emotional and physical health. The standard materials that are used to build housing and businesses are extremely hazardous to your health. Carpet, walls, floors, ceilings, roofs, cabinets, etc., contain high levels of benzene, formaldehyde and literally hundreds of different chemicals that have been linked to a vast amount of physical and mental health conditions like depression, asthma, cancer, anxiety, fatigue, insomnia and headaches.

Even the EPA, which is very reluctant to acknowledge the truth about any environmental health hazard, states that indoor air pollution in residences, offices, schools and other buildings is one of the most serious potential environmental risks to health.[1]

Air fresheners contain a variety of toxic chemicals such as benzene, formaldehyde and phthalates. Benzene and formaldehyde are linked to cancer and a variety of other conditions, and phthalates cause hormonal abnormalities such as interference with the production of testosterone, birth defects and reproductive problems. Even many air fresheners that are listed as all natural or unscented still contain these toxic chemicals. Phthalates are also found in a wide variety of other products such as cosmetics, fragrances, pharmaceuticals, vinyl, children's toys, sex toys, new cars and paint.[2]

The chemicals in dryer exhaust can cause a host of physical and/or mental health problems. This can be from your own dryer exhaust in your own home or from your neighbors that drift through the air and can contaminate a whole neighborhood. They contain toxins like alpha-terpineol, camphor, chloroform, ethanol, limonene, pentane, ethyl acetate, benzyl alcohol, benzyl acetate, which may result in some very serious central nervous disorders like Alzheimer's disease, attention deficit disorder, dementia, multiple chemical sensitivity, multiple sclerosis, Parkinson's disease, seizures, strokes, and sudden infant death syndrome. They may also provoke some other minor symptoms such as aphasia, blurred vision, disorientation, dizziness, headaches, hunger, memory loss, numbness in the face, and pain in the neck and spine.[3]

Perfume, cologne and other personal care products contain highly toxic chemicals to not only those who use them but also those around them sharing the same air space. They contain toxins such as benzaldehyde, benzyl acetate, ethyl acetate, methylene chloride and many more that are known to be carcinogenic, cause central nervous disorders, reduced motor activity, damage to the liver and kidneys, headaches, respiratory disorders, and many more.[4]

Your dish soap, laundry soap, disinfectants, floor cleaners, body soap, shampoo, toothpaste and any other personal care product or household cleanser are also hazardous to your health. They contain toxic chemicals like acetone, benzaldehyde, benzyl alcohol, alpha-terpineol, a-pinene, linool, methyl chloride, a-terpinene and many, many more, which are known to be carcinogenic, cause central nervous disorders, damage the liver and kidneys, damage the nervous system, induce asthma, leukemia, confusion, brain stupor and much, much more.[5] Many chemicals in cleaning supplies are also endocrine disruptors.

The chemicals in pesticides, perfume, air fresheners, cleaning solvents, cosmetics, natural gas, etc., alter metabolic functions, and disrupt hormones and neurotransmitters. They alter normal functioning of hormones and neurotransmitters and kill brain cells.

Cortisol, insulin, melatonin, estrogen, progesterone, testosterone, leptin, DHEA and a variety of other hormones have a very crucial role in the regulation and control of all body systems. An imbalance in hormones is very common in the general population due to a diet and environment contaminated with toxins. The human body was not designed to handle the onslaught of environmental toxins we all live with daily. The brain and the human body are extremely vulnerable to this sea of poisons and it leads to declining mental, cognitive and physical functioning.

The rise in cancer, respiratory disease, asthma, depression, arthritis, anxiety, hyperactivity, cardiovascular disease, musculoskeletal diseases, gastrointestinal disorders, hormonal problems, reproductive disorders, nervous system disorders, kidney disease, and even more minor problems such as headaches, stomach aches, nausea and rashes that people just accept as part of life are directly linked to environmental toxins.

We are only beginning to see the tip of the iceberg that these toxins have on our lives. Not only do toxins in the environment threaten nature and our planet itself, but they also have a profound impact on our mental, physical and spiritual health.

Pesticides

Pesticides and herbicides are one of the most detrimental and insidious environmental health concerns we face and are magnified by the fact that there is great resistance in our government and the general population to acknowledge the truth about how very dangerous these toxins are.

The wide use of toxic pesticides and herbicides, which are used in our society to eradicate bugs and weeds by individuals, agriculture and our government, exposes all of us to neurotoxins, carcinogens and endocrine disruptors that have detrimental effects on the nervous, immune and reproductive systems.

Pesticides were originally designed as nerve gasses for chemical warfare. They were designed to kill living things, and when it was discovered that they worked so well in killing people, they decided to use them in smaller doses to kill weeds, insects, rodents, etc. They attack the nervous system.

The chief target organ that is affected by pesticides is the brain.[6] When the brain is affected, symptoms such as loss of memory, loss of problem solving ability, inhibited intellect, paranoia, irritability, social withdrawal, schizophrenia, numbness, paralysis, poor coordination, weakness, auto immunity, headaches, dizziness, vomiting, chest pain and many more can develop.

One of the primary symptoms to develop from pesticide exposure is depression. The chief target organ of pesticides is the brain because pesticides seek out lipids and the brain is highly lipid with a high density of acetylcholinesterase, which is the target enzyme of pesticides. They inhibit the enzyme acetylcholinesterase. This enzyme controls the metabolism of our neurotransmitter acetylcholine. Acetylcholine is our primary "happy hormone." It is the basic chemical that makes the brain, all the nerves and the muscles work. Pesticides also inhibit the conversion of tryptophan into serotonin, which is another "happy hormone." Thus, if you have inhibited "happy hormones," depression develops.[7]

Organophosphate pesticides are taken directly into our nervous system (the brain, spinal cord and long nerves) and then transformed into chlorpyrifos oxon, which is actually 3,000 times more potent than the original compound. Then what is frequently done is to mix organophosphate pesticides with organochloride pesticides and then they inhibit the other happy hormones, norepinephrine and dopamine as well as serotonin.[8]

It should be very clear at this point as to why we have an epidemic of depression in our society. All of our "happy hormones" have been poisoned and inhibited. After our discussion on the importance of neurotransmitters like dopamine and serotonin in relation to alcoholism, we can see how this can lead a person to drink or drugs. When the neurotransmitters are inhibited, we self-medicate to bring them back up and try to feel better.

Pesticides are also a leading contributor to anxiety as well as a variety of other psychological disorders, cancer, migraines, pain for no apparent reason, respiratory disorders, impaired mobility, cholesterol disturbances, reproductive disorders and a whole list of other conditions. They also inhibit our other enzymes like ATPase (which is needed for energy), which can result in chronic fatigue; cholesterol ester hydrolase enzyme, which creates impaired cholesterol metabolism; and the enzymes that affect how the body and mind can handle stress.[9]

In addition to the brain, pesticides also affect the kidneys, heart, liver, lungs and reproductive system. They have mutagenicity abilities (meaning they can promote cancer cells) and teratogenicity abilities (meaning can cause birth defects).

Pesticides also include insecticides, herbicides, fungicides and bactericides. Most people are not even aware that they are exposed to these toxic substances on a daily basis and have no concept of the very harmful consequences they have on our health. Pesticides are found in almost every public place, such as the grocery store, schools, office buildings, hospitals, banks, golf courses, in neighbors yards, on your food and often in your own house. Evidence suggests that there is sufficient toxicity from residual pesticides in our food, air, water, homes and yards that can cause neurotoxic damage.

According to the World Health Organization, between 1 million and 25 million people suffer with pesticide poisoning each year.[10] It is estimated that as many as 20,000 people in the U.S. will develop cancer each year from the residue of pesticide on their food.

What is most horrific about these numbers is that these are people we are aware of, but the number is much higher when we include the enormous number of people suffering from pesticide symptoms unknowingly. People with psychological disturbances, depression, migraines, pain for no apparent reason, breathing difficulties, impaired mobility, cholesterol disturbances, reproductive difficulties and a whole list of other symptoms that are often the result of pesticide exposure.

If your body can't metabolize all the pesticides taken in at once, it stores it in various tissues, organs and fat and then leaks it out slowly weeks, months or even years later. Pesticides are difficult to excrete and become stored in fat cells and can remain indefinitely wreaking havoc on your body for years. So symptoms can be delayed and come on very slowly and, therefore, the exposed person may never connect the pesticides to the symptoms.[11]

Even if we avoid the use of pesticides and avoid places where they are present, they can still make it into our homes and destroy our health. I once had to move and throw away almost all my belongings because my neighbors who were a good quarter of a mile down the road sprayed herbicide all around their fence posts and it got in my house, on my clothes and all my belongings. I was so sick I could hardly sleep for an entire year. At times I didn't think I would survive this ordeal and my body has never recovered completely.

Common Symptoms from Pesticide Exposure:

- because of the disruption of our happy hormones, one of the most common symptoms is depression
- they can and often do mimic psychological disturbance
- loss of memory
- loss of problem-solving ability, mental flexibility and abstraction capabilities
- anxiety
- schizophrenia
- sensitivity to criticism
- delayed neuropathy with numbness
- intellect dysfunction
- paranoia
- irritability
- social withdrawal
- degeneration of the retina
- nausea
- headaches
- chest pain
- dizziness
- vomiting
- tingling
- numbness
- cramps

- chemical sensitivity

- chronic fatigue

- paralysis

- poor coordination

- weakness

- auto immunity

- breathing difficulties

- muscle weakness and pain, and loss of muscle control

- impaired mobility

- uncontrollable shaking

- hyperalertness

- apathy

- heart palpitations

- tachycardia

Endocrine Disruptors

Many of the common everyday chemicals found in our household cleaning supplies, as well as personal care products, pesticides, herbicides, plastic, dioxins, phthalates, PCBs, fuels, etc., disrupt the endocrine system. These chemicals are called endocrine disruptors or hormone disruptors. Everything from your apples to your toothpaste contains endocrine disruptors and other toxic chemicals.

Hormone/Endocrine disruptors enter the body through our food, air and water, attach to our hormone receptor sites, and impede normal functioning of the endocrine system, which results in a variety of abnormal reactions throughout the body.

The endocrine system is very important because it plays a crucial role in almost every function of the body. The glands of the endocrine system include the hypothalamus, pituitary, thyroid, parathyroid, adrenals, pineal body, pancreas and the reproductive organs.

It produces hormones that are used to communicate and send messages to all the different parts of the body. Hormones regulate metabolism, sexual development and function, mental processes, growth and maintenance, prenatal development, mood, tissue function and reproduction. The endocrine system works in coordination with the nervous system to keep the body functioning properly.

Environmental toxins put excessive demands on the endocrine glands and exhausts the system—particularly the adrenal glands. As we discussed at several other points throughout this book, the adrenal glands are the main system involved in the fight or flight stress response system. Remember how important the adrenal glands and pancreas are in relation to the many issues that the alcoholic lives with like blood sugar control and that striving to have them function adequately is crucial to maintaining sobriety. We'll be talking more about the endocrine system and its relation to addiction in chapter 12 when we discuss child abuse.

When your endocrine system is not functioning properly, you can't cope with stress effectively. This results in a vicious cycle where the weakened endocrine system creates more stress and the higher levels of stress continuously weaken the endocrine system even more.

The balance of the endocrine system is very delicate and it takes only very low levels of these toxins to upset this balance and result in a variety of serious and detrimental health problems that may include damage to the nervous, immune, metabolic and reproductive systems.

A subclass of hormone/endocrine disruptors is called xenoestrogens. These chemicals actually mimic our natural estrogens, which results in an increase in the level of estrogens in the body or they may obstruct our natural hormones from doing their jobs. Alternatively, they may also modify the manner in which our natural hormones are generated, discharged and metabolized.

Endocrine disruptors also have a major role in obesity, sexual disorders and severe hormonal imbalances in women. A vast number of women these days are suffering from hormonal imbalances and metabolic damage due to these hormone disruptors. It is these hormonal imbalances and metabolic damages that are largely responsible for the devastating symptoms of menopause and extreme PMS, premenstrual syndrome.

They are one of the roots of why we see so many men and women riddled with sexual health problems such as erectile dysfunction, low sex drive, infertility, decreased sperm counts, endometriosis, prostatitis, genital abnormalities, prostate cancer, and hormonal imbalances; and the number of people suffering from these problems continues to increase at terrifying rates.

Some contributing factors can be linked to work-related stress, anxiety, marital discord, past sexual trauma, concerns about sexual performance, alcoholism, smoking, nutritional deficiencies and diet, heart disease, lack of experience and confidence, or side effects from medications. However, many people continue to suffer with a variety of sexual disorders that have nothing to do with these factors and instead are directly linked to the presence of the high level of environmental toxins that we are all exposed to on a daily basis.

The hormones released by the endocrine system rule our reproductive and sexual development and functioning. When environmental toxins like endocrine/hormone disruptors enter our body, it can result in severe malfunctioning of the reproductive system and deterioration of sexual health. In some cases they may mimic our hormones like estrogen for the female and androgen for the males, which results in hormone levels that are too high. In other cases it blocks hormones from producing or functioning properly.

Everyone knows the powerful role of hormones in relation to sexuality. When hormone functioning is disrupted by environmental toxins, it can lead to all kinds of sexual health issues that won't respond to the best marriage counseling in the world or the newest most powerful drug therapy for erectile dysfunction or low sex drive.

What is most terrifying about these toxic chemicals is that the human body is not capable of breaking them down. Therefore, once they enter the body they are very hard, if not impossible, to excrete. Instead they accumulate, get stored indefinitely in our fat cells and recirculate through our body continually causing even more damage for years to come. The damage can be irreversible.[12]

Another frightening fact is that even though we can cut down our exposure to endocrine disruptors, unless major social change takes place, we will continue to be subjected to these toxic dangerous chemicals without our consent. These toxins are found everywhere we go, so it's literally impossible to escape them completely. This makes it very difficult to keep healthy even when we do everything in our own power to do so.

Heavy metal toxicity, like mercury, is another common environmental toxin that many alcoholics have in their bodies. The most common sources of contamination are found in pollution in our air, our water, acid rain, talc powder, fish, shellfish, shark, swordfish, broken thermometers, batteries, tuna, king mackerel, vaccinations, diuretics, suppositories, wood preservatives, adhesives, floor waxes, tattoos, fabric softener, hair dies, paint, plastics, chlorine bleach, laxatives, dental fillings, aluminum cookware, pesticides, fluorescent lightbulbs—even the so called CFL environmentally friendly lightbulbs—to name a few.

They disrupt the endocrine system, nervous system and immune system, and damage the pituitary, thyroid, hippocampus and adrenal glands as well as all the other organs and systems in the body. Additionally, they also disrupt and inhibit functioning of the crucial neurotransmitter in the reward pathway, dopamine, as well as serotonin, acetylcholine and norepinephrine.

Mercury toxicity is also believed to have a synergistic relationship with Candida. It is believed that Candida eats mercury for its own survival, just like it eats everything else. Others believe that because low-level mercury toxicity suppresses the immune system, it allows yeast to proliferate. Other experts tell us that mercury works like an antibiotic when it enters the body and wipes out all the healthy bacteria which allows Candida to take over and upsets the gastrointestinal tract.

It is also believed that Candida overgrowth develops as a defense mechanism as the body struggles to cope with mercury and other heavy metals. When mercury and other heavy metals are in the body, the cell walls of Candida bind to mercury and other heavy metals and prevent it from entering the blood stream. Candida is like a sponge soaking up the mercury. It's the body's own protective mechanism. So as long as there is mercury or other heavy metals in the body then yeast is going to proliferate.

Alcoholics should be tested for heavy metal toxicity, which can be done through blood work, hair analysis, or urine. Some of the popular methods of removing heavy metals from the body include chelation, cilantro paste, chlorella, glutathione, zeolite and clay baths.

MCS

One of the most insidious and serious health conditions to develop from environmental toxins is Multiple Chemical Sensitivity—also known as MCS, Environmental Illness or Chemical Injury.

Multiple Chemical Sensitivity is defined as an "acquired disorder characterized by recurrent symptoms referable to multiple organ systems, occurring in response to demonstrable exposure to many chemically unrelated compounds at doses far below those established in the general population to cause harmful effects,"[13] or "sensitivity to chemicals. By sensitivity we mean symptoms or signs as related to chemical exposures at levels tolerated by the population at large, that is distinct from such well recognized hypersensitivity phenomenon as IgG-mediated immediate hypersensitivity reactions, contact dermatitis and hypersensitivity pneumonitis. Sensitivity may be expressed as symptoms and signs in one or more organ systems. Symptoms and signs wax and wane with exposure."[14]

The symptoms of Multiple Chemical Sensitivity are vast and numerous and usually affect many organ systems. Enzyme pathways may be inhibited and liver detoxification pathways become overloaded. The blood brain barrier is affected and neurological, immunological, respiratory, endocrine, cardiovascular, genitourinary and gastrointestinal systems are likely to be affected with the central nervous system almost always being affected.[15]

Some of the most common reactions may include, but are not limited to: exhaustion, spaciness, mental confusion, cravings, depression, fatigue, headache, migraines, difficulty concentrating, irritability, short-term memory loss, lack of coordination, shaking, trembling, visual and verbal disturbances, muscle pain, difficulty breathing, rashes, anxiety, impaired mobility, itching, disorientation, confusion, food sensitivity, excessive drowsiness, constipation, diarrhea, earaches, heart pounding, hypothyroidism, learning disabilities, elevated blood pressure, increased pulse, and many more. Some symptoms may be quite severe and include sudden intense anger accompanied by unexplainable tears and crying, falling asleep, and an inability to think or speak coherently.

Dr. Rea, the leading medical specialist in MCS, calls it an environmentally triggered disease and explains that it may be acquired either by a one-time acute exposure or from low-level long-term exposures. As well as being chemically sensitive himself, Dr. Rea treats individuals with MCS in his clinic in Dallas, Texas. He points out that in 1987 the American industry poured 22 billion pounds of toxic chemicals into the air, food and water. He adds further that the well-being of man is a function of his environment; living in polluted surroundings adversely affects our health, and as the number of dangerous environmental pollutants continues to increase so do the numbers of people sensitive to these contaminants.[16]

The U.S. Department of Health and Human Services states that Multiple Chemical Sensitivity is an acquired chronic syndrome described as a severe toxic allergic like reaction to extremely low levels of chemicals in our environment. It has developed over the past four decades and is caused by overexposure to some 100,000 new, more toxic synthetic chemicals. Research contends that a victim's body becomes unable to cleanse its tissues of chemicals to which it is exposed, either in small doses over time or from a single tremendous dose.[17]

So what does this mean in lay terms? Well, basically it means that growing numbers of people, myself included, develop serious health problems from exposures to the common everyday chemicals we find in our environment. These chemicals can be items such as scented laundry soap or fabric softener, treated fabric, perfume, cologne, disinfectants, pesticides, herbicides, household cleansers, cigarette smoke, car exhaust, gas heat or other petroleum products, air fresheners, bleach, shampoos, toothpaste, food supply, new carpet, remodeling materials, or cosmetics to name a few.

Some people are able to get injections or sublingual drops that neutralize reactions to chemicals, but this approach is not very effective for many people, only the mildly sensitive. The main treatment modality is avoidance. However, the problem is that complete avoidance of chemicals is not possible. It's like living in a minefield continuously.

Individuals affected with MCS are forced to make profound changes in lifestyle and diet, and endure multiple losses in life as they knew it, including their livelihood, identity, friends and sometimes even family members. Most of those afflicted are no longer able to be in environments that contain common everyday chemicals, which are found almost everywhere. Therefore, this means that most public places are off limits to them, their social life becomes extremely limited and there are very few places if any that they are capable of obtaining employment. It becomes increasingly difficult to function in this chemicalized world at all.

How does all this relate to alcoholism? Well as in all the issues we've talked about so far, once again when we look over the list of symptoms associated with exposure to environmental toxins, we not only see why many physical illnesses develop but once again we see the typical profile of the alcoholic. Environmental toxins have a profound impact on the brain and nervous system and result in a variety of psychological and physiological symptoms. Many alcoholics unknowingly have Multiple Chemical Sensitivity. These symptoms can be a major trigger that drives an alcoholic to drink as they try to self-medicate to feel better.

Once again we also see that environmental toxins have a profound impact on the all-important "neurotransmitters," dopamine, serotonin, etc., that are involved in the addiction process. Environmental toxins make the neurotransmitters go haywire and deplete them. They are all over the place. Remember, our main goal in recovery from alcoholism is to keep the neurotransmitters in balance. When neurotransmitters are out of balance, then cravings for alcohol and/or drugs occur.

For example, if an alcoholic who is in recovery works as a pest exterminator or spends time on a golf course that are notoriously polluted with herbicides or has their apartment fumigated for cockroaches, then their neurotransmitters are inhibited and symptoms of anxiety, depression, irritability and confusion develop and then they have cravings for alcohol and/or drugs to get relief.

The same applies to everyday common chemicals in your home. Every time you sprinkle air fresheners on your carpet, wash your clothes, scrub the floor, take a bath, put on your makeup, get new carpet, remodel your house, get a new car, paint your finger nails, paint the walls, take clothes to the dry cleaners, clean the bathroom, spray your hair with hairspray and even brush your teeth, you are exposed to toxic substances that throw your neurotransmitters out of balance and can lead to cravings for alcohol and/or drugs.

Additionally, Dr. Theron Randolph, the grandfather of environmental medicine, who we talked about in the food allergy connection, also discovered that some people are biochemically susceptible to experiencing a pleasurable, euphoric, addictive high when exposed to environmental toxins.[18] Chemicals stimulate the reward pathway in a similar manner as alcohol and/or drugs, and just like when you ingest an addictive substance, once the environmental toxin is out of your environment, you then experience the same type of physical and emotional crash where you feel extremely low, depressed, anxious, confused, or hyper—which results in a craving for alcohol and/or drugs to get relief from the discomfort. Environmental toxins bring you up high and then send you crashing down, thus keeping the process of physiological addiction active.

Once again, you might be saying, "What, Cynthia? Why haven't I heard of this? Surely our government would protect us from these things. Don't we have agencies in place to take care of this kind of thing?"

The biggest and most serious problem we face is that agencies such as the EPA and FDA who are supposed to protect our health do not do so. The laws and regulations we have in effect do not protect the consumer; they protect the manufacturer of the chemicals and pollutants. Chemicals and drugs rule this country and those manufacturing them have phenomenal power and influence over our governmental policies. They keep the truth from you. It is hidden, lied about and covered up.

Cindy Duehring, a sufferer of MCS—deceased at the age of 36, after a long struggle with MCS complications—was a leading researcher and writer at Environmental Access Research and I took this quote from Environmental Neurotoxicity in her article titled, "Screening for Nervous System Damage from Chemical Exposure."

> It was a most dangerous illusion that our society has brought forth, in the false belief, that the chemical ingredients in our everyday home and office consumer products, from cosmetics and perfumes to cleaners and carpets, have been tested for health effects to protect the public. Most of the chemicals have never been tested and are not under any regulation. There are three new chemical compounds introduced in the United States every day. Pre-marketing testing of compounds as potential neurotoxicants have serious deficiencies. Many of these neurotoxic compounds came into use before the passage of the Toxic Substance Control Act in 1976 and remain untested and are still not required to be tested.[19]

The prevalence of MCS in the population may be as high as 15 percent at this time,[20] and yet there is incredible backlash from the medical and chemical communities who try to deny and discredit the existence of this devastating illness. Not only MCS, but all physical and mental health conditions that are a result of environmental toxins are vehemently denied and fought against by the medical community, government agencies, chemical manufacturers, etc.

As I see it, they refuse to acknowledge it because to do so would mean that global change would have to take place. We would have to stop manufacturing chemicals and find a new way to live in the world. Companies manufacturing pesticides and other toxic chemicals would lose billions and billions of dollars. If we eliminated the diseases and health conditions that result from these toxins, then the medical community and pharmaceutical companies would also lose billions of dollars. Pharmaceuticals cannot fix the damage that is done to the human body from chemicals, so more money down the drain for them. As we discussed in a previous chapter, our medical universities, hospitals, and much of our medical research is supported by the pharmaceutical industry, so they will not support the medical society if they do not do what they want them to do. What they want them to do is deny that chemicals are toxic to the human body and Multiple Chemical Sensitivity does not exist. Most of the modern day living conveniences everyone is accustomed to are created with environmental toxins, so these would have to be given up or alternatives for these conveniences must be found.

If we must stop manufacturing all the chemicals that have a detrimental effect on human health, everyone has to change. Every individual on the face of this earth would be impacted in one way or another. To acknowledge the truth about environmental toxins and MCS could actually destroy the entire financial structure of the country, which is already hanging by a thread. The truth of this issue would be detrimental to the economy, therefore, it is denied However, to continue to ignore it and try to put our head in the sand, has even greater consequences on human life and health and the planet itself.

What we see playing out here is the exact scenario that we saw for decades in the tobacco industry. Minimizing, rationalizing, justifying and blatant lying, cheating and deceiving to protect the interests of those who have the most money to lose, until eventually the truth could not be hidden anymore. We can only hope that some day we will achieve the same awareness for chemicals and environmental toxins as we did for tobacco, but the tobacco industry was not as widespread as the chemical and pharmaceutical industries and our economy was not dependent upon their profits, so it will likely take a much longer time to get people to see this light. Basically the chemical and pharmaceutical industries, the medical society, the government agencies and society in general are all engaging in mass delusion and denial, because the consequences of this truth are catastrophic.

The lackadaisical attitude of many of our government agencies and politicians, their total lack of regard for the environment and their almost laughable environmental policies are not only appalling but also very frightening. They don't seem to get the critical point that destruction of the environment ultimately leads to destruction of the human being.

Reduce Your Exposure to Chemicals

It's impossible to avoid environmental toxins like endocrine/hormone disruptors completely because they are everywhere in our food, air and water; however, you can drastically cut down your exposure and reduce their presence in your life by making a variety of lifestyle changes that include the following:

1. Eat organic and eliminate sugar and caffeine.

2. Use earth-friendly and natural household cleaning products. Baking soda, hydrogen peroxide, lemon and vinegar are great non-toxic alternatives and can be used for just about anything. You can also find a variety of natural products at your local health food store.

3. Wear only natural clothing fibers and organic clothes if possible. Synthetic fibers and non-organics are treated with high levels of formaldehyde and even petroleum. About $3 billion is spent on pesticides for cotton fields each year worldwide, with over 600,000 tons of pesticides and chemical fertilizers on the U.S. cotton fields alone.

4. Throw away your perfume and cologne. Avoid people who wear them.

5. Use natural, unscented laundry soap and fabric softener. They also contain chemicals contributing to asthma, central nervous disorders, immune dysfunction, etc.

6. Use non-toxic alternatives for pest control. Eliminate the use of pesticides or herbicides in your home and yard.

7. Don't use air fresheners.

8. Don't get new carpet. New carpet is high in formaldehyde, benzene and a variety of other chemicals that can really destroy your health. Hardwood and ceramic tile are good, healthy, green living alternatives.

9. Use non-toxic and all natural personal health care products. Replace your body soap, feminine napkins, shampoo, toothpaste, etc., with natural choices.

10. Don't use bleach or chlorinated household products such as paper towels, toilet paper, coffee filters, etc. Scientific studies have linked chlorine and chlorination by-products to cancer of the bladder, liver, rectum and colon, as well as heart disease, artherosclerosis, anemia, high blood pressure and allergic reactions. Bleach alternatives and

unbleached products can be found at your local health food store. Peroxide can be used instead of bleach.

11. Do you have a job where you work around toxic chemicals? Get a new one.

12. Build your house or remodel with green building materials.

13. Move to a location that has cleaner air and is away from agriculture and industry.

14. Use a shower filter or bath ball when showering or bathing. More chlorine is absorbed through the skin during a shower than it is when you drink it.

15. Don't drink tap water. Buy a high-quality water filter or purchase water out of a filtration machine or water from the health food store that is in glass bottles.

16. Don't wear your shoes in the house. When you go into a building that has pesticides or a yard with herbicides, it gets on your shoes. You then track the pesticide into your house, where it actually becomes more potent and toxic than it was outside.

Living an environmentally friendly or green lifestyle is the wisest and most beneficial action you can take to safeguard not only your physical and emotional health but also your entire life.

To educate yourself more thoroughly on the topic of environmental toxins and their impact on our mental and physical health, you must read the following books: *Our Stolen Future* by Theo Colborn, Dianne Dumanoski and John Peterson; *Chemical Exposures: Low Levels and High Stakes* by Nicholas Ashford and Claudia Miller; *The EI Syndrome* by Dr. Sherry Rogers; and *An Alternative Approach to Allergies* by Dr. Theron Randolph.

The best doctors to address Multiple Chemical Sensitivity and health issues related to environmental toxins are called clinical ecologists or a doctor of environmental medicine and they can be found at the American Academy of Environmental Medicine.

Eleven

Hypothyroidism

"The pure and simple truth is rarely pure and never simple."
~Oscar Wilde

Another very common biochemical trap found among alcoholics is hypothyroidism. The symptoms that result from this disorder can also be an underlying factor in relapse, as it too impacts neurotransmitter functioning and is responsible for a variety of disruptive physical and emotional symptoms. This was one of the first conditions my doctor of environmental medicine found when I first went to see him, and I immediately began treatment.

The thyroid is a small butterfly shaped organ and is one of the main glands involved in the endocrine system. It is found in the front of the neck and is responsible for a variety of vital body functions. It produces hormones that regulate and affect just about every function in the body and is most crucial for body metabolism. The thyroid converts the food we eat into energy. Thyroid hormones impact body weight, energy levels, muscle strength, skin condition, heart rate, menstrual cycles, cholesterol levels, memory, emotions, mood and much more.

When the thyroid doesn't produce enough of these crucial hormones, then hypothyroidism occurs and results in a variety of psychological and physiological symptoms. Some of the most common symptoms that occur are fatigue, depression, anxiety, constipation, weight gain, forgetfulness/short-term memory loss, irritability, and myalgias or arthralgias, but other frequent symptoms may include listlessness, intolerance to cold, heart palpitations, cold hands and feet, menstrual irregularities, vascular headaches, premature gray hair, slow pulse and reflexes, flaky dry rough skin, puffiness of face and eyes, unsuccessful dieting, coarse lifeless hair that falls out easily, loss of sexual desire, high cholesterol, muscle and joint pain, and weakness.

Hypothyroidism can occur for a variety of reasons. In order for the thyroid to produce one of its main hormones called thyroxin, it needs the amino acid tyrosine. As we learned earlier, most alcoholics are deficient in amino acids; thus one of the reasons hypothyroidism is so prevalent among alcoholics. Additionally, Candida overgrowth interferes with and mimics thyroxin in the body; thus wrecking havoc on proper functioning of the thyroid gland. The thyroid is also very sensitive to environmental toxins like endocrine disruptors, which impede normal functioning of the gland.

The thyroid gland has a very complex and delicate interaction with neurotransmitters. Yes, those neurotransmitters, dopamine, serotonin and GABA that are so crucial in the addiction process. Neurotransmitters are needed for the modulation and syntheses of the thyroid-stimulating hormone; while on the other hand, the production of serotonin is dependent upon the thyroid. Additionally, hypothyroidism alters the manner in which the brain uses these neurotransmitters.

Here again, as in all the other conditions we've discussed thus far, we see that common pattern emerging for the alcoholic. First of all, we have a condition occurring that impacts important neurotransmitters and the reward pathway. As we learned earlier, deficient or out of balance neurotransmitters often lead to cravings to drink or drug, and then relapse. Secondly, the symptoms of hypothyroidism such as depression, anxiety, fatigue and restlessness are some of the most common symptoms experienced by alcoholics in recovery and continue to put them at risk of relapse as they attempt to find relief by self-medicating with alcohol and/or drugs.

Hypothyroidism often goes unsuspected and untreated. As much as 40 percent of the population may be suffering from hypothyroidism because it is frequently undetected by conventional blood tests, which is the most common medical procedure used for diagnoses. Blood tests are unreliable for diagnosing hypothyroidism. They only detect it when it is an extreme case and most cases of hypothyroidism are sub-clinical.

My doctor used what is called the "Barnes basal temperature test" to diagnose my hypothyroidism. This test is named after the late Dr. Broda Barnes of Connecticut who created it. Dr. Barnes spent 44 years in both university labs and private practice studying hypothyroidism and published more than 100 scientific papers on this subject. He also wrote a comprehensive book entitled *Hypothyroidism: The Unsuspected Illness* about his discoveries, if you'd like to learn more about it.

In his studies, he found patients where even though their thyroid blood test and physical examination of the thyroid was within normal limits, still exhibited clear-cut hypothyroid symptoms. He concluded that the most accurate assessment of thyroid function is obtained by evaluating ones metabolic rate, as exhibited in the basal body temperature and the resting pulse rate.[1]

My blood work showed that I didn't have a thyroid problem. However, the first time I saw my alternative health doctor, he took my pulse and it was only something like 35 and that wasn't even the resting pulse. A normal pulse is 65–80. He couldn't believe it and said he didn't know how I was functioning at all. I then followed the testing procedure described below and found my pulse and body temperature were always running low.

A temperature and pulse that consistently runs low may be an indication of hypothyroidism. Generally a pulse running 65 or below indicates lower thyroid function. The normal basal body temperature runs between 97.8 and 98.2 degrees Fahrenheit. A temperature running below 97.6 indicates the possibility of low thyroid function.

The Barnes basal temperature test is a simple, do-it-yourself test that you can do at home. It is accurate and requires nothing more than an oral thermometer. Here's what you do.

At bedtime shake down a mercury thermometer to 94 degrees Fahrenheit and place it on the nightstand, within easy reach. Do not use a digital thermometer for taking your temperature because they are not as accurate. When you wake up in the morning, make sure you stay in bed quietly and take the thermometer and place it securely under your armpit. Hold it in place for 10 minutes and then write down what the thermometer reads. During the 10 minutes you're waiting, take your pulse for one full minute and record what this result is also.

Do this exact procedure each morning for several weeks. Make sure you do not get up to go to the bathroom or anything else. It must be done before you have any activity. You must be in bed for a minimum of two hours before reading your temperature and the reading will not be accurate if you move around or get up. Do not use an electric blanket or other electrical devices in your bed. Do not sleep on a waterbed to perform this test. A waterbed will elevate your temperature artificially.

It has also been found that a woman's body temperature varies with the different phases of her menstrual cycle. The second and third days of her menstrual cycle are when the most accurate/reliable temperature can be found. Therefore, it is recommended that you make note on your records with red pen on the days you were menstruating and make sure you perform your test during this week.[2]

If your basal temperature consistently runs below 97.8 or your pulse runs below 65, you may have hypothyroidism. Take your results to a competent health care provider who is knowledgeable with the Barnes basal technique and discuss your findings and treatment options with them. Once again, this won't be your typical general practitioner. You'll need to look again for a doctor of environmental medicine, a doctor of orthomolecular medicine or a naturopathic doctor at the American Holistic Medical Association, the American Academy of Environmental Medicine, the American Association of Naturopathic Physicians, American Holistic Health Association or www.orthomolecular.org.

Treatment with a natural thyroid preparation, available only from your physician, rather than a synthetic drug is the best treatment for most people with hypothyroidism. The thyroid produces two hormones, one is T3 and the other is T4. Synthetic drugs like Synthroid only contain T4. T4 is converted by the body into T3, but for many people the body can't adequately make this conversion. Natural thyroid, such as that found in Armour thyroid or from a compounding pharmacy, is derived from porcine and it contains both T3 and T4 and is easier for the body to synthesize.

Twelve

Child Abuse

"The truth is heavy, therefore, few care to carry it."
~Talmud

Child abuse has profound physiological, spiritual, emotional and social consequences that are carried with the victim for the rest of their lives. There are more than 3 million reports of child abuse and neglect each year, and that's only the cases being reported. Most child abuse goes unreported.[1]

That means there is a staggering amount of abuse taking place in our society. Child abuse continues to be overlooked and minimized in our culture because there is still a pervading dysfunctional and destructive belief that it is acceptable to use physical violence, verbal aggression and exploitation in the process of child rearing,[2] which originated in and continues to be encouraged within religion. Additionally, most of society fails to recognize the depth of damage that is incurred.

It's no secret that most abused children grow up to be alcoholics or addicts, and most alcoholics and addicts have had an abusive childhood, and science now reveals that there is a biochemical reason this occurs. It used to be believed that the scars of child abuse were exhibited only in the psychosocial arena or through the development of defense mechanisms that become maladaptive and self-defeating in adulthood; and that in itself is detrimental enough, however, scientific findings now tell us that it is much deeper and more serious than even this.

Abuse was thought to be similar to a software problem that could be reprogrammed, where as now neurobiology tells us it is more like a "hard wiring." Because child abuse takes place during a crucial period of brain development, neurobiology now reveals that trauma such as physical, emotional and sexual abuse and neglect have a profound impact on the structure, function and chemistry of the brain that may result in irreversible damage.[3]

Neuroscientist, Dr. Martin Teicher, associate professor of psychiatry at Harvard and director of the Biopsychiatry Research Program in Belmont, has found in his studies that abused children have abnormal brain wave patterns. He tells us that the more severe the abuse is, the more powerful the impact on the brain function will be. The relationship that the child has with the abuser is also important. Abuse perpetrated by a family member is more detrimental than abuse perpetrated by a clergy member or babysitter.

Teicher and other neuroscientists have found that abuse damages important brain structures like the cortex, which is related to rational thinking. Some of the most dramatic damage is seen in the limbic system. The limbic system is the "primitive midbrain region that regulates memory and emotion." It contains two deep lying brain structures, the amygdala and hippocampus.[4]

The hippocampus determines what information coming in will be stored in the long-term memory. It is essential for processing emotions and memories and is the control center for most of the body's hormonal systems. Trauma to the hippocampus also results in memory loss, which may explain why many abused children forget their abuse soon after it happens.

While the amygdala's primary job is to "filter and interpret incoming sensory information in the context of the individual's survival and emotional need and then help initiate the proper response." The amygdala assists us in being able to take quick action when facing a dangerous or threatening situation such as jumping out of the path of an oncoming semi. Ongoing abuse causes the amygdala to alert us to danger even when a threat does not exist. Neuroscientist, Dr. Bruce Perry, says, "A maladaptive amygdala makes an abused child recoil in fear at the drop of a hat."[5]

The hippocampus and amygdala are found to be smaller in abused individuals. Additionally, both of these areas of the brain are crucial for learning. An association has also been found in that the greater the reduction in size of the hippocampus, the more severe the dissociative symptoms will be exhibited.

Dr. Teicher also tells us that these changes in the brain take place in attempt to adapt to an unsafe environment and ensure evolutionary survival. He even goes as far as to include sexual promiscuity, which is frequently seen in abused woman, as one of these adaptations. Although these changes are effective in the short term, in the long term they result in a variety of detrimental physiological, behavioral, cognitive, social and psychological consequences that may be permanent.

Damage to these important brain structures results in a variety of psychological and physiological symptoms like post traumatic stress disorder (PTSD), dissociative identity disorders (multiple personality disorder), antisocial behavior, borderline personality disorder, irrational fear, aggression, increased risk of suicide, sexual promiscuity, impaired ability to concentrate and learn, and self-destructive behaviors.

Now here's an extremely crucial component of child abuse that relates to the neurotransmitter connection we've been discussing throughout this book. All this damage to brain function and structure is also associated with serious changes in brain chemistry. When a child is exposed to continuous and overwhelming stress early in life, such as abuse, it alters the production and release of their stress-regulating hormones like cortisol and essential neurotransmitters like epinephrine, dopamine, serotonin and GABA. Survivors of abuse typically have lower than normal levels of important neurotransmitters like serotonin and dopamine, and GABA receptors are altered.[6]

When a child lives with ongoing traumatic stress like abuse, the brain stimulates the release of high levels of neurotransmitters and stress hormones. Since the abuse is ongoing, their brain is releasing these neurotransmitters in excessive amounts on a continuous basis, which ultimately causes great damage. Remember in chapter four when we discussed what happens when neurotransmitters are stimulated excessively? Over time as this continues, the neurotransmitter receptors become unresponsive or "desensitized" and eventually the brain no longer produces and releases adequate levels of neurotransmitters for the brain to function properly; thus the abused child becomes an adult who suffers with anxiety, depression, mood disorders, hyperactivity, as well as impaired attention span, etc.

The abused child is used to having high levels of those crucial neurotransmitters involved in the addiction process and are conditioned to engage in other behaviors that will keep them released. So they eat sugar, smoke cigarettes, drink caffeine, and get into alcohol and drugs to maintain those levels. Since these substances only boost the neurotransmitters temporarily, they continually need more. Essentially, abused children are biochemically set up to become an addict.

In addition to that, we learned in the hypoglycemia chapter that when were under stress, this releases sugar into the blood stream. So, that means the child living with abuse is having sugar pumped into their system pretty much all the time. Thus, this sets them up for Candida overgrowth, sugar addiction, hypoglycemia, adrenal exhaustion and all the other health problems associated with excess sugar.

Additionally, these excessively high levels of neurotransmitters and stress hormones also damage and inhibit the growth of neurons in the brain.[7] When the stress persists for a long time, the neurons shrink in size and will even die. Neurons are cells that send and receive electro-chemical signals to and from the brain and nervous system. Neurotransmitters are the chemical messengers used in this process. The neurons are also where the neurotransmitter receptors reside. Without an adequate supply of neurons, neurotransmitters cannot be released or received properly. Communication from the brain to the nervous system and other parts of the body malfunctions.

Here again we have the all-important issue of the reward pathway and those crucial neurotransmitters dopamine, serotonin and GABA that lead to addiction. Why do so many abused children grow up to be addicts and alcoholics? Because their neurotransmitters have been damaged, depleted and put out of whack by the abuse. Malfunctioning neurotransmitters result in feelings of depression, anxiety, fatigue, irritability, hyperactivity, fear, PTSD and much more.

The brain of adult survivors of abuse is like a laptop that's been dropped on the floor. Their internal wiring is all over the place. Chemical messengers aren't produced in sufficient numbers or they produce too many, they aren't connecting properly, and they miscommunicate. Abused children grow into adults who have neurotransmitters that have gone haywire and results in a variety of uncomfortable, sometimes crippling physiological and psychological symptoms. They attempt to balance out, calm down or rev up the neurochemicals in the brain with drugs and alcohol.

Other studies suggest that low levels of serotonin may lead to abusive behavior and it is believed that this may be why some abused children go on to be abusers while others don't. Abused children who grow up to be abusers themselves may not be the sole result of learned behavior. It may also be the result of long-term changes in brain chemistry, particularly serotonin.[8] However, it's important to keep in mind that not everyone with low levels of serotonin turns out to be an abuser and this phenomenon probably has several different contributing factors, which include learned behavior and sometimes the child identifies with the abuser as a way to simply survive, as a way to connect with the abuser in some way or in an attempt to possess their power and strength.

The child who identifies with the abuser then grows up to reenact abuse on others.

What's really interesting about these scientific findings is that researchers have discovered that if intervention takes place, some damage to the brain can be reversed. For example, it is believed by leading physicians treating psychological trauma that "positive experiences that contradict a traumatized child's negative expectations are critical to helping the brain to readjust itself." For example, "just saying to a child that you are sorry the event happened changes brain chemistry."[9] If a child is removed from the abusive environment and provided with a loving and nurturing environment, then some healing may occur.

Unfortunately, this is not usually the scenario with child abuse. Most children do not get rescued from child abuse. They must endure it for a lifetime, and in order to adapt to this hostile environment, the brain is altered and they develop coping mechanisms that become maladaptive in adult life and then engage in their own destructive behaviors such as alcohol and drug addiction and relationships with abusive people. Although it is now believed that brain changes can take place even in adulthood, the more time that passes between the actual abuse and the initiation of intervention, the more deep-rooted the neurological damage will be.

To make matters worse, people who have been abused tend to develop a variety of self-defeating beliefs about themselves and the world. They view bad events in a self-blaming way, which undermines self-esteem and encourages depression and helplessness. Unfortunately, it is believed that this type of thinking may have a negative impact on brain chemistry as well, and thus sets them up in another vicious cycle of interfering in neurotransmitter functioning even more, which only amplifies and perpetuates the negative thinking pattern.

As we discussed above, the excessive and continuous release of stress hormones is associated with a variety of negative effects on the body and mind. Another one of the main systems impacted by the excessive and continuous release of stress hormones is the stress response system of the body.

The primary system involved in the body's stress response system is known as the HPA axis, which involves a complex interaction between the hypothalamus, pituitary and adrenal glands. It is responsible for controlling essentially all the body's hormones, nervous system activity, storage and expenditure of energy, as well as regulating the immune system, controlling reactions to stress and a variety of other body processes like digestion, mood and emotions, and sexuality.

When you're under stress, the hypothalamus releases a hormone called corticotrophin-releasing factor (CRF), which then flows through your pituitary gland and stimulates the release of adrenocoricotrophic hormone (ACTH), which then stimulates the adrenal glands to release cortisol. This process makes you alert and gives you the energy needed to deal with the stressful event.

In a normal circumstance, once the threat (the stressful event) passes, then the hormones recede. However, in the case of child abuse, the threat never passes, therefore, the HPA axis never stops releasing hormones and eventually burns itself out, resulting in a hypothalamus, pituitary and adrenal glands that don't function adequately.

It's also important to note here that several neurotransmitters like dopamine, serotonin and norepinephrine are needed for regulating the HPA axis and, as we discussed above, these neurotransmitters are first being excessively stimulated and then not being produced and released sufficiently so this leaves the HPA axis even more vulnerable to malfunction.

A malfunctioning HPA axis is associated with a variety of psychological and physical symptoms like panic attacks, chronic anxiety, insomnia, PTSD, ADHD, depression, chronic fatigue syndrome, fibromyalgia, irritable bowel syndrome and alcoholism.

Dr. Putnam, another leading researcher in child abuse, tells us that in fearful circumstances like abuse, stress floods the brain with cortisol repetitively and excessively. Over time this repetition damages the brain and the adrenal glands. In an attempt to adapt to this situation, the brain then lowers the threshold at which cortisol is produced to a dramatically lower level; however, the system remains in a hypersensitive state.[10] This results in a variety of psychological and physiological symptoms such as those seen with posttraumatic stress disorder.

When we are under attack or threatened, cortisol redistributes the energy in our body, but excessively high levels lead to high levels of fear and anxiety.[11] Cortisol also damages the hippocampus, which as we learned is detrimental to memory and cognition, and may damage or alter the hormonal system. Severe damage to the hippocampus is believed to lead to dissociation and in extreme cases result in dissociative identity disorder, also known as multiple personality disorder.

Dr. Bruce Perry explains that typically when we're exposed to acute stress, the neurophysiological changes are rapid and reversible; however, when the exposure to the stressful situation is ongoing and intense, as it is in child abuse, the changes are not reversible. The stress response system of the body becomes "sensitized." It now reacts to stressful situations in a much more sensitive manner. It is believed that this phenomenon is similar to the changes that take place in neurotransmitter receptors like that seen in sensitization to cocaine. These changes result in symptoms like hypervigilance, increased startle response, affective disorders, anxiety and PTSD.[12]

A child living with child abuse is in a constant state of fight or flight. Their adrenal glands never get a break as their body is continually releasing high levels of stress hormones like cortisol. This often leads to adrenal exhaustion or at the very least depleted or malfunctioning adrenal glands. The adrenal glands are no longer able to perform their jobs as needed for the body and brain to function optimally. As we learned earlier in the chapters on sugar, caffeine, nicotine and hypoglycemia, the adrenal glands have a crucial role in maintaining blood sugar, producing hormones, managing stress and fatigue, and many other important body functions that can result in cravings for alcohol.

When the adrenals are exhausted, they no longer produce enough cortisol. Cortisol is crucial for many body functions like glucose metabolism and blood sugar maintenance, regulating blood pressure, immune function, and inflammatory response. When there isn't sufficient cortisol in the body, the individual is susceptible to autoimmune disorders, chronic pain syndromes, chronic fatigue, asthma, allergies and more. Again in an attempt to self-medicate the many symptoms that occur as a result of a malfunctioning adrenal gland, the abused individual often reaches for drugs and alcohol.

It is believed by neuroscientists that a variety of factors such as the nature of the trauma, the degree to which body integrity is threatened and the family support system after the trauma has a great impact on how severe the neurological damage will be and the extent of symptoms that an abused individual may experience.[13] Someone who endures a life-threatening abusive situation or one that is highly degrading is likely to exhibit more neurological damage than abuse that occurs in a less threatening more benign setting. Alternatively, if the abused individual receives support and validation from other family members after the abuse, they are likely to be less traumatized than the individual who is dealing with a family that denies, represses or hides the abuse, or blames the abused.

The age in which the abuse occurs also seems to influence which set of symptoms the abused person presents with, because different areas of the brain are developing at different ages. It is believed that abuse that occurs before the age of four may result in different symptoms than those exhibited in children who are abused later in childhood.[14] This explains why there's such a wide variety of symptoms found in abused individuals and why some people exhibit more symptoms than others. Unfortunately, for those who've been abused their entire life beginning in infancy and ending when they leave home as a young adult, the damage is pretty extensive and may include the whole gamut of possible symptoms.

I have only touched the surface here on the extent of the neurological damage that occurs as a result of child abuse and neglect. Volumes have been written and the depth of this issue is staggering; thus it is beyond the scope of this book to cover it in detail. I have given you an overview and what this tells us is that all the so-called psychological symptoms like anxiety, depression, fear, irritability, mood disorders, fatigue, etc., that are so typical for survivors of child abuse are actually physiological in nature. This also illustrates how deeply intertwined the mind and the body really are.

However, abuse also creates a variety of problems in the social, emotional and spiritual arenas that can and often do lead to drug or alcohol addiction. These areas have been covered pretty extensively in the self-help field and, therefore, there is no need to go into them in great detail again here. My goal at this time is to call attention to the brain chemistry aspect and highlight a few other important areas.

Child abuse in any form violates a child at their core. It shatters their personality, identity and spirit, which results in a confused and fragmented sense of self.[15] It is the ultimate act of betrayal and abandonment that wounds and scars every fiber of their being. Nothing is left unscathed and this trauma is carried with them for a lifetime. This should be of grave concern to all of us, because these damaged children grow up into adults who teach our children, administer law enforcement, minister to our families and run our governments, etc.

Children who were abused grow into teens and adults that feel flawed, inferior, worthless, hopeless, inadequate, dirty, overwhelmed with deep shame, depressed, anxious, extreme loneliness, helpless and afraid. They have low self-esteem and self-worth, aggression or anger control issues, feel like a failure, are severely lacking in coping and social skills, and have difficulty with intimacy and relationships. They are often unconsciously drawn to partners with similar characteristics as their parents and then reenact the abuse over and over. They experience a constant state of internal deprivation with deep feelings of loss, isolation and emptiness.[16]

It is no wonder that so many victims of abuse turn to drugs and alcohol to feel better. When you don't feel good about yourself there's no motivation to do what's healthy for your body and mind. It seems inevitable they would reach for relief and artificial stimulation through drugs, alcohol, sugar, caffeine, cigarettes, etc.

With so many issues working against them, survivors of abuse literally don't feel capable of functioning in the world. Alcohol and drugs are used as a coping mechanism. It gives them courage when they're afraid; company when they are lonely; a false sense of control and power, which was taken away from them in childhood; it reduces the dysphoria; and anesthetizes the emotional pain. It is also used to keep memories of the abuse from surfacing.[17]

When you don't feel loved, nurtured, connected and worthwhile, this too has a very powerful negative impact on neurotransmitters. Being nurtured is a necessary component to thrive and provides healthy stimulation to neurotransmitters. So although these particular issues we're speaking of at the moment are emotional and spiritual, they are deeply interconnected with the physiological and perpetuate the vicious cycle of damage to brain chemistry.

Additionally, when the survivor of abuse becomes involved in the use and abuse of drugs and alcohol, they usually engage in behaviors that violate their morals and values. This results in deeper feelings of shame, guilt and confusion, which drives them even further into alcohol and drug use to cover up these feelings. I think this was illustrated very clearly for you in my own life.

Addicted survivors of abuse who don't address their abuse issues are at high risk of relapse or bouncing back and forth between different addictions.[18] When an alcoholic or addict gets sober, all these feelings and memories they've been repressing and "numbing out" come rushing into consciousness. Just because you get sober does not mean you magically develop self-esteem and stop feeling worthless, ashamed, and inadequate, etc. On the contrary, with drugs and alcohol out of the picture, all these negative feelings are magnified. It takes time and work.

Additionally, they don't suddenly know how to handle their anger, practice assertiveness, build healthy intimate relationships or develop effective social skills. They may still blow up when they get angry, can't function in social situations, don't know how to get their needs met and avoid intimate relationships. These things must be learned.

Even when survivors of abuse are no longer under the influence of drugs and alcohol, they may still engage in behaviors that are confusing and violate their conducts of behavior with acts like promiscuity or relationships with abusive people. They can't understand why and this incites more feelings of shame and guilt, which may lead to a drink in an attempt to cope.

Since their identity was shattered, never fully developed and/or is deeply attached to their drug and alcohol abuse, when they get sober, they don't really know who they are or how to fit into this world. They feel more fragmented, disconnected and lost, which results in lots of confusion. To have successful recovery with sobriety, there must be a successful recovery of self.

If we look at my life as an example, we can see how this all plays out. As a child, I first started reaching out to sugar and then cigarettes, then alcohol and then drugs to cope with, numb out and repress all the emotional turmoil I lived with daily. My original identity was lost. She had a rag stuffed in her mouth and was locked in a closet with her hands tied. Anytime she attempted to emerge she was beaten, ridiculed, stifled and used. I essentially learned that who I was, was unacceptable. She was not allowed to exist.

So the identity I developed was very fragmented and evolved out of the abuse, my parent's distorted perception of me and then my addictions. I had no real sense of self. I existed only to serve my parent's needs. There was no praise, admiration and cuddling for being a beautiful little girl, for drawing pictures, doing good in school, for new skills I learned, etc. There was no encouragement to be who I was. The only time my parents were "happy" with me was when I was doing something for them or taking care of them, and even then it was never good enough. So that's who I became—someone who was used and not good enough. That was my first piece of identity to form.

In my early teens, evidence of serious brain structure, neurotransmitter and adrenal system damage was clearly exhibited with the severe anxiety attacks, chronic pain and depression that began to consume me. It became impossible to function without prescription drugs and even they couldn't keep it under control. This too required heavy self-medication on a continuous basis.

For as long as I could remember, I felt deeply flawed, depressed, empty, inadequate, defective, worthless and consumed with shame. Getting through the day without being high or drunk was unbearable. I didn't have a clue how to fit into this world. I felt like an alien who was completely inadequate in social situations and couldn't maintain a relationship. Drugs and alcohol made it possible for me to function. So this too became a huge piece of my identity. Drugs and alcohol were very much a part of who I was. I was someone who drank and did drugs. It was something I was good at and I didn't feel good at many things. So in an unhealthy way, it gave me pride that I was severely lacking in.

I had been sexualized by every important man in my life, so I began sexualizing myself at a very early age. It was the only way I knew how to interact and connect with a man. This too was something I was good at and in a twisted way gave me pride as well, and became a very big piece of my identity. Additionally, a damaged HPA axis caused me to have an excessively high sex drive, which drove me to fill my physiological needs at the expense of my emotional needs.

In my active using and addiction years, I engaged in a lot of promiscuity, which I shared with you earlier, provoked a great deal of shame and anguish for me internally and thrust me deeper and deeper into addiction. It was one of the many vicious cycles ruling my life. The more I used, the more I violated my values; the more I violated my values, the more I had to use. There was layer after layer of shame and anguish to cover up.

When my son was born, I then had a new piece to my identity of being a mother. I loved being a mother, it was the only good piece of identity I had; however, it was in complete contradiction with my other pieces of identity; thus the result of great conflict. I couldn't be a good mother when I was drunk and using. I couldn't be a good drunk when I was being a good mother. I couldn't be as drunk and high as often as I wanted and I couldn't be free to have sex when I wanted. This began another vicious cycle and internal battle that resulted in even deeper shame. I desperately wanted to be a good mother, yet I desperately needed to be drunk and high. I vacillated back and forth between the two, continuously trying to find a way to succeed at both, but feeling like a miserable failure in every way.

By the time I made it to rehab, my identity consisted of a highly sexualized drunk and addict, someone who allowed herself to be used, and a mother. That was all I had to work with. It's not that I didn't have other aspects to my identity, but I wasn't in touch with them. They were buried and had to be nurtured and developed when I got sober.

As soon as I got sober and discovered there was another way to live, that part of me that was stuffed in the closet with a rag in her mouth began to emerge and she was ecstatic to be alive; however, this resulted in a lot of confusion and more internal conflict that took many years to sort out. Over time my identity expanded to include a sober person, an intelligent woman, a member of AA, a better mother, a secretary, a college student, etc., and I began to feel good about myself, but that other damaged self was always trying to take over.

I literally felt like I was in pieces. There seemed to be two selves. The one who allowed herself to be used, who sexualized herself and had relationships with unavailable/abusive men, and the self who didn't want any of this and was working very hard to change. Since being used, not good enough and sexualized were at the core of my development, they were the hardest to override. As you'll hear later in this book, I battled with that piece of my identity for many years into sobriety before putting her to rest.

Additionally, almost immediately after getting the drugs and alcohol out of my system, memories of my sexual abuse began to surface. I was still in my 30-day treatment center when flashbacks started to occur. Memories of my physical and emotional abuse had never been buried, they were in my consciousness daily, but the traumatic aftermath they created was no longer anesthetized with alcohol and drugs. The raw brutality, loss, grief and betrayal of it all was now felt in full effect and I was flooded with overwhelming memories and feelings I didn't know how to handle. I was consumed with questions like "why" and "how," and I felt robbed.

My saving grace here was that my rehab counselor immediately guided me in the right direction that allowed me to address these issues effectively and reduce their potential for triggering relapse. If you remember back in chapter three in the story of my life, I was attending classes, seminars, workshops, reading books, attending groups and private counseling to work on all my abuse issues.

Although it took me many years to make significant healing in this area, the fact that I had awareness was what empowered me and eliminated the abuse as a risk factor for relapse. With awareness came understanding for myself and my behaviors, with understanding came forgiveness of myself and motivation to work on my issues. Awareness and understanding also began to lift the veil of shame and with that came a sense of freedom and the ability to develop a healthier identity.

When I would read a book about adult survivors of abuse or attend a workshop, I identified so deeply that it was as if the book or workshops were written specifically about me. Another lightbulb came on and I was astounded to learn that there was an explanation for all the craziness in my life. Suddenly my entire life made sense and this information alone was incredibly healing.

So in summary, the main point I'm trying to highlight here is that although it is essential to address the biochemical aspects of alcoholism and balance neurotransmitters, even if you make a lot of progress in healing your biochemistry, the abuse issues still have the power to sabotage recovery if they too are not addressed.

If a survivor of abuse does not gain awareness and understanding of their abuse issues after they get sober, then they will remain in the grips of the trauma and its aftershock. It is the unconscious factors operating in the background that leave them at risk of relapse.

On the other hand, as we saw in my own life, I was working very hard on my abuse issues, doing everything humanly possible to stay sober and still struggling. I was making great progress with sobriety, but something was missing. That missing piece was the biochemistry and neurotransmitter aspect and it wasn't until I included that in my treatment plan that I was able to get over the hump. Both are crucial for successful long-term recovery.

Since we know the profound impact that child abuse has on brain chemistry, it is also my belief that when you engage in behaviors like counseling, workshops, groups, seminars and books that help you heal your child abuse that the validation, support and understanding that accompanies these activities is not only beneficial on the emotional level but it also helps balance out the neurotransmitters and heal brain trauma as well.

I know in my own experience as I became enlightened about child abuse issues it was so mind-boggling and powerful it felt like brain cells, neurons and neurotransmitters were firing so strongly in my head it was as if my brain was rearranging itself. The information was staggering and innovative in my mind because I had never heard it before and it changed my life completely.

Another issue for the survivor of abuse, if they are entering traditional treatment for addiction or AA, is that many of the methods used are counterproductive. Angry, forceful confrontations that are frequently used to break denial can push those with abusive backgrounds further into resistance, because they feel they're being violated again. The whole powerlessness concept is threatening because they were unable to control what was done to them as a child so it's terrifying to think they have no power as an adult. The structure and tone of treatment and AA tends to be punitive, shaming, rigid and blaming, which resembles the atmosphere they grew up in. Traditional treatment methods often make the survivor of abuse feel revictimized.[19]

Considering the fact that the majority of people entering treatment for addiction have been abused, this gives us another clear indication as to why traditional treatment is not successful for so many people. It is my opinion that those survivors who do feel comfortable in AA and traditional treatment do so because, as we learned earlier, survivors of abuse are often unconsciously drawn to situations and people that simulate their dysfunctional family system. It's familiar to them. On some level they feel comfortable in AA and yet on another level it incites great internal conflict. That was the case for me and the longer I stayed sober and the deeper I worked on my childhood abuse issues, the more uncomfortable I became with certain aspects of AA. Treatment for alcoholism and drug addiction needs to empower the individual and that is not the case with AA and mainstream rehabilitation centers.

It's also important to note here that although this chapter is talking specifically about child abuse, that any high-stress traumatic event in life has the potential to alter and damage the body's stress response system and brain chemistry. Other events like natural disasters, kidnapping, civilians in war or those engaging in combat, prisoners of war, a car wreck, plane wreck, a terrorist attack, chronic health conditions or other similar scenarios where someone is in crises or traumatized and unable to escape could have the same results and make one vulnerable to addiction.

Thirteen
The Neurotransmitter Connection

"Truth is the cry of all, but the game of the few."
~George Berkeley

When we take a look at all the issues I've presented in this book thus far, we see the one thing they all have in common is that they all have a powerful effect on brain chemistry. Alcoholism is not a mental disorder, a character defect, a lack of willpower or a spiritual disease. It is all about neurotransmitters and biochemistry. There are several different biochemical issues going on simultaneously that feed into one another and perpetuate a vicious cycle that keeps the alcoholic or addict from achieving or maintaining sobriety when they are not addressed.

These biochemical issues are usually present in the body before addiction to alcohol or drugs develop and are the catalyst that pushes one into the addiction cycle and then perpetuates the cycle as well. We develop addictions in a misguided attempt to normalize our brain chemistry. We're trying to feel normal through self-medicating. Our neurotransmitters are out of balance or deficient and our brains are missing what's necessary to feel like most people feel normally.

Do we develop defects in character, psychological symptoms, loss of spiritual connections and lack of willpower? Yes, we do, but they are all a result of the drinking and drugging, not the root of it. When under the influence of drugs and alcohol we violate our values and morals and engage in behavior that may be hurtful, dishonest and shameful. We lie, cheat, steal, treat people badly, betray and develop a variety of dysfunctional coping strategies like rationalizing, denial and justification. With years of continued alcohol or drug abuse our morals and values change. We become someone that we really aren't. At this point, our own behavior perpetuates the cycle of addiction as well.

The psychological symptoms like depression, anxiety, irritability, etc., as we clearly illustrated earlier are not the cause of alcoholism, but the result of many physiological factors like Candida overgrowth, food allergies, nutritional deficiencies, environmental toxins and neurotransmitter imbalances. As time goes on and we begin to feel powerless in our ability to stop our behavior and without knowledge of the true root of the problem, we begin to lose our willpower. All of this has a profound impact on us spiritually. Additionally, for those of us who lived with child abuse and neglect, damage to willpower, neurotransmitters and spirituality was activated quite early.

Neurotransmitters and biochemistry is the crucial component that traditional alcohol and drug treatment programs is missing and is needed for long-term sobriety. They have the emotional and spiritual aspect covered, but they don't address the physiological, and this is why the success rate for long-term recovery from alcoholism and drug addiction is so low and why cravings to drink and drug continue. Some people can manage to maintain sobriety with the spiritual approach alone, but they are the minority and do so at great cost.

In order to achieve successful long-term sobriety without cravings, the biochemical issues must be addressed and neurotransmitters must be replenished. The key word here is "long-term." Yes, some people can get a few weeks or months or even a year or so under their belt with the 12 steps, however, the majority of people don't make it "long-term." The reason is that biochemistry sabotages the recovery path. Those that do make it, fight constant cravings for alcohol and struggle with a variety of psychological symptoms. Staying sober is a daily battle. When you address brain chemistry, the battle is gone. There are no more cravings.

After I had about five or six years of sobriety, I was searching for a book that I could give to a man in my life who was struggling with addiction, that could teach him some of the things I knew about addiction, when I stumbled upon a book called *Seven Weeks to Sobriety* by Joan Mathews Larson. At the time

I didn't know there was a "biochemical" or "biochemistry" to addiction. I didn't know my knowledge actually had a name. I only knew that diet, hypoglycemia, environment, hypothyroidism, nutrition, Candida, etc., were components of the addiction process. It was in this book that I learned there was an actual word for what I knew, "biochemistry," or "biochemical."

Once again I was dumbfounded. Here it was, a treatment plan that addressed almost everything that it had taken me years to piece together myself presented all together in one place. I couldn't believe that such a wonderful resource existed and no one in traditional treatment was even aware of it.

In Joan's book, she tells us that alcoholism is biologically predetermined by body chemistry and has found there are three main types of alcoholics. Allergy addicted, Omega 6 Deficient and II ADH/THIQ. In the allergy addicted alcoholic, the alcoholic is allergic to alcohol; in the Omega 6 Deficient, they are deficient in the essential fatty acid Omega 6; and in the ADH/THIQ, the individual is born with an alcohol dehydrogenase liver enzyme that enables the alcoholic to metabolize large amounts of alcohol without negative effects and the brain makes endorphin like tetrahydroisoquinolines from alcohol.[1] I found I fit the allergy addicted profile perfectly. Remember the very wise Dr. Silkworth that initially told Bill W. that he had an allergy to alcohol? He was absolutely right. Bill W. was so very close to the truth.

I'm not going to go into deep detail about this aspect as each of these are described in great detail in Joan's book and there's no point in me rewriting Joan's material. I strongly recommend that you pick up a copy and devour every word of it. My goal right now is to just call attention to the fact that this spectacular resource exists. However, keep in mind that no matter which type of alcoholic you are, the physiological process of addiction and impact on neurotransmitters is the same.

Joan has a treatment center in Minnesota called the Health Recovery Center where they treat alcoholism with diet, nutrition and changes in lifestyle that address the physiological issues I have presented for you in this book. Joan offers a comprehensive treatment plan that will help you identify which type of alcoholic you are, support your body through detox and then heal the biochemical issues through nutritional supplementation and diet. It provides the body with the nutritional support it needs to correct the body chemistry, balance neurotransmitters and eliminate cravings for alcohol.

Since that time, I have read a lot of other resources on the biochemical connection and it is all this information combined that has become the compilation of what I've presented in this book and what I call the neurotransmitter connection.

I think all this material about neurotransmitters, spirituality, abuse and the interconnection of it all is the most exciting and fascinating topic in the world. Even though I've known this stuff for years, as I've written this book and put all my thoughts and knowledge into one place, it has solidified and brought the material together for me in my own head in a whole new way.

We've learned that neurotransmitters can be out of balance for many different reasons. They are influenced by factors such as poor diet, nutritional deficiencies, genetics, environmental toxins, Candida, high levels of stress, child abuse and neglect, and drugs and alcohol.

As Joan tells us, you may be born with a particular body chemistry that sets you up for addiction. It is pre-programmed in you on a physiological level. Additionally, you may inherit a deficiency in nutrients and neurotransmitters and be born with neurotransmitter imbalances. Then you start eating white sugar and other refined foods, more nutritional deficiencies develop and neurotransmitters and other essential functions get more out of balance. If there is child abuse, which there so frequently is, this also causes depletion and damage to the neurotransmitters.

When the symptoms begin to build, you seek relief in drugs and alcohol. Drugs and alcohol provide a temporary fix, but ultimately they damage the neurotransmitters even more and much more severely. The longer you continue to use drugs and alcohol, the more damage that is done. The more damage that is done, the more symptoms and misery that build, the more relief is needed. Thus, the vicious cycle is set into motion.

To stop this roller-coaster ride, all behaviors that result in excessive and artificial stimulation of the neurotransmitters must be eliminated. You must change your diet, lifestyle and behavior to ones that support balance in neurotransmitters. Excessive stimulation of the reward pathway in the brain must stop. The brain must become accustomed to normal levels again, so receptor sites and neurons can normalize.

Neurotransmitters are not only at the root of alcoholism, addiction and cravings, but they also contribute to many of the other conditions that alcoholics live with, such as anxiety, depression, fatigue, irritability, weight issues and sleep problems. They play a very important role in many common health conditions we see in society today such as obesity, depression, fatigue, migraines, attention deficit disorder, hyperactivity, autism, anxiety, obsessive compulsive disorder, chronic pain, behavioral problems, Parkinson's, Alzheimer's, dementia and many others.

After extended alcohol or drug usage, the neurotransmitters have been damaged extensively and the brain no longer functions adequately. When you give up the drugs and alcohol, not only do the excessive levels of neurotransmitters disappear, but now you actually have less than you did before. The brain no longer releases enough of them to perform its job and, remember, one of the main jobs of neurotransmitters and the reward pathway is moderating mood, providing feelings of pleasure and making you feel good. Without adequate neurotransmitters you don't feel normal, balanced or happy.

It takes time for the neurotransmitters to adjust and balance out. If you continue to eat sugar and other refined foods, consume caffeine, smoke cigarettes and be exposed to high levels of environmental toxins, your neurotransmitters can never recover and normalize. These substances continue to provide excessive stimulation to the reward pathway and perpetuate the physiological process of addiction.

However, the good news is that if you remove all these substances, give your brain time to heal and replenish the neurotransmitters, they will rehabilitate themselves the majority of the time. In some cases, such as severe and extended child abuse or certain very powerful drugs, extended periods of drug abuse, or damage from some environmental toxins, it is believed that there can be some permanent damage to neurotransmitters and functions of the brain and nervous system that is not reversible.

In my own situation I have found this to be true to a certain degree. I have been able to rehabilitate my neurotransmitters enough that I cured my alcoholism, however, I have other health problems related to neurotransmitters that as of yet, I've not been able to heal. Don't let this discourage or frighten you, because most people can make enough significant progress to achieve long-term sobriety. Remember I lived with severe emotional and physical abuse, sexual abuse and neglect, and started using at a very young age, so my neurotransmitters had an extensive amount of damage, and as soon as I followed the protocol I'm sharing with you in this book, my alcoholism was no longer an issue in my life.

However, here's a very important point to keep in mind, if you're thinking of continuing down your journey of alcohol or drug abuse. The longer you stay at it, the more damage you do to the neurotransmitters. The harder your drug of choice, the more damage you will do to the neurotransmitters. So recovery for someone who has used softer drugs will have an easier road to recovery than someone who used hard drugs; someone who has drank or used for a shorter period of time will have an easier recovery path than someone who has been at it for decades. Additionally, someone who doesn't have child abuse or neglect in their past will have an easier time in recovery than someone who does—because their neurotransmitters have been damaged since they were a child.

So, one of the most important keys to long-term sobriety is the brain must become accustomed to not having such excessively high levels of neurotransmitters. We must support the brain and body with nutrients so that it's not physiologically excruciating to stay sober. The reward pathway and those crucial neurotransmitters, dopamine, serotonin, glutamate and GABA need to be balanced. Normalizing brain chemistry through diet, nutrition and lifestyle choices is what's needed for successful sobriety.

The first crucial step for balancing neurotransmitters is to stop giving them excessive stimulation. No sugar, refined foods, processed foods, smoking or caffeine. Environmental toxins must be removed from your living space and a diet that reduces Candida overgrowth and addresses hypoglycemia must be followed. The second step is to replenish the neurotransmitters with proper diet and supplementation.

One of the reasons so many of us are deficient in neurotransmitters is because our diets are deficient in protein and healthy fat. We've all been taught that meat protein and fats are not healthy for us and that isn't true. Healthy fats are essential for the production of neurotransmitters. Healthy fats are found in food like nuts, seeds, avocados, olive oil, walnut or sunflower oil, coconuts and fish. Without quality protein in the diet, we don't receive enough amino acids. If you don't consume amino acids, you don't produce neurotransmitters. Amino acids are the building blocks of those essential neurotransmitters—serotonin, dopamine, GABA, and glutamate, etc.—involved in the reward pathway and the process of addiction. Protein is found in highest concentrations in meat, including red meat, nuts, seeds, eggs, dairy products and beans.

It's important to note that animal proteins and their byproducts, which include red meat, poultry, fish, eggs, yogurt, cheese and milk are the only proteins that are complete proteins, meaning they provide the body with all of the essential amino acids it needs. All other sources of protein are incomplete, meaning they only contain some amino acids or levels that aren't high enough to be beneficial. In order to provide the body with adequate levels of amino acids, which as we discussed is crucial for the alcoholic, foods that are incomplete proteins must be combined to achieve complete proteins. However, most foods that are incomplete proteins such as grains and beans are also high in carbohydrates, and the alcoholic wants to keep carbohydrates minimized to keep neurotransmitters and blood sugar in balance and Candida overgrowth under control.

Some people are concerned about eating meat, but meat is only a problem when eaten in excess without other healthy foods and fats in the diet, and when prepared improperly or eaten in conjunction with other refined foods and sugar. Meat has gotten a bad wrap when it didn't deserve it. It isn't meat that causes high blood pressure, weight gain, heart disease and all the other conditions that it is blamed for. It is sugar, unhealthy oils, white flour and other refined foods, additives, preservatives, hormones, antibiotics, and pesticides in the food. I eat meat three times a day and I have very healthy levels of cholesterol and blood pressure. However, it should be organic. Meat that isn't organic contains antibiotics, pesticides and hormones, which will aggravate Candida and cause further damage to the endocrine and nervous systems and deplete neurotransmitters. Vegetables should be organic as well, for the same reason.

Most people on a diet high in meat, such as the Candida diet, find they lose weight and their blood pressure and cholesterol levels actually get lower even though they are eating more meat. However, if you do have high blood pressure or cholesterol, you will want to be sure to monitor your progress and communicate with your physician. If you have kidney disease, you should also consult with your health care provider before eating a high protein diet, because this can be difficult for the kidneys to handle if they aren't functioning properly.

However, each of us should try to eat less fatty cuts, don't cook meat with oil and don't fry. Read your meat packages and choose meats with lower percentages of fat. If the labels are confusing, ask someone in the meat department to help you. When preparing your steak, roast, chicken or turkey, trim excess fat before cooking. Remove all skin. Deep-frying adds a lot of fat to your food in the preparation process and so does pan-frying. Baking or broiling without oils is best. When you do fry, use healthy oil like olive oil. Stick with whole cuts of meat like a steak, chicken breast or sliced turkey, rather than buffalo wings or chicken fingers. Although bison is a red meat, it is lower in fat and cholesterol than chicken or turkey, so a very healthy choice.

Balance your meat protein with a small amount of complex carbohydrates and an abundance of low carb vegetables. Foods that are high in carbohydrates or high on the glycemic index, even complex carbohydrates, if eaten in excess can also deplete neurotransmitters. Particularly for those who already have malfunctioning neurotransmitters.

Eating fresh foods is always the preferred form, because they contain more nutritional value than any others. Frozen food would be the second choice, and canned food should always be the last choice. Additionally, vegetables should be steamed instead of boiled because steaming helps the vegetable to retain its nutrient value, while boiling pulls it out.

So, once again, we learn that the healthiest diet for an alcoholic is one that is high in protein and low in carbohydrates. There are some body types that really need meat protein as part of their diet, and the alcoholic is usually one of them.

Common prescription drugs on the market that are used for depression, anxiety, Parkinson's, hyperactivity, OCD, etc., work by altering the neurotransmitters in the brain; when you hear a disorder described as a "chemical imbalance" the chemicals they are referring to are neurotransmitters. However, the problem with prescription drugs is that in the long run they actually make the problem worse. They deplete the neurotransmitters even more and create even more imbalance. Amino acids give the body what it's missing naturally. They heal and restore balance to the neurotransmitters.

However, once extensive neurotransmitter depletion has occurred, as it has with the alcoholic or drug addict, it is very difficult to replenish them through diet alone. A balanced amino acid supplement is usually required along with their specific cofactors. Remember, amino acids are the building blocks for neurotransmitters. This is especially crucial in the early stages of recovery. The body needs to be supported with specific nutrients during detox and early recovery.

After detox and several weeks of stability, it would probably be wise to have some neurotransmitter testing performed. A simple urine test can tell you which neurotransmitters you are deficient in and what supplements you'll need to take to correct the imbalance. I recommend neurotransmitter testing by NeuroScience. They are the leading authority in neurotransmitter issues and provide a simple urine test you can perform in the privacy of your own home that will identify your imbalances and provide you with a detailed protocol with recommendations for supplementation and dosages that are required to correct them.

Knowing which neurotransmitters are out of balance is important because they work together and sometimes one is the precursor to another. For example, glutamate is derived from glutamine, which is an amino acid, and GABA is derived from glutamate; so if you're deficient in glutamate, you may also be deficient in GABA.

Sometimes it may be impossible to keep neurotransmitters in balance without ongoing supplementation. As we learned earlier, environmental toxins, stress, Candida, diet, etc., all have a negative effect on and deplete neurotransmitters; and some of these factors, like environmental toxins or excessive stress, may be out of our control and continually throw our neurotransmitters out of balance. If the neurotransmitter deficiency is the result of genetics, it will probably be necessary to continue to replenish them through supplements as well.

As we talked about numerous times throughout this book, another system that is frequently malfunctioning or depleted in the alcoholic is the adrenal system. All systems in the body work in conjunction with one another and affect each other and certain neurotransmitters also impact adrenal functioning. Adrenal testing should also be performed to find out how well they are still functioning. If they aren't functioning adequately, additional support may be necessary; suggestions will be provided with the test. The most effective testing for adrenal function is a saliva test. Once again, I recommend NeuroScience, and this too can be a simple test performed in the privacy of your own home.

If you don't want to do any of these tests at home, you'll need to find an alternative health care provider who is educated in neurotransmitter testing. Once again you'll need to look to the sources I have mentioned at other points in this book that provide a database for each state.

As we learned earlier, the alcoholic is deficient in a variety of vitamins and minerals and these must be replenished in the body as well, as discussed in the nutritional deficiencies chapter. All vitamins, minerals and amino acids work together and need each other to make the brain function as it should. When this is done successfully, the chances of achieving long-term recovery increases drastically.

When you stop artificially stimulating the reward pathway and allow your neurotransmitters to stabilize, cravings for alcohol and/or drugs simply disappear. When cravings disappear, then staying sober is no longer a struggle.

Another way to help stimulate neurotransmitters you are deficient in is to engage in activities that stimulate neurotransmitters naturally. Exercise, prayer, meditation, activities like yoga, time with nature, nurturing relationships or any activity that feeds you spiritually will stimulate neurotransmitters in a healthy manner. It's also important to get adequate sunlight, as it too will stimulate neurotransmitters, as evidenced by people who get depressed in the winter when sunlight is minimal in some parts of the country. Getting enough sleep is also crucial for balanced neurotransmitters. However, on the flip side, malfunctioning neurotransmitters may disrupt your sleep and cause insomnia, so the sleep issue is a two-way street.

The neurotransmitter connection explains all the mysteries of alcoholism. It illustrates clearly why some people can drink alcohol without becoming addicted. Why some people develop alcoholism early in life and for others it is later in life.

Some people become addicted because their body wasn't producing enough neurotransmitters to begin with, because they were born with something they inherited. While other people who live with an abusive family feel so bad emotionally and physically that stimulating the pleasure pathway becomes a way to cope and feel good and their neurotransmitters are altered from the abuse itself. Some people are born an addict waiting to happen on the biochemistry level, while other people don't have a biochemistry that sets them up for it. Their genes, biology, chemistry, heredity, etc., does not leave them predisposed. People who have normal levels of neurotransmitters are not as vulnerable to addiction.

On the other hand, some people are set up biologically, but never have what I call an "inciting incident." I borrow the term "inciting incident" from the world of screenwriting. Unless you've studied screenwriting, you're probably not aware of it, but in every movie you watch there is an "inciting incident." It happens usually within the first ten minutes of every movie.

The "inciting incident" is the life-changing event that occurs in the story that sets the movie into action. Without an "inciting incident" there would be no story to tell. It is the catalyst that propels the movie forward and carries it all the way to the end. It is the crucial point at which the hero of the story is confronted with a major conflict that alters their life as they knew it and they must resolve it. It forever changes the course of their life.

For example, in the movie *Die Hard*, the "inciting incident" is when terrorists take control of a building that holds McClane's wife inside it. Some other examples are in *When Harry Met Sally*; Harry makes a sexual move on Sally. In *Pretty Woman*, Edward gets lost and stops to ask a prostitute for directions.

Sometimes an "inciting incident" is so powerful it hits you like a sledgehammer, while other times it is subtler like a soft summer breeze. However, in screenwriting the "inciting incident" always occurs early in the movie; in addiction it frequently starts early in life, however, it may not occur until later in life. In addiction the "inciting incident" can be a variety of things. It can be child abuse, loss of a parent, eating sugar and refined foods, environmental toxins, death of a spouse, loss of a job, or any major loss. Let's use my life as an example to take a look at this concept more fully.

Alcoholism ran rampant on my father's side of the family—although they may deny it, in my opinion my father and grandfather were both alcoholics. My mother, although she is unaware of it, has a severe Candida problem and likely has neurotransmitter deficiencies. She has suffered with anxiety attacks and agoraphobia since she was 17.

So to begin with, I was born already predisposed to alcoholism carried over from my father and mother. First of all, I was subjected to physical, emotional and sexual abuse very early in life. I was also subjected to neglect, which meant I wasn't getting adequate nutrients in my diet and, therefore, I developed a variety of nutritional deficiencies. My neurotransmitters were probably deficient when I was born, then damaged and depleted even more with the abuse and neglect. There were several "inciting incidents" in my life that put me on the path to alcoholism very quickly.

Let's hypothesize for a moment. Suppose I was born with an alcoholic predisposition but my parents were wonderful loving parents and met all my needs beautifully. Under these circumstances I may not have been on the road to alcoholism so quickly, because the "inciting incident" of child abuse and nutritional deficiencies would not occur. However, let's say, as many unaware parents do, they fed me a diet high in sugar and refined carbohydrates, which led to the development of a sugar addiction as a child and in my teen years led me to move on to drugs and alcohol. In this circumstance the "inciting incident" would have been the unhealthy diet rather than the child abuse.

On the other hand, let's say they were nutritionally aware parents and they weren't abusive. All my emotional and physical needs were met adequately and I ate a healthy diet that didn't include sugar and refined foods and we never used environmental toxins in our home. Under these conditions there is no "inciting incident", so it's possible that I could have grown into an adult without becoming alcoholic even though the predisposition was there.

Continuing on with this example, let's say I've grown up into a fully functioning adult without any active addictions, but I moved into an apartment and they send out an exterminator to eliminate a cockroach problem. The cockroach problem won't go away and they repeat the process several times. At this point I develop a bunch of psychological and physical symptoms. Pretty soon I start having cravings for sugar, carbohydrates or alcohol, or I'm so miserable I start drinking or drugging to feel better. I've now had the "inciting incident" that activates the predisposition that was waiting quietly in the background all these years.

Alternatively, let's say instead of moving into this apartment, I went away to college and because I wanted to join in and be part of the crowd I started going out and having drinks with my college buddies. Before I knew it I was out drinking every night and couldn't control myself. I began drinking every day. In this case, the "inciting incident" is I began drinking just to fit in socially, but my predisposition that was lingering in the background was immediately set into motion.

Let's pretend for a moment that as a teenager both my parents were killed in a car accident and I'm devastated. As a way of coping I begin to drink or take drugs and immediately I'm thrust into active addiction because my predisposition has been lurking quietly in the shadows.

However, let's go back and pretend that my parents were never killed, I never ate sugar and garbage food, I never had an apartment infested with cockroaches, and never went to college. Instead, let's say I got married and had children. I had a happy fulfilling life in which alcoholism never presented itself. Then 20 years later my husband has an affair with my best friend and leaves me, or he gets killed unexpectedly in a car accident or one of my children dies in a swimming pool. In my anguish and pain I start having a drink here and there to find some comfort. Pretty soon I find I'm drunk all the time and can't leave it alone. The predisposition that was dormant for all these years is set into motion at this time.

In one last scenario, let's say I was born with a predisposition to alcoholism but suppose my parents were incredibly loving, met all my needs adequately and when I was six months old they become environmentally aware and ate a healthy organic diet. I never developed any nutritional deficiencies or ate refined white sugar or processed foods. I never had any major exposure to environmental toxins. When I grew up, I followed in their footsteps and become an environmental activist and bought my own health food store. I was strong enough to resist social pressures and never engaged in social drinking. I married a fantastic man and we had several children and grandchildren and I never had any tragedy in my life. I lived a blessed life until I died naturally at the age of 96. Under these circumstances it is entirely possible that even though I was born with a predisposition to alcoholism, that it never became active because my neurotransmitters were balanced out in every way and I never experienced an "inciting incident".

Let's look at my son's life as another example of how this plays out differently for everyone. My son was born with an alcoholic mother and an alcoholic father, so he was biologically predetermined for alcoholism. As a child he was sexually abused by my brother, which set him up further for addiction. Although I wasn't aware of it at the time, my son showed signs of severe Candida overgrowth and food allergies when he was a baby and a young child, which were probably acquired from me during birth. He was an addict waiting to happen.

However, I got sober right before he turned five and we began a road of recovery. I believe if this hadn't happened, my son would have probably followed in my footsteps and became an addict when he was a child. However, I changed his diet by removing sugar, caffeine, white flour and all additives and preservatives, eliminated foods he was sensitive to, switched to organics, cleaned up environmental toxins from our home, and he made great improvements in his health. We engaged in years of counseling and took many steps to heal the emotional damage from his child abuse. We were very close emotionally and he obeyed most of my rules without a lot of rebellion.

Although, like most children, he wanted to fit in, so he would sneak sugary foods when he was away from home. As a child, he didn't have the self-discipline skills to keep away from sugar and other refined foods or understand the seriousness of this issue. He saw everyone else eating it and wanted some too. His sugar addiction was never arrested, because there was no way for me to control his diet every minute of every day. Parents of his friends thought I was being mean by denying him sugar and would give it to him behind my back and lie to me. I worried what may happen in the future, because I could clearly see addictive behavior in him in regard to food. Even though he was biologically predetermined and had been abused as a child, drug or alcohol addiction didn't happen in his younger years, because of the changes I had made in our life.

However, when he turned 17 and got closer to being an adult, he was then spending more and more time away from home. He was eating sugar and being exposed to environmental toxins all the time and he met friends who were smoking and doing drugs. Although I had worked hard and done everything in my power to help him heal emotionally, he still had some issues with self-esteem and, like all teenagers, he went through the natural phase of rebellion.

As a child he had felt confined and deprived because I wouldn't let him eat as he wanted, so now he rebelled by eating everything he was never allowed to have. Like any young man, he wanted to fit in and he was very vulnerable to peer pressure. As an adult, his sugar addiction progressed on to cigarettes and marijuana very quickly. He began smoking cigarettes and doing drugs around the age of 17 and within a year was a full-blown addict to marijuana and nicotine. The biological predetermination he was born with was now set in motion in response to the "inciting incident" of peer pressure and teenage rebellion.

However, he had several things going for him that most addicts don't have. Underneath it all he had a good relationship with me and he had years of knowledge about diet, nutrition, Candida, environmental toxins, addiction, etc. Although he was trying at the time to deny the truth he knew, it had been his foundation for a long time. He knew what was right and what he should be doing, but he had to go through his own experiences to own it as his own truth and not just something I taught him.

After a few years, his rebellion phase began to pass and he could recognize that the dysfunction in his life and the symptoms he was having were really a result of Candida, environmental toxins and diet. At age 20, he was only out there for about three years when his symptoms became so severe they gave him no choice but to change. He had some pretty intense withdrawal symptoms for a couple weeks and was quite sick as he detoxed chemicals out of his body; but he was able to get back on track relatively easy by eliminating sugar, caffeine and cigarettes, and following an organic Candida diet, stabilizing his blood sugar, and cleaning up his environment. He has now been clean for almost six years without any cravings or struggle at all.

Okay, so see the pattern here? The "inciting incident" for me was the physical/emotional/sexual abuse and neglect as a small child, but the "inciting incident" for my son was peer pressure and teenage rebellion, while for other people it could be something else that comes later in life. For some people who are born with a biochemical predisposition that have a good childhood, their alcoholism may not be triggered until later in life when they turn to alcohol for another reason. Perhaps their job puts them in many social positions where drinking is the thing to do, or perhaps someone gets a divorce and they turn to alcohol to comfort their pain, or they face the death of a loved one or a spiritual dilemma. The addiction develops later because the predisposition is there in the wings, waiting. If nothing puts it into motion, then no one knows there was a predisposition. Once the "inciting incident" occurs, then addiction is set into motion and the vicious cycle ensues.

The "inciting incident" for many people is child abuse. Abuse is an extremely powerful "inciting incident". As we illustrated earlier, it has profound ramifications on an individual physically, emotionally and spiritually. That is why so many people with alcoholism or other addictions have an abusive childhood. However, depending on the circumstances, it may not come into play until later in life.

Most professionals in the biochemical field believe that alcoholics are born with a biochemical predisposition that sets up the individual for addiction and I agree; however, I believe it is still possible to develop alcoholism or addiction if there isn't one. As we learned earlier, neurotransmitters can become deficient, unbalanced and/or damaged in a variety of ways; therefore, the biochemical issues can develop at any time in life. A person could be born without any predisposition, however, soon develop neurotransmitter dysfunction in response to their diet, environment, stress or upbringing. A biochemical shift may occur.

Because most of society engages in eating an unhealthy diet that is high in sugar and encourages Candida overgrowth, and is exposed to large doses of environmental toxins and excessive levels of stress, this leaves pretty much everyone at risk of damaged, unbalanced and depleted neurotransmitters. If a child is living with physical, emotional and/or sexual abuse, it will damage the neurotransmitters as well and cause severe emotional and spiritual trauma that sets up the whole addiction process. If you develop nutritional deficiencies from eating a poor diet, it can lead to addiction. So even if you're born without a predisposition already set in place, a diet high in sugar and lacking in nutrients, exposure to toxic chemicals, the development of food allergies, child abuse or any other high stress traumatic event could still damage your neurotransmitters and thrust you into the vicious cycle of alcohol or drug addiction process as you attempt to cope and medicate uncomfortable physiological symptoms.

At this point you may once again be thinking, "Wow Cynthia, why haven't we heard about this? Why isn't this common knowledge? Why aren't treatment centers embracing this valuable knowledge and using it?" I have scratched my head and asked myself the same question many times. To be honest, it's all very puzzling and disturbing to me. I don't really understand. When I was presented with the truth, it immediately opened my eyes. My response was, "Wow, isn't this wonderful and amazing." I felt like I was let in on the biggest secret in the world and I was eager to embrace it. I was appalled that this incredible information was not readily available to me.

The truth of the matter is that this information is out there, but it's hidden from you, so you need to know where to look. Unfortunately, most people don't know where to look. Another surprising fact is that this is not a new concept. It is a sound, scientifically proven and well-documented approach in the field of addictive biochemistry and orthomolecular medicine and what many people are not aware of is, that to some extent, it's been around since the time of Bill W., the founder of Alcoholics Anonymous, but has continually been rejected by mainstream medicine.

In the 1960s, Bill W. met a physician, Abram Hoffer, who taught him about the concept of megavitamin therapy. Bill was intrigued with this concept and came to discover that many of the symptoms like depression, anxiety, tension, etc., that alcoholics in recovery struggled with were related to hypoglycemia and vitamin B3, and that they could be controlled with diet and supplementation. He attempted to distribute this information widely throughout the AA community through a series of pamphlets called The Vitamin B3 Therapy.

However, these communications stirred a great deal of controversy throughout the entire AA community and most notably from the AA International Board, which consisted of members of the medical community that Bill himself had appointed, who felt that Bill was not a physician so he could not speak about such matters. Bill was not allowed to continue his work and was forced to stop sharing the information in AA meetings. He was stifled by the very community he had built and this valuable and life-changing information was ignored and dismissed.

It is heartbreaking to think of the profound and revolutionary changes Bill W. could have made in the field of alcoholism if he had been allowed to continue his work in this area. If he were permitted to combine the biochemical aspect with Alcoholics Anonymous, the results could have been nothing short of astounding. Once again we see how close Bill W. came to discovering the truth.

Unfortunately, to this date, nothing much has changed in the treatment of alcoholism or addiction in decades. Once again, many of us in the natural health field believe that is because traditional mainstream treatment centers are controlled by the medical community, and the medical community is ultimately controlled by the pharmaceutical companies; and they have no interest in recognizing the effectiveness and success of orthomolecular medicine and the biochemical approach, because it does not enhance their pocketbooks. As we discussed in other areas of this book, that means they would lose billions of dollars and they have no interest in curing any disease.

As Dr. Tullio Simoncini, a pioneer in the curing of cancer, tells us, "When a scientist has an effective and revolutionary idea, the medical institution attempts to suppress his work because he threatens the interests of the ruling class. No matter how effective the therapy in question is, their aim will be to destroy him."[2]

It's also important to note, that the fact that neurotransmitters and the reward pathway are at the root of addiction is not my opinion or a theory or concept that I created. It is what science has found to be true and even NIDA, the National Institute on Drug Abuse, and some universities are teaching this basic concept. In the back of this book, you'll find a link to the National Institute on Drug Abuse website and another site called The University of Utah in my bibliography. I encourage you to visit these sites and learn more about the science of addiction. The difference between NIDA and those of us in the natural health field is that they fail to understand that these issues can be addressed successfully with diet, nutrition and lifestyle changes, as I have outlined in this book.

There are only two treatment centers that address alcoholism through the biochemical approach and they are considered alternative treatment centers. You may find a few centers here and there that have incorporated a few pieces of orthomolecular medicine like nutrition or hypoglycemia, but they don't get the whole picture.

The truth about alcoholism is pretty radical. It challenges not only the current belief system, but reality on many different levels. It means that a new mind-set will have to be embraced and global change will have to take place. Our society does not embrace change or accept new concepts very easily or readily. It will cling onto the old for dear life at all costs. Truth is often denied even when it is undeniable and hits right between the eyes.

Contrary to popular belief, most people don't like the truth or really want to hear it. The truth is accepted only by a few. When confronted with it, most people will deny it and walk away. Change is uncomfortable, scary and threatening, and people will attack the truth speaker before attempting to believe and change. All we need to do is take a look at history to see that this is true.

For many years we believed the world was flat and that we were the center of the Universe. Christopher Columbus was ridiculed and Galileo was shunned. People refused to believe these truths that contradicted the reality they were comfortable with.

We've burned witches at the stake for being different or misunderstood by the majority of the population. Women were not allowed to vote and had to fight for years to achieve that right.

It was not all that long ago that our society thought it was acceptable to have African Americans as slaves, and it took a civil war to change this way of thinking. Still today you will find some people who stubbornly cling to racist ideology.

Not that many years ago being gay was considered a mental illness. Although we've made great strides in this area, people are still fighting to change the stigma attached to this.

For decades the tobacco industry vehemently denied that nicotine was addictive and caused cancer even when we had facts to prove otherwise. It has only been a few years since they finally owned up to this truth and did so only after being pushed into a corner with nowhere else to go.

Even when the truth is blatant and shocking, such as the senseless loss of life in the Vietnam War or the Iraq War, many refuse to admit their mistakes and acknowledge the truth.

Unfortunately, we can see that denying truth and refusing to change is a pattern in our culture. Once society holds a particular reality, it takes decades to embrace a new one. To accept a new reality one must let go of what is comfortable and familiar and move into unknown territory. Most people would rather stay with the status quo. They won't move out of the comfort zone unless forced to. People in power will fight vehemently to keep the truth from being revealed and protect their own interest regardless of the consequences. The closer the truth gets to being out, the harder they will fight to discredit it. People who have already seen the light literally have to battle those who refuse.

Additionally, when facing the truth is a harder road than living with the lie, many people often choose the lie. To accept the truth about alcoholism requires making major life changes that are not by any means easy. It's much easier to attend meetings, fight cravings, take prescription drugs and endure frequent relapses than it is to adopt a healthy diet and lifestyle that is free from sugar, caffeine, cigarettes and environmental toxins.

Sadly, when we look at the impact that alcoholism has on our society, we see that the consequences of ignoring this truth are deadly.

Fourteen

Leaving AA

"Some minds remain open long enough for the truth not only to enter but to pass on through by way of a ready exit without pausing anywhere along the route."

~Elizabeth Kenny

Let's go back to my life story for a minute and get caught up. In chapter three the last thing I mentioned about my journey through sobriety was that I found a new doctor and learned all the things I've just presented to you. Let me point out that all this information I just presented didn't come to me all at one time. I was piecing it together bit by bit over the years. I would stumble upon one book and then another and then another. At the time I didn't have a book like this one that had combined all this material in one place. The very first things I learned were that I must quit eating sugar, stop smoking, stop drinking caffeine, follow a hypoglycemia diet, clean up environmental toxins and reduce Candida overgrowth. At the time, I didn't understand the whole neurotransmitter issue or know there was even a name for what I had learned. That information came a little later.

The first thing I did was remove sugar from not only mine but my son's diet and I was absolutely astounded. As soon as I removed sugar from my diet, the crippling anxiety attacks I had been suffering with most of my life magically disappeared. Instantly! Just like that. I could not believe that after all these years it was something so simple. In disbelief I tested the theory over and over again and it never failed. If I ate sugar, the anxiety attacks came back immediately with a vengeance.

Now, I'm not saying this was an easy task either. My addiction to sugar was as severe as my addiction to alcohol and drugs and the process of recovery proved to be the same. I went through a similar grieving process when giving up sugar as I did the drugs and alcohol. Once again I had to let go of something that had been part of my life for so long. I rationalized and justified my behavior. I used it compulsively in spite of the negative effect on my life. As I mentioned in the chapter on food allergies, I actually wrestled my friend to the floor for a Twinkie and I fought with myself many times before achieving success. I struggled and fell off the sugar wagon several times before getting it right. Even though I knew I would suffer immensely from eating it, I just couldn't stay away from it.

However, it didn't take as long to succeed with this addiction, because once I could clearly see the cause and effect relationship, I could no longer stay in denial about the impact it had on my life, and this motivated me to stick with it. Additionally, once you start taking sugar out of your diet and begin to feel better, when you eat it again, the effects are much more severe and disabling. Just like when you stay off the drugs and alcohol. When they are removed from the body, the brain begins to recover, and when you put it back in the body, then it is a horrible shock. Once again illustrating the addictiveness of sugar. Within a couple months, I arrived at a point where the joy and benefits of eating sugar no longer existed. The misery was so intense that once again there was no choice in the matter. I was done with it.

Additionally, remember my son who had been held back in first grade because of his learning disabilities and hyperactivity? The one who was literally bouncing off the walls and extremely difficult for me to handle. After taking sugar out of his diet, he immediately became a new person. His hyperactivity was instantly gone. He could now do his schoolwork, concentrate, sit still, listen to instructions and he wasn't bouncing off the walls anymore. Our relationship improved drastically because we were no longer strung out on sugar and driving each other crazy. Naturally, as a child who had been eating sugar all his life, he would often sneak sugar from friends and neighbors and every time he did, his hyperactivity would return. However, the majority of the time he wasn't getting it, so he remained balanced most of the time.

As I continued to learn more about this whole biochemical issue of addiction and became more aware, I then discovered that other things would set off my anxiety attacks and my son's hyperactivity. I discovered that a big glass of orange juice would skyrocket me into a severe anxiety attack or shoot my son off into orbit because of the high level of natural sugar it contains. I also realized that when I sprayed my hair with hairspray I would be crippled with anxiety, irritability and mental confusion. I learned that a food allergy to wheat was a main trigger for my depression and so was hypothyroidism. When I addressed these issues, my bouts of depression disappeared.

At this time, I also quit smoking, gave up caffeine, removed all processed and refined foods from our diet, started eating organic, and removed environmental toxins from our living space. Giving up cigarettes was another major battle. I had been smoking three packs a day since I was 15, and I was now 28. A friend in AA shared with me that he had quit smoking by chewing on toothpicks, so I tried that and it really helped. He also gave me a lot of emotional support and I called him whenever I had intense cigarette cravings and he would talk me out of giving in. Once I got through the initial withdrawal, the process got much smoother because I wasn't eating sugar or drinking caffeine. My cravings for cigarettes disappeared very quickly because I didn't have sugar and caffeine triggering the addiction process.

That was 21 years ago, and to this day, I still follow this lifestyle. From that time on, staying sober was no longer a struggle. I never had cravings, desires or struggles to drink or drug again.

After learning about sugar, food allergies, diet, caffeine, hypoglycemia, hypothyroidism, Candida and environmental toxins, and seeing the drastic difference it made in my son's life, and mine, I became outraged with the mental health system. I had been suffering needlessly all these years with anxiety attacks and depression. I had been from one end of the mental health system to another and not one single person in the mental health field had a single piece of this knowledge that can change people's lives. I found this to be an appalling crime. It was then that I decided to go to college and become a mental health counselor. At the time, all I had was a high school education, so I enrolled at Youngstown State University and began another new journey.

This was in the 80's and at the time alcoholism was still considered a disability and, therefore, made you eligible for certain social service programs. I received financial aid from the Bureau of Vocational Rehabilitation to go to college. I feel the need to mention this because I had a fantastic social worker at BVR who was another important figure in my life for many years. Without his support I would not have been able to achieve my educational goals, and for this I am deeply grateful and hold him fondly in my heart as well.

When I learned this information about Candida, sugar, cigarettes, caffeine, hypoglycemia, environmental toxins, etc., I tried to share this knowledge with my fellow AA friends. I was so excited about what I had discovered and thought they would be thrilled to hear about it too, but sadly and surprisingly they were not. I was met with skepticism and criticism. My information was completely ignored. None of them really listened to anything I said. They refused to even examine or consider how it might be a factor in their life. They were completely closed-minded. They got defensive. "All you have to do is go to meetings," I was told. "You're going to get drunk," I was told.

Give up sugar, cigarettes and caffeine; you've got to be kidding. It was just too challenging to their reality. I very quickly realized that it was a futile attempt, so I stopped trying to inform them. However, now that I knew what I knew, I no longer shared the same bond with them. It drove a wedge between us. I couldn't sit in the AA meetings and watch them puff away on one cigarette after another, shove sugar-laced donuts down their throat, pound down one cup of coffee after another, engage in numerous sexual liaisons and claim freedom from addictions. My belief system and values had changed and I couldn't be a part of this.

In addition to that, after I stopped smoking and my body cleared itself of the poisons, I would get sick whenever I went into an environment with cigarette smoke. This is a phenomenon known as unmasking. When you start removing toxic chemicals from your environment, you do what is called unmasking. It's similar to what happens with alcoholism. Once you stay sober for a while and then you drink, your body's reaction to it will be severe because you've been away from it for so long. The same applies to chemicals and foods that you're allergic to. When you take them out of your system, you can then no longer tolerate them the way you once could. The body can no longer be exposed to these substances without becoming sick.

This was 20 years ago, so at the time smoking was permitted everywhere. Everyone in AA smoked and the rooms where the AA meetings were held would be so filled with smoke you could hardly see to the other side of the room. Every time I went to an AA meeting, I would have trouble breathing, get headaches, my throat would feel like it was swelling shut and I would just feel sick all over all the next day.

Additionally, over time as I sat in the meetings and listened to the philosophy that they preached, it started to sound like nonsense to me. It felt rigid, shaming and abusive. We no longer shared the same truth. I started to feel oppressed instead of empowered by their limited view. I no longer found comfort and hope in their words.

Due to the combination of these three issues, I began to cut down on my attendance at AA meetings and functions. This was a very difficult and painful time for me, because I loved AA and my AA friends. I was terribly hurt and disappointed, but slowly I began to pull away and go on my own path. This of course, prompted even more criticism on their part. When I did attend a meeting, I was met with, "Where have you been?" "Why aren't you coming to meetings?" and "You're going to get drunk."

In my entire life I had never felt like I fit in anywhere except a bar, until I found AA, but now I felt I like I didn't fit in there either. I was no longer one of them. Eventually we no longer had anything in common and I no longer felt accepted or welcomed by them. It was a terrible loss.

It was a very scary time as well. The last thing in the world I wanted was to get drunk or high. It had been pounded in my head so many times that if I quit going to meetings, it was inevitable I would get drunk. Although I really didn't believe this anymore, I was afraid to trust my own truth. So leaving AA was a very gradual process. I tested the waters very carefully to see what would happen.

To be honest, I was terrified. I was in uncharted territory and I didn't have a compass. There wasn't anyone I knew that had taken the path I was taking. It was unheard of at the time. There was no one to follow and I felt completely alone. The really funny thing is that even the woman in AA who gave me that first book called *The Missing Diagnosis*, which began my journey into all the biochemical aspects of AA, hadn't taken the journey I was on. She still attended AA faithfully and even she told me I was going to get drunk.

So at first, I just cut down to one meeting a week, and then it was one a month. When the world didn't fall apart and cravings to drink or drug did not return, I then progressed to every other month or so. Still the world did not fall apart and still no cravings to drink or drug returned. Eventually I came to trust myself and knew I wasn't going to get drunk. It took about a year to walk away completely.

No cravings to drink or drug have ever returned. Staying sober was and is not a struggle in any way anymore. As a matter of fact, it was no longer an issue in my life at all. I never even thought about it and still don't.

There was one AA person that I maintained contact with when I left and that was my beloved counselor, Hal, from rehab. He was the only person who didn't tell me I was going to get drunk. I'm sure that he carried this fear for me in his own mind, but he never put it out there for me. He never embraced the biochemical information I tried to share with him, but he continued to accept me and the fact that I was following a different path. He didn't criticize or preach. I deeply appreciated that and respected him even more.

For many years after I left AA we continued to get together for an occasional visit in his office or a walk around the block. He lived in the same town as my ex-husband and one time when I was picking up my son from a visit at his father's house we stopped in unexpectedly at Hal's house and had a beautiful visit with him and his wife. I believe that was the last time I saw him. Eventually I moved away from the area and lost contact with him. However, even though it's been years since we talked, I hold deep affection and gratitude for him in my heart. I truly believe he saved my life. This is true for all the AA people who touched my life as well.

However, here's the important thing to keep in mind. Although I left AA, I did not abandon recovery. I just followed a different path than I followed before. My recovery path included following the hypoglycemic diet, treating Candida, keeping sugar, caffeine, cigarettes and environmental toxins out of my life, eating organic and taking dietary supplements.

In addition to that, although I no longer embraced many of the principles that I learned in AA such as powerlessness, I did still continue to pray, meditate, build my character, practice honesty, heal my childhood abuse issues, go to counseling when needed, give back to others, and seek personal, emotional and spiritual growth on many levels. The world of psychology and traditional treatment has many great gifts that are essential to the process of recovery as well. It was the combination of all these things that gave me the struggle-free sobriety.

Recovery from alcoholism is about much more than abstaining from alcohol. It's about building a new life, a new identity and new values. The recovery path also involves addressing all addictive behaviors, healing relationships and childhood trauma, developing a new self, deepening your relationship with that self and spirituality. Thus far we have only touched briefly on these secondary aspects, so at this time I feel it's crucial that we discuss each of them in further detail and give them the attention they deserve.

Fifteen

Healing Childhood Trauma

"But such is the irresistible nature of truth, that all it asks, and all it wants, is the liberty of appearing." ~ Thomas Paine

As we learned in chapter 12, the incidence of childhood abuse in people with alcoholism is extremely high and plays a major role in the addiction process. When alcoholics who have abuse in their past get sober, they are left with a lot of issues to resolve, and if they are not addressed, they put the alcoholic at high risk of relapse.

It is my belief that when you address all the biochemical aspects of addiction that balance your neurotransmitters that this will help heal some of the physiological child abuse damage, but not all; and there is damage on the relational, spiritual, psychological, social and emotional level that needs to be addressed in other ways. There are a variety of ways that child abuse may impact your recovery in addition to neurotransmitter or brain chemistry issues.

When the adult abused as a child gets sober, all the hurt, shame, grief, pain, sadness, anger and even rage that was hidden behind the alcohol will present itself in full force. They have stuffed it and hid it behind the alcohol. Feelings and memories that have been stuffed away for years will surface and can be overwhelming.

Spending time with family members who were responsible for the abuse can, and often does, trigger memories and unresolved feelings around the abuse. After a visit with the family, you may walk away with intense emotional pain and shame. If the family members are addicts and are still using, it's very easy to get sucked back into the dysfunctional cycle, particularly when emotions are running high.

Additionally, people who have been abused as children have a great deal of difficulties in their interpersonal relationships. They are often attracted to people like their parents where they reenact the abuse over and over again and develop a pattern of relating that is unhealthy and destructive. They have trouble getting their needs met, don't know how to communicate effectively and are afraid of intimacy.

On a spiritual level, it alters their concept of self and how they fit in this world. They don't know who they are and where they fit in. It leaves them with feelings of internal deprivation and emptiness. Their identity is conflicted and fragmented.

Each of these aspects are very important secondary issues that can sabotage recovery from alcoholism if not learned to deal with effectively. As I mentioned in several other areas of this book, I attended a lot of private counseling, groups, seminars, workshops, etc., and read a lot of books for healing child abuse; and I think they are an essential tool to get the ball rolling, because they provide awareness and validation. That in itself encourages a certain level of healing. However, it is a lower level, and there must be deeper healing to make real progress.

If you engage in traditional psychotherapy and read the child abuse recovery books, it is often suggested that the abused individual end their relationships with dysfunctional/abusive family members. Another popular approach is to confront family members about the abuse. Although I took both of these steps in my path for recovery, I have a couple words of caution for anyone making this consideration.

This should be a very personal choice—what's right for me may not be right for you. What's right for you may not be right for your friend or other group members. Do not allow anyone to push you into something that doesn't feel right or you may not be ready for. This is a huge decision that will have major consequences on the rest of your life and one that should not be made lightly or hastily. There are a lot of factors to take into consideration and each one should be weighed out carefully.

First let's talk about whether you end the relationship. Here are some questions you should ask yourself (and be sure to be honest). It's very easy for abused individuals to not see their relationship realistically and to idolize the abuser. They sometimes confuse hope with love. They are willing to accept crumbs. It is best to make this list with someone who can be objective and help you look at it more honestly.

1. What are you getting out of the relationship today?
2. Is there something of substance in the relationship or is it superficial?
3. Is it a healthy relationship in any way?
4. Are there enough healthy components to justify staying?
5. How does the relationship make you feel emotionally?
6. Does the relationship meet any of your needs?
7. Do the benefits outweigh the abusive aspects?
8. How dysfunctional and abusive are they today?
9. Do you need a complete ending of the relationship or a partial separation?
10. Are you constantly seeking their love, affection and/or approval to no avail?

The answer to these questions will help you determine what steps you should take next. If you have a relationship with the abuser that leaves you feeling empty inside or tore to pieces every time you spend time together and you're not getting anything at all out of the relationship, then you're not losing much by severing it. However, on the other hand, if the abuser is a little softer around the edges now and you feel that the benefits you receive are higher than the negatives, then you may choose to continue the relationship.

Some people who feel the relationship with the abuser is salvageable are able to continue the relationship by setting firm boundaries on what is acceptable behavior at this time and limiting the time spent around them. It's a very individual experience and only you can decide whether it's best to sever or not.

Here are a couple key points to keep in mind:

- You can sever your physical connections with your family members, but the spiritual connections never end. No matter how much time passes, you will still be connected to them on some level and you'll probably be aware of that connection. However, that does not mean you should or have to spend time with them. You can love them from afar. Family is the most important thing in life, but sometimes it's best to let them go and create a new one.

- Regardless of how much you were hurt, how angry you are, how little you receive from the relationship, how much you want to end the relationship or how right the decision is, it will be a painful and difficult process. Even when it's the best thing for you to do, it is a major loss and will be accompanied by grief. It leaves a hole in your life.

Now in regard to confronting the abuser, there are many things to be aware of before making this decision as well. The first and most important point is that before confronting, you must already be prepared for the possibility that your relationship will end and ready to deal with that.

It is extremely rare that dysfunctional/abusive family members will acknowledge their abuse or say they are sorry. As a matter of fact, the chances are very good they will shun you. Keep in mind that dysfunctional families hate the truth speaker. If you speak the truth about your family, they will probably end the relationship with you out of fear and shame. In many cases, depending on how deeply enmeshed the family system is, it's not only your parents that will cut you out of their life, but your siblings as well. The truth speaker is usually ostracized, so that no one has to face it and life can continue as it always has. You are viewed as a traitor and must be eliminated. If you're not prepared to lose the relationship, you should hold off on confronting until you are.

Even if the abuser doesn't end the relationship, it is very rare that this scenario will end good or in the manner in which you would prefer. You must be ready to face whatever may transpire. At the very least, they are probably going to attack you and/or deny it ever happened. Therefore, it is essential that you make the decision to confront with realistic expectations.

You should not go into a confrontation with the hope that they are finally going to admit their wrongs and apologize. There should be no expectations of getting anything from them, because that's probably not going to happen and will only leave you deeply disappointed and feeling revictimized. If by some miracle they would own up or offer an apology, that would be an extra bonus. The purpose of a confrontation with the abuser is simply to speak the truth. To honor yourself and your truth. To stand up for yourself. To validate your experiences. To say out loud, "What you did to me was not okay." Your attitude should be, "Someone in this damn family needs to speak the truth."

Here is how the process unfolded in my life.

I had many different abusive family members to contend with and each one of these relationships was handled differently. There was my birth mother, stepmother, father and then my brother who abused my child. I shared with you in chapter three that each year I was sober I grew more and more aware of my family's dysfunction and more dissatisfied with the relationships. Each of these relationships caused me a great deal of internal conflict and emotional pain, because the memories of the abuse and the scars they left on me became a very big elephant in the living room. There came a point in each relationship where I couldn't ignore these feelings. I simply couldn't stand it anymore and there was no way to go on without talking about them. However, that point was at different times of my life for each one of them.

My birth mother was the first one on the list. If you remember in my story, the last time I saw her was when I was 19. I don't think I ever saw her again until a couple years after I got sober, so I was older than 27. At this point, I was trying to sort things out and build healthier relationships. I took my son and we went to see her. I tried for a while to see if a relationship could exist with her, but I struggled immensely with the same old feelings I had before. I still felt dirty, ashamed and extremely nauseas in her presence. Even just a phone call would incite the same feelings. In all fairness, I must say that she did attempt to reconnect with me, but I couldn't do it. After all these years, nothing had ever been said about what transpired between us in my childhood. There were so many questions and so many unspoken dirty secrets. Everything was just swept under the rug like it never occurred. Eventually there came a point when I couldn't take it anymore.

I decided to confront her about the abuse, neglect and abandonment, see what her response would be and take it from there. Since I really never had any relationship with her at all, I really had nothing to lose. The risks were low. I felt that maybe after I got everything off my chest that I may be able to maintain some type of relationship with her, but that was not the case.

Doing it in person was too threatening for me, so I wrote her a letter where I listed all the atrocities I remembered that had been committed against me, how they made me feel, the impact they had on my life and how I felt about it today. I explained that this was interfering in my ability to have a relationship with her today.

Surprisingly, she called as soon as she received the letter. However, she denied that any of the incidents had ever occurred and didn't own up to anything. The biggest issue revolved around her abandonment of me. Instead of taking responsibility for the fact that she let my father take me away without any fight at all and never attempted to come and see me even once afterwards or offering me any kind of comfort for how devastating it was for me, she turned herself into the victim. She focused on her pain instead of mine. What I needed from her at that time was simple acknowledgement of the devastation of losing my mother. She focused on trying to get me to give her comfort for how painful it was for her. I have no doubt there was pain involved in the situation for her, but it was not my responsibility to comfort her pain or absolve her guilt.

I was the child. I was the one abandoned. The focus and acknowledgement needed to be on me and my pain first and then we could move on to her.

Additionally, even though she hadn't been with him for decades, she idolized and defended the crazy perverted boyfriend that had abused me so severely throughout my years with her. She flat out denied his abusive acts and her involvement in it. Her loyalty was with an ex-boyfriend instead of her own daughter who was making an attempt to revive the relationship. I needed explanations, not denial. It was another slap in the face and added insult to injury.

It was way too much to handle, my head was reeling and I ended the conversation telling her that I didn't know how I could continue a relationship with her under these circumstances. It was confusing and difficult at the moment, because she didn't want to hang up. I could feel her clinging to me with fear. It seemed that on some level she wanted me in her life, but she wasn't able to do what needed to be done to get me there. That was about 17 years ago and I've never talked to her since. I let go of her that day. I think of her from time to time, but I have just never been motivated to reach out for contact. It's what's best for me. She has never made any attempt to contact me either. Several years later I heard through my cousin on that side of the family that my mother tells people that the reason we don't have a relationship is because I went to some counselor who brainwashed me into believing I was abused as a child. When I heard that, it only validated my position of keeping away from her even more.

Shortly after the confrontation with my birth mother, things came to a head with my father as well. As I mentioned at other times in this book, the wounds with my father were very deep and our relationship consisted of nothing but me trying to get love and affection that he didn't give. The longer I stayed sober and the more I grew emotionally, the less tolerant of him I became. I continued to feel dirty, ashamed and nauseas in his presence as well; so I avoided contact with him as much as possible, because a visit with him would leave me an emotional wreck for days. However, I still couldn't quit banging my head against the wall and every now and then I would still find myself in his living room trying one more time. He was married again to a new woman and it was the same scenario—she entertained me while he slept or tinkered out in the garage. She was a good enabler too, and tried really hard to involve him in the visits to no avail and to cover and compensate for him. He still never made any attempt to see me. Any relationship that existed between us did so because of my actions, not his. I received absolutely nothing from this relationship. The only thing he ever gave was rejection, abuse, criticism and ridicule.

Then one day something happened that broke the camel's back. I went to my father's house to visit him and he had bought a parrot as a pet. We were sitting at the kitchen table and I was trying to engage in a conversation with him, but he was completely ignoring me as usual. His wife kept trying to draw him in, but he was completely absorbed in his bird.

I sat and watched him in disbelief and horror while this bird sat on his shoulder and he was actually kissing it, hugging it, loving it, rubbing against it and talking to it affectionately. I had never witnessed my father express any love in any way, so this was a shocking sight and it was the final straw.

Now, I'm a bird lover myself, so I have nothing against birds, but in my entire life, my father had never given me one ounce of love or affection. I thought he was incapable, but there he was, giving it to a friggin bird, while I sat across the table empty handed and longing for it. When I said good-bye that day, I knew I would never be going back. It felt like something broke inside me. I was done trying to get my father's love.

Shortly after that, I put a letter together for my father. Confronting him in person would never be possible, as I was terrified of him. Once again, I made a list of all the atrocities he had committed against me, how it impacted my life and how it affected me today. Although unlike my birth mother, the goal of this letter was not to try and work anything out. I had let go of him and the hope that he would love me and I was saying good-bye. I had no desire to try and heal this relationship because it was impossible. I spoke the truth and then told him I wanted nothing to do with him in the future. I sent the letter off and I never saw him again. He never responded in any way. His wife sent me a letter and scolded me for treating my father so badly and I wrote her back telling her it was none of her business and please stay out of it.

That was about 17 years ago as well and we have never spoken again either. Several years later, I heard through the grapevine that he was sitting in the local bars of our hometown one night drunk and boo hooing about all the terrible things I said to him and telling everyone I hated him. I sent him another letter and told him I did not hate him, I hated what he did to me. I also told him that the people in the bar did not have the answers to our relationship and if he ever wanted to talk about it that he should come to the source and give me a call. He, of course, never took me up on that offer.

The third and most difficult confrontation took place with my brother who sexually abused my son and right along with that came my stepmother, because she was very tied in with him. In addition to working on healing my own sexual abuse, I had also spent the last five years working on helping my son heal. I had learned that the response the abused child gets from the non-abusers is one of the most important aspects as to how the abuse will impact the child. As you know from my previous discussion of this story, I did not validate my child or give him the kind of protection I should have when he reported it to me.

Although I was quite a bit late, I felt that I needed to backtrack and do all the things that should have been done in the first place, in order to give my son the best chance of recovery.

I had already had many conversations with my son about the abuse and he had been taught that if anything like that ever happened again with my brother or any other person that he should tell me immediately. I had apologized to him for not protecting him when he was younger. I told him that I made a very big mistake and didn't do the things I should have done because I was an alcoholic at the time. I assured him that none of it was his fault and that my brother was very wrong and this behavior is never acceptable. I encouraged him to talk about the abuse openly with me so that he wouldn't internalize the shame any further. Even though my brother no longer lived in the household, my stepmother had been informed several years ago that my brother was not to have any contact at all with my child. Every time my son spent time with my stepmother, I would question him when he came home on whether he ever saw my brother. For several years she honored this request without incident.

My son still spent a fair amount of time with my stepmother. He frequently went for visits on the weekend and he loved spending time with her. Then one day I went to pick up my son after he had just spent the weekend with her and my brother was hanging out in the backyard. I was very angry and asked her what he was doing there. She was hanging clothes on the line and acted as if she didn't know what I was talking about. "Oh, he hasn't been here that long," and went about her business as if nothing had happened. I was outraged.

I had been considering for some time confronting my brother and reporting him to child services, but I was afraid to take the step because of what consequences I may see from my stepmother and other siblings. I also still worried about the impact that my brother's mental disability had on his behavior and I still wasn't sure how aware he was. However, when I saw him there that day, I decided it was time. I confronted my brother right there and then. I was able to do it in person with him because he wasn't as threatening to me and it was brief. I don't remember all the exact words, as my heart was pounding out of my chest and I was quivering from head to toe, partly out of fear and partly out of rage over the situation. I told him that he should never have contact with my son again and that he should stay away when he was there for visits. I informed him that I believed what my son had told me and that I knew he had abused him.

It was the look in his eyes that day that gave me the courage and motivation to take the next steps. I walked away feeling sick to my stomach because it was the first time I saw a perpetrator instead of my brother. He had a cocky, arrogant air about him and I saw something in his eyes that I don't know how to explain, but it was at that moment that I realized he had at least some awareness that his behavior was wrong and I knew he was still a threat not only to my son but to other children. He had the same wicked look on his face that my father used to have when he enjoyed beating me and he seemed to be deriving pleasure from watching me squirm. He seemed to be basking in the fact that he had gotten away with it and there was nothing I could do about it. I also arrived at a stark realization that it really didn't matter how aware he was, his behavior had to be stopped.

Life was never the same for any of us after that day. Shortly thereafter I called in Children's Services and made a report. They came to our house and interviewed my son. They investigated my brother but, of course, he denied it. I knew there wasn't really any legal action that could be taken at this time, because too many years had passed and there was no evidence. However, I felt it was necessary for several reasons. It helped to validate to my son on a deeper level that I could be trusted and would protect him, it would help purge the shame that he carried over the situation, it made a statement to my brother about my position on the matter and it would be on record that my brother was a child molester in case any reports came in the future—and I was pretty sure they would. During this time, I also learned from an old friend that my brother had also molested one of my father's girlfriend's daughters, and even though my father knew about it, he too did nothing about it and covered it up.

My brother was now married and had children of his own. My sisters each had children that he had access to. The wife of my brother was mentally challenged as well, so going to her with the information wasn't the best option. I went to her mother, my brother's mother-in-law, and told her what happened to my son and that she should keep an eye on her grandchildren. She brushed me off and told me she was a doctor and if anything like that was going on she would recognize it and she was certain that it wasn't. I also told my sisters what happened and that they too should watch out for their children, but it didn't seem to register.

When my son told his story to the investigator from Children's Services, a few more facts were presented that he had not shared before. It appears the abuse went beyond just oral sex, although my son has blocked some of it out, there are a variety of memories that indicate penetration probably occurred. Even worse than that, he revealed that his grandmother, my stepmother, had actually walked in on my brother abusing my child on at least one occasion and maybe more and pretended she didn't see it.

During the years when I was still drinking, after we had confronted my brother and I stopped having him babysit for me, when she was supposed to be babysitting for me, unbeknownst to me, she was leaving my son alone with my brother at his house and he was coming to her house when my son was there and she would leave them alone together there as well.

Keep in mind that through all these years my stepmother insisted to me that the abuse never occurred and protected my brother. Granted, if I had not been inebriated all those years, I would have been clearheaded enough to be more thorough in my attempts to protect my son; however, another side of the coin was that I was operating on the assumption that my stepmother would also protect him, but it appeared to me that she handed my child to my brother on a silver platter.

At this point, I was already outraged by the fact that she had recently flat out betrayed my son and me by allowing my brother to be at the house when my son was there. It was blatant disrespect and lack of regard for both my son and me and I was in the process of trying to decide how I was going to handle this when this new piece of information came to light. Once again here was the straw that broke the camel's back.

Over the years of my sobriety, my relationship with her was slowly deteriorating. The more healing I did and the healthier I became emotionally, the less connected I felt to her and the more I disengaged from the family. Because of her Jekyl and Hyde pattern when I was a child, I never trusted her completely. I was always waiting for the knife in the back. Her love continued to feel fake or that it stemmed out of guilt rather than true connection. I had a lot of unresolved anger and hurt over her use and abuse of me when I was a child. I sometimes felt that the only reason she was still in this relationship was because of my son. I often contemplated confronting her as well, but I loved her and didn't want to lose the relationship.

Unlike my relationships with my birth mother and my father, I did actually get something out of my relationship with my stepmother. She often gave me emotional as well as a little financial support from time to time and showed me affection. My son loved her deeply and their relationship was important to him. Whatever steps I took were going to have a serious impact on that relationship as well and I didn't want him to lose her. I had more of an emotional connection with her than either one of my birth parents, but I could just never shake my doubts and fears about her sincerity and trustworthiness, and the longer I was sober, the more these fears and doubts presented themselves. My ex-mother-in-law told me once when we were having a fight that my stepmother talked about me behind my back and said horrible things, but then clammed up and I didn't get the whole story, so this fueled my fears even more.

I had been struggling all these years with my feelings towards her and here it was staring me right in the face, the fear that I had always worried about was a reality. She couldn't be trusted. She betrayed me again. She stuck the knife in my back like she had done so many years ago and I didn't even know it; not only that, she had betrayed my son as well. I was devastated. There was now no other choice but to confront her, I couldn't go on like this anymore, and I had to protect my child. I wrote her a letter, but delivered it to her in person. I handed it to her and told her to read it and that I would call her later to discuss it. I hugged her and I left knowing that I may never see her again, but still holding on to hope that we may find a way through this.

Once again I listed all the atrocities that she had committed against me as a child and as an adult, with special attention to the issues of betrayal that had just occurred around the incident with my brother and how they made me feel. I expressed to her all the feelings, doubts, fears and questions that I struggled with in our relationship. My goal in this letter was not to hurt her or sever the relationship. I was hoping that by some miracle we would be able to talk about them and find a way to salvage the relationship, but that didn't happen. She shut down completely and refused to speak with me about any of it.

I called her a few days later as I said I would, but the line was busy. The line was busy for weeks to come every time I tried to call, no matter what time of day or night I called. After a while I gave up and waited to see if she contacted me. She never did. Weeks and then months went by. Even though I knew this kind of reaction was a possibility, I guess it still surprised me to some degree, but I believe I had my answer. Her behavior clearly demonstrated how important I was to her. It seems all the fears and doubts I had about her sincerity and depth of love were valid. If she had loved me as she said she did, we would not have been in this position. Apparently something I said scared the hell out of her, because she was hiding like a coward. I grieved deeply, but accepted our relationship was over and let her go.

About a year later, I had a major crisis with my health and thought I may die. When I was in the midst of this ordeal, I was feeling very afraid and alone; I missed her and gave her a call out of desperation. She pretended she didn't know it was me. She pretended she couldn't hear me. Then she finally said, "What do you want?" I told her something like I was hoping we could talk about the letter, and she said, "You know that none of that stuff was true."

I said, "No, everything in that letter was absolutely true."

She said, "No, it wasn't."

I said, "I guess we have nothing to talk about then."

She said, "I guess not," and we hung up.

That was about 15 years ago and that was the last time we ever spoke. I realized then, without a doubt, that my worst fears were true. She did not love me. These were not the actions of someone with love in their heart.

A couple years later, the chief of police from my hometown called me in, because they needed a new report from me on my son's sexual abuse. My brother had been arrested for sexually molesting his own children and my sister's and the police were gathering as much ammunition against him as they could. Penetration had most definitely occurred and they had the evidence they needed. He was sent to prison. My son and I took some vindication in justice being served.

When I severed with my stepmother, I contacted both of my sisters and told them that what had transpired between me and my stepmother had no bearing on my relationship with them and that my door was always open to them. However, I never heard from either one of them again. My other brother that I was very close with was now out of prison, but living with my father, so I couldn't just call him up. I had tried several times to see him after he got out of prison, but for some reason he was not interested. This broke my heart, but I had no choice but to let him go. I heard through the grapevine that he was struggling with adapting to freedom.

About eight years ago he was visiting my old best friend that I grew up with and they called me up. I was ecstatic to hear from him and we reconnected as if no time had ever passed between us. I had given him my email address and he said he was going to give it to my parents, because he was sure they would want to hear from me. I told him that I was sure that wasn't the case. Then one day out of the blue, emails started showing up in my email account from my stepmother that weren't addressed to me. Over and over I would get a bunch of those silly chain mails that at the time were notorious for carrying viruses. I was in the process of setting up my online businesses and only had one computer at the time and they were bogging down my system. It appeared that my brother had given my stepmother my email address and she had added it to her address book and then forgot about it. Now every time she sent out a mass email to everyone in her address book, I was getting an email from her.

I sent her a brief, but polite note, stating that I was running a business online and these chain mails were bogging my system down and notorious for carrying viruses, so could she please stop sending them to me. I wasn't interested in trying to reconnect or anything, but I couldn't resist my curiosity as to how she would respond to me, so I very casually asked her how she was, mentioned that I had finished college and told her that my son was becoming a beautiful young man. I told her she was welcome to let me know how she was doing if she wanted, but if not that was okay too. The chain letter emails stopped instantly, but I never got a response from her. I told my brother about this incident and he was surprised, because she never mentioned it to him. He and I maintained contact by phone for a couple years, and then one day when I called his number, it was no longer in order.

A little later I then moved out of state and we lost contact. I have tried numerous times to reconnect with him. I've searched for him in the phone book on the Internet, but there was no listing for him. I've left messages for him in several different places that I've been trying to reach him. I recently sent him a card through my former best friend when I was growing up, but there hasn't been any word. I hope someday we can reconnect again and I continue to hold him in my heart.

So, as you can see, it was really essential for me to confront and end the relationships in which I did and when I did. Why on earth would anyone want to continue a relationship with people like this? It was necessary for my sanity and serenity. For me, it was abusive and suicidal to continue a relationship with them. Even still, it wasn't a decision that was made lightly in any of the situations. It took a long time and it was a process. You can't just read the recovery books and do what they say. You have to take the steps when you are ready and when it's right for you. Your process may be very different than mine. You must make a decision based on your circumstances.

Being ready doesn't mean it will be easy or pain free. I was literally terrified with each confrontation, and even though I didn't even have a lot to lose, it was extremely difficult and the grief, loss and pain were immense. However, I don't have any regrets. The truth had to be spoken and I couldn't continue a relationship with them as it was. It was the best thing I could do for myself and my son, but doing the right thing is often not very easy or comfortable.

Forgiveness

Honor thy mother and father, we are often told, regardless of how they have treated us. In an abusive family that is a bunch of crap. Your mother and father are not worthy of your honor if they are beating, neglecting, raping or harming you emotionally. If anyone else were treating us in this manner, we would be expected to walk away and it would be considered a crime; however, in the case of parents, we are expected to overlook it.

Lots of mental health professionals, new age gurus, self-help mentors, religious leaders, etc., preach about the need for forgiveness. Forgive and forget you may be told; but in the case of child abuse, this is something that is very difficult for many to achieve. There's nothing wrong with forgiveness; however, before we push people to forgive, we first need to educate them about what forgiveness means and how the process of forgiveness works.

For people who've been abused or people who've been wronged on a very deep level it can sometimes be very difficult to forgive, because it is invalidating. It feels like we're saying, "Hey, this was okay." You will often hear proponents of forgiveness say that forgiveness means to "let go of your anger and resentment," and that is true, but that is not all it means. The reason forgiveness is so difficult for so many people lies in the "definition" of forgiveness and all its "unspoken" implications.

The definition of forgiveness in the dictionary depends upon which one you're looking at, but here are some of them:

1. To grant pardon for or remission of (an offense, debt, etc.); absolve

2. To give up all claim on account of; remit (a debt, obligation, etc.)

3. To grant pardon to

4. To cease to feel resentment against: to forgive one's enemies

5. To cancel an indebtedness or liability of

6. To pardon an offense or an offender

7. To excuse for a fault or an offense; pardon

8. To renounce anger or resentment against

9. To absolve from payment of (a debt, for example)

10. Stop blaming or grant forgiveness

11. To stop being angry with

12. To stop being angry about [1]

That's quite a list and, as we can see, it is a little confusing and is likely to stir up some more anger and resentment from someone who's been hurt or harmed deeply. If we look up the definition of absolve, excuse and pardon, we see words like overlook, release from obligation, relieve from penalty, release from liability, let it pass without punishment, to free from guilt or blame, and it becomes even more confusing and complicated.

More importantly is that the majority of our society's interpretation of "forgiveness" does not mean "let go of anger or resentment." It is linked to many other unspoken elements, including its religious underpinnings. What most of us have grown up to understand as forgiveness means to "let off the hook." It's as if we're saying "it's okay what happened." Our current understanding is that the person being forgiven won't be held accountable and receive no penalty and even more importantly is that the person being forgiven will feel justified in what they did, or that they got away with it without any consequence.

"Letting go of resentment and anger" I can do, but to say what was done to me is "okay" is downright insulting, appalling, unacceptable and a crime in and of itself. So, our first goal in helping people to achieve forgiveness is to help them understand what it truly means.

Because the word forgiveness has so many negative associations and different interpretations, I think we actually might be better off if we found a new word to use for this process, perhaps it would be more effective to use the words "let go." However, for the purpose of this discussion, we will continue with the term forgiveness, and work on finding a more acceptable definition.

A new definition may be better understood if we talk about what forgiveness "isn't."

- Forgiveness does not mean to condone.

- It does not let them off the hook.

- You are not saying that what was done to you was okay.

- There should be a penalty, but there probably isn't.

- The offender is still responsible for what they did.

- The offense is not excused.

Forgiveness means that I understand why you did what you did, even if you don't, and I no longer allow it to have power over my life. I won't invest physical, emotional or spiritual energy in anger and resentment over it. I let go of you and the offense completely. What you did to me was not okay; however, I have compassion for you and will not hold onto this anger and resentment and let it eat me alive.

This does not mean that you can never feel anger about this situation again. There may be times in your life when certain circumstances will trigger your anger again. The key here is to acknowledge it, feel it and let it go. The anger and resentment are only harmful when we hold onto them for an extended period of time, when they have outlived their usefulness. Anger can be a great motivator. Use it to your advantage. Use it as learning tool to grow and advance. Anger will help you keep yourself protected from abuse in the future. Learning to say, "No, I won't allow you to treat me that way," is a healthy benefit of anger.

Forgiveness is a Process

The other most important factor we need to help people understand is that forgiveness is a process. Most people cannot jump immediately from pain and anger to forgiveness. There must be a period of time when the offended person feels and acknowledges their anger, hatred, outrage, sadness, hurt, grief and resentment and allow them to be. It is completely natural and normal to feel anger and resentment when someone has harmed you.

It is only by fully experiencing these feelings that you are able to let go of them. Your anger, resentment, sadness, outrage, etc., need to be validated, acknowledged, honored and respected. You are certainly entitled to feel them. You are completely justified in feeling them. What else could you possibly feel?

What was done to you was an atrocity. However, you should not hold onto them for the rest of your life so that they destroy your life. It is your life they destroy, not the abusers.

These feelings need to be purged and released. One of the best ways to begin this process is to express them with someone safe like a counselor or a friend. Writing them in a journal is also very effective. Don't hold back, censor or edit your writing. Just allow whatever it is you feel to be written with complete honesty. You can rip it up later and no one else ever has to read it, unless you prefer.

As we discussed above, expressing the feelings to the offending person in a confrontation is also a popular and effective means of purging, however, that's not always possible. It may open you up for more abuse, the abuser may be dead or you may feel too vulnerable to confront them face-to-face. So for some, this method may not work. It is my opinion that the deepest healing and purging occurs through intimate relationships and we'll discuss that aspect in further detail in chapter 16, but feeling and expressing your feelings is very important as well.

Expressing these feelings once may and most likely will not be enough. It may take many times in many different ways before they are resolved. Forgiveness for my family came for me, but it took many steps and many years to get to this point. Before, during and after the confrontations with my family it involved intense grieving periods, in which I thought I might die from the sadness. I expressed my feelings to my parents, to my counselor and in a journal many times. I revisited these feelings over and over with my counselor and my journal.

I had intense rage, anger and grief that I released by beating my mattress with a plastic baseball bat over and over. This was extremely effective. Probably the most effective technique I used and I recommend it to anyone. There is something incredibly freeing about involving physical energy with emotional energy to release it. You've probably heard of child abuse recovery groups engaging in this kind of activity while they are together using bataka bats, but I found it too threatening to do in a group. I needed to do it at home in privacy, to let it all hang out in its ugliness. I swung the bat so hard and so much physical energy was involved that I would literally fall on the floor in exhaustion after a session and my body would hurt for days. Another technique I used was getting in my car with the windows up and the radio as loud as it could go and screaming at the top of my lungs. Sometimes I screamed so much I lost my voice for a couple days.

This process continued for several years with many bouts. I cried buckets and buckets of tears over the hurt my family caused me. I would ask my counselor if it would ever end and she said "yes," but I truly didn't know if it would, but then eventually one day it did. It was all purged.

No one can tell you when you have felt enough or when it's the right time to forgive. No one can force someone else to this point or encourage them to go faster. It is something that has to happen on its own, in its own time, deep within the offended person. To tell someone they should forgive before they are ready is another violation. It invalidates their experience and their feelings. They must be allowed to feel what they feel for as long as it takes.

You can't just say, "Okay, now I'm going to forgive you." Forgiveness comes in time as you work through your feelings. If someone tries to "superficially" forgive because that's what everyone told them they should do, then that's even worse. Their pain, anger, grief, resentment, outrage, etc., gets buried and festers into deeper problems.

The pace of forgiveness also depends on the circumstance. If someone admits they were wrong, says they are sorry and attempts to make restitution, then forgiveness can be pretty easy. However, when you have someone that has committed unthinkable atrocities against you, looking you in the face, saying I never did anything wrong to you and if I had it to do all over again I'd do it the same, the road to forgiveness is going to be a little longer.

Forgiveness does not mean that you have to continue a relationship with them. I once had a friend who told me that I hadn't forgiven my parents because I didn't want a relationship with them. She said that if I had forgiven them, I'd want to be around them. That absolutely is <u>not</u> true. You can let them go, send them on their way, wish them all the best, but not want to see them again.

Traditionally forgiveness is something you give when someone admits they're wrong, has sincere regret and asks for forgiveness. It's not just given for any reason. Although I believe forgiveness can be given if the offended person chooses to, even if the offender has not taken these steps, it is my belief that in order to continue a relationship with the abuser, they must admit they're wrong and ask for forgiveness. There should be sincere remorse and a desire to do better in the future.

In order to continue a relationship with an abuser, they must acknowledge the hurt, say they're sorry and make some attempt at restitution with a sincere heart. Depending on the severity of the offense, this could take some time. Trust will need to be rebuilt. The one who was abused will need to feel assured that it won't happen again. In my case, it simply would be sadomasochistic to continue a relationship with my parents. I received very little or nothing emotionally from them. They hadn't admitted anything and never said they were sorry, instead they were denying and blaming me. They were all still active addicts and/or abusers. They continued to cause me great pain. It was impossible to have any kind of healthy relationship with them.

I am not an unreasonable person or lacking in compassion and understanding. It is very understandable to me how things could have unfolded in my childhood as they did. There are many explanations that my family could offer that would make sense. They could have said, "I was young," "I was immature," "I was overwhelmed with life," "I was abused as a child and didn't know any better," "I made a terrible mistake," or they could have simply said those two very magical words, "I'm sorry. I don't know why it happened, but I'm sorry." Saying I'm sorry is really not a very hard thing to do. It really is not asking very much. If they can't give at least that little bit, then there is really no relationship here to save.

However, I have forgiven my family. I have compassion and understanding for them and their plight. I don't feel anger, hatred or resentment anymore. However, I don't desire to have a relationship with them. I rarely think about them. When I do, I feel sad for them, for us, for what could have been, for what I don't have, for what I lost. I sometimes feel pity for them, because they don't even have awareness of any of these things.

I occasionally ponder in a weird kind of awe this question: "How can they let this kind of relationship exist?" My relationship with my son is the most important thing in the world to me. If there is any kind of rift between us, I work to resolve it immediately. If my son came to me and said, "Mom when I was a child and you did (x), it really hurt me," I would hold him and hug him and kiss him and tell him I'm sorry and try to explain why, and then do everything in my power to make up for it.

As a matter of fact, we have had this experience. As evidenced in my life story, I certainly was not a perfect parent by any means. I was an active addict for many years and even in sobriety I made many mistakes and engaged in behaviors that were hurtful and inappropriate as I worked my way out of my dysfunctional family patterns. It took me a very long time to learn how to be a good parent; my son is 25 and I'm still learning. However, the more common scenario that has occurred between us is this:

I go to him and say, "Remember when I did (x) when you were a child?"

He says, "No, not really."

I say, "Well, I'm really sorry anyways."

He says, "It's okay."

I acknowledge all of my mistakes and take full responsibility for them. I worked hard to make restitution and heal my relationship with my son and I encourage him to let out any feelings he may have towards me from his childhood, even though it is uncomfortable to hear them.

If my parents loved me at all, they would have made at least some attempt to do the same for me and we would have a relationship today. It is their responsibility to fix this, not mine. I gave them every opportunity to work this out and make it right, but they have not done so. There has been nothing. In all these years, there has been no attempt to connect with me at all. I think their behavior says it all.

Yes, we can have compassion and understanding for why the abusers behaved the way they did and forgive them; however, if they still behave in that manner, offer no acknowledgement of the crime or offer no apologies or restitution, it is not acceptable to remain in the relationship, because under these circumstances it continues to be abusive.

Understanding the process of forgiveness is very important for alcoholics for a couple of reasons, even if by some miracle they haven't been abused as a child, because as alcoholics we tend to engage in lots of behaviors that we will need forgiven for. In our active addiction years, we cause a lot of emotional pain and damage that may leave our loved ones with a variety of scars. We need to understand how forgiveness works so that we can help our loved ones get through the process. Not only because we want to be forgiven, but also because it is what is best for them. It will help our loved ones heal and improve the quality of our relationship.

We can't expect our spouse and children who we've neglected for years, called horrible names in a drunken rage or worse to be able to forgive us overnight simply because we got sober. In order for wounds to heal and be forgotten, they need to be acknowledged. Their feelings must be validated to help them let go of the pain. A lot of people avoid talking about damage they've done out of shame or because it's uncomfortable. They think it's better not to bring it up because it's easier, but that is not the answer. Yes, it is uncomfortable to face, but it's essential to move on and remove the power it has over the relationship. There isn't anything that can't be forgiven and forgotten if the right steps are taken. Never underestimate the power of the words, "I'm sorry," but also be sure to back it up with action. Saying "I'm sorry" is the first step in the process; however, there is still a lot of work to be done.

Sixteen

Relationships and Intimacy

"From error to error one discovers the entire truth."

~Sigmund Freud

Not everyone coming into treatment for alcoholism or drug addiction is quite as messed up in the relationship department as I was. For me, the damage was pretty extensive and it took a long time to work it out. However, dysfunctional relationships tend to be the rule rather than the exception when it comes to alcoholism and addiction, and most people have a good deal of issues in this area that need attention. The extent of damage that one has in this area is dependent upon a variety of factors, such as what kind of childhood you had; if the childhood was abusive, how severe it was; how long you've been an alcoholic; and what kind of skills you managed to acquire prior to becoming an alcoholic and hold onto afterwards.

The majority of people in treatment have grown up in abusive homes, which has left them with many emotional scars that hamper their ability to form healthy relationships. Additionally, alcoholism feeds dysfunctionality. It impedes and often obliterates intimacy and communication, which are essential core components of having a relationship. An active alcoholic is not capable of meeting the emotional needs of their partner adequately, which makes the relationship emotionally abusive even when it is unintentional.

If you remember in chapter three, I shared that the only suggestion I didn't follow in recovery was in regard to the "no relationships for a year" rule. There is some wisdom in this rule, but for most people it's just not realistic and there's no point in setting people up to feel like a failure in this respect. Yes, in an ideal world, it really would be best not to have any relationships for the first year so that you can stay focused on yourself, your needs and staying sober, but we don't live in an ideal world.

People coming into recovery are raw, their emotions are wild, they're scared, vulnerable, horny, want to connect with others and have sexual needs. We are relational beings and to try and put that on hold during such a vulnerable time is really difficult and sometimes impossible for most people.

Relationships are a risk to recovery, because deep emotional pain can be a trigger to drink or use, especially in the early phases of sobriety, until you have learned to deal with your emotions better. If the relationship ends, and it most likely will, because relationships developed early in recovery don't tend to last, then the loss and pain you are left with puts you at high risk of self-medicating. However, if you have a sincere desire to stay sober and you are committed to your recovery, then that will reduce this risk; and if you're following a recovery program that includes biochemical repairs, then your risks are reduced even more.

A more realistic and healthier way to handle this aspect of life is to teach people in recovery to start dealing with their feelings without the use of drugs or alcohol as soon as possible. Learning to cope with feelings without the use of drugs and alcohol is the name of the game in sobriety. However, the worry is that it takes time to develop these skills and it won't happen overnight, so for many people the knee-jerk response to emotional pain is to go back to the familiar, which is drinking or drugs. On the other hand, the only way you can build effective coping skills is by actually putting them into action. It is through experiences that you learn and grow. You can't learn to ride a horse by sitting on the sidelines and watching, you must actually engage in the activity. The same applies to relationships.

If you can stay out of a relationship for a while, yes it is a good thing to do, but if you find this impossible, then don't beat yourself up for it and just take the necessary precautions to keep it from interfering with your sobriety. Because here's the thing, no matter how much time you have sober, deep emotional pain can be a possible trigger if you don't know how to deal with your feelings effectively; so you might as well learn now, because you ultimately have no choice.

In the 21 years I've been sober, once I made biochemical repairs, there have only been two times when the thought of drinking crossed my mind. Each time was the result of intense emotional pain I was experiencing as the result of a relationship. These were not actual "cravings" to drink, they were only fleeting thoughts. I thought, "Boy I'd like to get drunk and not feel this pain I'm feeling." I had a desire to be numb. However, acting on these thoughts was never considered. It just wasn't an option.

I handled both of these situations by acknowledging these feelings, recognizing that they could be dangerous thoughts if not handled properly and dealing with them head on. I made an appointment with my counselor and worked through my feelings by talking them out and exercising. I didn't give the thoughts permission to grow into something bigger and they passed quickly without turning into an actual threat. Developing effective coping skills like these for dealing with not only relationships but life in general is crucial for successful recovery, and the sooner you can begin to cultivate these skills, the less risk to your sobriety.

However, there are a couple key points to keep in mind. In early sobriety you're not thinking clearly and you're riding an emotional roller coaster, so you're not likely to be making the best choices in the world for potential partners. Over time you'll be attracted to different people and make different choices. Feelings and emotions can be very intense in early recovery because when you give up alcohol and drugs you begin to really feel for the first time. It may feel like true love, but you'll probably find out shortly that it isn't. Try not to expect too much or get your hopes up too high. Don't be looking for the "forever" thing.

Keep in mind that any relationship you have in the first year or two of sobriety is not likely to be long term. As you change and grow, your preference in partners will evolve as well. If you are involved with another alcoholic in recovery, this will apply to both of you. You may go through many relationships in early recovery. Most alcoholics don't know how to communicate and maintain a healthy relationship. Many of them have not ever seen a healthy relationship and don't know how to have one. It takes time and practice to learn these skills.

Although the relationships you develop in early sobriety are not likely to be long term, they serve as a vehicle for you to arrive at a better place. They are like a classroom where you can experiment with new behaviors and skills and provide you with an environment to heal and grow. The only way to learn how to have a relationship is to have them and you may have a lot of them before you finally get to a healthier point.

Additionally, many people coming into recovery are already married or in a committed relationship, so it's not realistic or healthy to expect them to neglect or walk away from these relationships during this time. Adjustments and compromises will need to be made that allow the recovering person to do what needs to be done for their self while still remaining committed to their relationship. The alcoholic may have to take some time to be selfish and focused on their sobriety, however, this needs to be done with the cooperation of their partner, not at their expense.

The damage that alcoholism can do to a relationship is extensive and severe, and during early recovery it will probably be a rocky road. The partner of the alcoholic has their own hurt, anger, resentments, etc., that they need to deal with. It will take time to work through the damage that has been done. It's a high-risk time for infidelity as well. The damage may leave both partners with resentments and unresolved feelings that have put a wedge between them. Neither one of them may feel like the other understands them and what they're going through. The bonds developed with other people in recovery are very intense. You connect very quickly and deeply and, although not the preferred behavior, it's pretty commonplace for married people to stray off the reservation during this time with a fellow alcoholic.

So whether you're single or married, in early recovery there is a great deal of work to be done in the relationship arena. There needs to be education on what a healthy relationship consists of and how to build one, individual and couples counseling, groups, expressing of feelings, learning to communicate, building intimacy, learning to get your needs met, negotiating, talking it out, getting honest etc.

Additionally, many people, both single and married, have sex and/or relationship addictions that accompany their alcoholism, and thus engage in a pattern of unhealthy relationships. Men often have sex included in their addiction and women often have relationship addiction issues. Women can have sex addiction issues as well, but it's more common for them to be addicted to the whole relationship. Breaking these patterns is hard to do in the early phases of recovery, although an essential part of the path down the road.

Most treatment centers address the needs of couples by providing them with groups and counseling while the single people are left fending for themselves. However, there are many resources available to the single person that can be used to get through this period. As I mentioned earlier in my story, my life pattern had been to go from one relationship to another and that was the first thing I did in sobriety as well. If you remember, the first thing I did was hook up with the attractive Scottish man and there were many relationships in the first couple years.

They never posed a threat to my sobriety because I took advantage of all the tools that were available to me, by educating myself with books, seminars, classes, workshops and counseling. I immediately began to put the principles to use in my relationships. Yes, I was hurt at times, but I was learning to deal with these feelings as a sober person. I used my friends in AA, my groups and my counselor to work out the feelings rather than turn to drugs or alcohol.

Every relationship was a learning experience and each time I came away a stronger person with better relationship skills and I knew myself a little better. I was slowly learning what I wanted and needed in a relationship and how to navigate these waters. Learning is a process—you take a few steps forward and you fall down, you take a couple steps backwards and then forward again—sometimes you soar and other times you crash and burn. With each relationship, I had more awareness and a stronger resolve to achieve a healthy relationship.

My struggle was certainly not unique for people recovering from addiction. Although you may not hear other people talk about it as openly as I am doing here, out of shame or lack of awareness; issues like mine are rampant for those in recovery. There were all kinds of relationship dysfunction and sexual behavior going on, not only in AA but in rehab itself. When I was in the alcohol treatment center, some individuals, even those that were married, were slipping into each other's beds at night for a midnight rendezvous or even the closets and empty offices for a quickie.

Casual sex among single and married people alike is rampant in the 12 step community and people change relationships like they change socks. Partly this is due to the fact that everyone's emotions and brains are still under the influence of alcohol and drugs as they detox, but unfortunately, a lot of people are just not addressing their sex and relationship issues. They fail to see the relevance or don't have a desire to change this behavior. Many people just showed up for meetings and that was the extent of their recovery. They continued to use or be used by other people and engage in unhealthy sexual and/or emotional relationships without desire or intention to change. Some people even use the meetings as their meat market for preying on vulnerable people. Most of them were pretty easy to spot; however, some were a lot more slick and slipped under the sleazebag radar with ease. Some people even manage to manipulate the principles of the program to justify their behavior.

I had a relationship with a married man in AA who told me that there was nothing morally wrong with his behavior because he had worked it out with God. His sponsor had told him that he had sexual needs that had to be fulfilled and God understood this. Additionally, his sponsor told him that as long as he didn't feel guilty for his behavior there was no risk to his sobriety, so it was okay to lie and cheat on his wife, unless he felt guilty. I actually heard this kind of rationalization from quite a few men in AA. This seemed to be a common philosophy that many male sponsors passed along. Although I kept falling on my face and engaged in a few affairs with married men in sobriety, I was trying really hard to break this pattern; what made it even more difficult was the large number of married men who actively sought me out and pursued me. The number of married men in 12 step programs engaging in infidelity is astounding, not to mention the ones outside the program. If I had accepted the advances of every married man who approached me, I would have been a very busy girl.

In my younger years I thought it was flattering and exciting, but as I grew healthier emotionally it began to disgust me. Did I have a friggin neon light on my forehead or something, I wondered. I couldn't understand how they kept ending up in my life. Sometimes I already had a couple dates and weeks of bonding on the telephone before they revealed they were married. It was maddening.

Even when you have a true desire to change your behavior and are actively working very hard on these issues, as I was, if you've been badly damaged from childhood abuse, it takes years and even decades to resolve them and there will be lots of fumbling in the dark until you find your way. This was the case for me and it was the source of a great deal of pain and conflict for many years in my sobriety, long after drugs and alcohol were no longer an issue.

Sometimes I would make better choices and get involved with a good solid man who really wanted a relationship. I would tell myself this was the person I should be with, and I would try really hard, but I couldn't stay with these men. I'd break it off and fall on my face with someone unavailable, who couldn't meet any of my needs and caused me deep emotional pain. The more pain they caused me, the more I wanted them and the harder it was to break away from them.

As a society, we have a hard time understanding why women are attracted to abusers. As someone who's been there, I can tell you it is because they simply can't stop themselves. Until deep healing has occurred, there is an underlying force at work that is stronger than any rational or logical thinking. The other side of the coin is that it is not a black-and-white situation. The abuser is a complex individual and like all human beings has good qualities as well.

The last time I mentioned my ex-husband to you was before I got sober. After I got sober, I never had a desire to go back to him again and our cycle of getting back together ended. He continued to drink and do drugs, which was a major point of contention in our relationship as parents. I had to enforce strict rules so that he wasn't driving around with my son in the car while he was drunk or high. He resented these rules and this caused a lot of strain and conflict in our relationship and he vacillated in and out of my son's life over the years, because a lot of times he wasn't willing to abide by the rules. He disappointed, let down and hurt my son emotionally many times over the years, which resulted in a pretty poor relationship for them. We were often angry with him for not being the father we wanted him to be. He was often angry with us for pushing him to be responsible and become a better father. However, I tried hard to work with him to maintain some kind of relationship with my son and in spite of everything we remained friends on some level, had respect for one another and cared for each other till the day he died.

He developed many chronic health conditions as a result of his drinking and smoking. There was heart disease, high blood pressure, heart attacks, pancreatitis, a stroke and ultimately a brain aneurysm that killed him at the ripe young age of 47. Although, we had been divorced many years, I was surprised by the impact his death had on me and realized that when you have a child together, you remain connected on levels you're not even aware of. It was very sad and I grieved deeply for a good year. I miss having that one person in the world you can call and say "hey our son is doing this or that" and I have deep sorrow for the fact that my son lost his father, even though he wasn't the perfect model.

At one point, Robert, my lover from rehab, came back into my life one more time. He had relapsed and was caught in the grip of addiction quite severely once again and I became trapped in the mission to save him once again. Naturally he was engaging in a variety of addictive behaviors like sex with a variety of women, lying and using, which ultimately resulted in me getting my heart broken once again. After catching him in a major lie concerning another woman, I ended our relationship for the last time. However, no sooner did I end this relationship and I was immediately in another even worse situation with another married man.

I later heard through the grapevine that Robert had so many DUIs that he literally ran from the police to the airport and boarded a plane back to the UK to avoid arrest. We didn't speak for several years after that, but I often thought of him and once out of curiosity I hunted him down by telephone. He was now living in Scotland and he was still drinking. I saw him in a new light now that several years had passed and his hold on me was now broken, and I realized it was a mistake to contact him. I got angry with him very quickly for selfish drunken behavior and severed the connection again. That was 10 or 11 years ago and we've never spoke since then. However, as I mentioned before, when you share a life-altering experience like recovery together, you are bonded together forever. I still carry him in my heart.

Over and over this was the pattern for me. I repeatedly got involved in relationships with men who were unavailable in one way or another and then struggled terribly to get out of them. Over and over I banged my head against the wall trying to get my needs met. I'd no sooner get out of one and then I'd be in another one. Sometimes I could get out quickly and other times it took months or years.

Give me a room full of a hundred emotionally healthy men where everyone of them wanted to have a relationship with me and one person who didn't or was a user and an abuser, I would want the man who didn't want me or the user/abuser every time and I'd do everything in my power to make him want me.

Although it sounds like I wasn't making any progress in this area, I really was. It may be hard to see, but growth was happening. I didn't used to be aware that I even had any needs and I never attempted to get them fulfilled. I was simply willing to accept whatever little crumbs the man was willing to toss me. I would accept any behavior that was thrown at me. I would put up with anything in order to hold on to a relationship. I allowed myself to be used and abused and never said a word. That was no longer the case. I was aware of my needs and I was at least attempting to have them fulfilled. I was learning to assert myself and express my needs. I would speak up when behavior was abusive or I was being used and walk away. Unfortunately, each time I walked away, I chose another man who was still a man like my father and not willing or capable of meeting my needs and this is where I got stuck. No matter how hard I tried or wanted to, I couldn't change the type of men I was attracted to.

It was a long, slow process that unfolded in segments. Within the first month of sobriety, there were no more one-night stands or meaningless sex that left me feeling empty, so that was the first and easiest step. After the first year of sobriety, I was able to break the pattern of having more than one relationship simultaneously to meet my needs, however, married men still continued to be a huge problem off and on for several years. Finally, after a very humiliating and destructive relationship with a married man, there came a major break for me in this area as well. I no longer wanted married men. However, last but not least, the men who were unavailable emotionally, who didn't want commitments, were players, ones that were active addicts, who were users and abusers were still irresistible to me.

Even after five, six, seven, ten years of sobriety, after reading every book on the market for recovery, healing child abuse and relationships, attending all the workshops, classes, seminars and groups, continuous one-on-one counseling, engaging in all the activities and techniques that are supposed to heal child abuse issues and enable a woman abused as a child to seek healthier relationships, it just didn't happen for me. Over and over I found myself involved in a relationship I didn't want to be in, that didn't meet my emotional needs and caused me great emotional pain. No matter how hard I tried, I couldn't stop being attracted to men like my father.

Even after I had years of stable sobriety, was balanced, emotionally healthy and very self-disciplined in every other area of my life and was in graduate school studying to be a mental health counselor, I couldn't stop this unhealthy behavior and break this cycle even though I despised it. I could clearly see my unhealthy pattern and dysfunction and yet I couldn't break it. "My God, what is wrong with you?" I would ask myself over and over. I knew better. I wanted better, but I just couldn't stop myself. It was agonizing, embarrassing and humiliating for me.

I went from one counselor to another trying to understand why I couldn't stop being attracted to men who used and abused me and put a stop to it, but couldn't find the answers. Literally, I think I had seen almost every mental health professional in the county. No one could help me. They were at a loss, because I had worked hard to change and followed all their instructions. The internal conflict and emotional pain that this behavior caused me was so great and the swinging back and forth between contradicting values and behaviors were so extreme that this lead a couple of the counselors I saw to believe that I might have DID, Dissociative Identity Disorder, also known as Multiple Personality Disorder, which is pretty common in women who have been severely abused as a child, as I was.

I researched this possibility thoroughly, and for a while I thought they might be right. I most certainly had severe PTSD (posttraumatic stress disorder), which usually accompanies DID. When I read the experiences of other DID women, I could relate completely to their feelings and experiences. There certainly seemed to be two me's. There was clearly a me who did not want these relationships and a me who could not resist them. I lived a double live. By day I was a loving mother, excelling in college and a competent mental health professional, but by night engaged in this vicious battle of being attracted to men who violated everything I stood for. It was like I was Clark Kent and Superman, but my Clark Kent violated my values and caused me great emotional distress. There was no controlling her. She would take completely over and run the show and she was much stronger than I was.

However, there was one key factor missing that led me to believe I didn't truly have two distinct personalities, and that is the loss of time. In all the material I read, every DID woman experienced a great deal of loss of time. When one personality took over, then the main personality would not be present and when she came back in control she didn't know what happened during the hours that the other personality was in control. I never had any loss of time. I was always fully aware when the other self took over so this didn't seem to fit the criteria for textbook DID. A couple of my counselors said that this just meant that I had "conscious" personalities. Meaning both of them were present at all times. However, there were other counselors who disagreed with this conclusion and thought that the label didn't fit me completely. They felt I was engaging in dissociation, had a severely fragmented sense of identity and pieces of me were compartmentalized, but not true separate personalities.

Although, I don't really know for certain what the case was, I went with the fragmented sense of identity rather than the DID, because it felt more like the truth; however, since I did fit the definition of DID in several ways, I remained open to the possibility and actually worked on integrating my identity as if I actually did have DID.

In many ways I did feel that I was two different people. I experienced battles with myself as if I were dealing with another person. I did refer to this aspect of myself as "she" or "her." "She" kept trying to take over and "she" caused me immense internal conflict and pain. "She" had different values and behaviors than I did. It often felt like I was an observer rather than a participant or in a dream state when engaged in these relationships, which is a sure sign of dissociation.

If you remember in the chapter on child abuse, I talked about how my first identity formed into someone who sexualized herself, someone who was used and not good enough. This was at the core of my development and I came to believe this is why it was the most difficult hurdle for me to overcome.

This piece of my identity, known as "she," didn't know how to stop allowing herself to be used or how to stop sexualizing herself. She, in some ways, craved it and basked in the experience. It was the only way she knew how to connect to a man. It made her feel alive and exhilarated. To get her to stop this behavior was like asking her to stop being who she was. She had to become someone else. She felt stifled and repressed when I didn't allow her to behave as she wanted.

For many years "she" was much stronger than I was. She was the one who had been in control most of my life, until I got sober. I could gain the upper hand for a while and that's when I would make great progress, but she would sabotage everything and come back in and take me a few steps backwards. I battled with this piece of identity that wanted relationships with abusive men for many years and "she" did not go down without a fight. There was no stopping her once she got a good stranglehold on me. I was often beside myself and completely distraught by her behaviors.

When I had five or six years sober, we met a new man, we'll call him Michael to protect his identity, who became a very significant person in my child abuse recovery and integration of my fragmented identity in many ways. He, of course, was an active alcoholic, in the advanced stages of alcoholism. Naturally this meant he engaged in all the usual alcoholic behaviors, like lying, cheating, stealing, using and abusing. Just like my father he was aloof, distant, selfish, emotionally cut off, terrified of intimacy, never expressed his emotions and rarely showed affection.

He was exceptionally attractive physically and we had an intense sexual bond like either of my identities had never had before and "she" fell head over heels in love almost instantly. Actually I was quite attracted to him as well; however, as I learned the extent of his drinking and his intentions, I tried to put an end to it right away, but "she" wouldn't have it.

Not too long into the relationship he stated right up front that he "just wanted to have a good time" and was not looking for a "commitment." I respected him for being honest and immediately said, "Okay then, let's get out of here," and promptly ended the relationship, however, these words were music to "her" ears. This only made her want him even more and began the vicious battle of trying to make him want her.

There "she" was on the damn phone calling him up. She'd start the relationship back up. I'd end it. She'd start it. I'd end it. We went back and forth like this for an entire summer. At one point the relationship ended for an entire year. During that year there were a couple other brief affairs to deal with the rejection, but the connection to and longing for him didn't stop. She yearned and yearned for him. When we would pass him in town, it tore her to pieces. Then one day out of the blue, he called and it started all over again.

At this time I was still working on my issues with one of the counselors, Daryl, who felt I had DID. She too became one of the most significant people to have ever touched my life. I worked with her on my childhood issues for over a decade and still give her a call even now from time to time when an issue resurfaces. She too helped me learn a great deal about abuse, relationships, commitment and intimacy and played a pivotal role in my healing.

I would repeatedly show up in her office, completely distraught, because I was once again back in this relationship I did not want to be in. She shared with me her belief that the only way to heal and stop having these relationships was by actually accepting where you are at the time and allowing yourself to completely immerse yourself in it. She suggested that I accept, for the time being, that this was where I was at and allow the "unruly one" to have her way. She felt the only way "out" was to go "through it."

This was a pretty radical belief and contradicted everything I had learned about recovery from child abuse thus far. However, it really made a lot of sense. I had tried everything else and it didn't work. The consensus for healing from child abuse is that you must run from these kinds of relationships and avoid them at all cost. There was great shame in my inability to achieve this goal and I didn't know what else to do.

At first I resisted my counselor's belief, and continued to try and stop the relationship, but it became very clear I wasn't going to succeed, because this relationship was much more powerful than any I had ever had before. The grip it had on "her" and she had on me was bigger than both of us. It was irresistible in ways like never before. I simply lost control, completely; there was just no stopping "her." It was impossible to drag her away. He hit all her emotional triggers and was the perfect man in her eyes for all our dysfunctional needs.

Around this time, I had also read a book by Harville Hendrix called *Keeping the Love You Find* and it had a very similar approach as to what my counselor was suggesting. I highly recommend you pick up a copy of Harville's book and give it a good read. His teachings revolve around how relationships help us heal our childhood wounds.

Harville tells us that our choice in mates is made on an unconscious level and that the unconscious has an agenda of its own. That agenda is to "heal the wounds of our childhood." We are unconsciously attracted to mates who possess the same characteristics as our parents.

"What we unconsciously want is to get what we didn't get in childhood from someone who is like the people who didn't give us what we needed in the first place."

Harville also tells us that the answer to this dilemma is not to keep finding new relationships, but to work out the issues within the relationship. We must learn to respond to and interact with one another in a different way. Each partner needs to become aware of his or her unconscious needs and wounds and help each other heal.[1]

The only problem I faced with this theory was that my partner wasn't willing to make a commitment to healing me, but since I was incapable of being attracted to a loving and committed mate, I decided to use the same principles by starting where I was at and working with what I had.

So I quit fighting with "her" and allowed her to have the relationship. I surrendered to the craving and allowed her to wallow in it completely. "At least he wasn't married," I assured myself. However, I had ground rules. I said, "Okay, we'll do this, but here's the deal." I worked like a parent in the background overseeing a child's work. I guided, instructed and sometimes forced "her" to grow, learn and change. Anytime he engaged in behavior that was unacceptable or abusive, she was forced to take the necessary steps to stick up for herself and/or leave the relationship until he behaved appropriately. She had to learn to speak up, express her needs, say no when she wanted to and tell him when his behavior was unacceptable.

At this point, it was no longer clear whether he wanted a relationship or not. He was still saying the words, but his actions were saying something different. He said he didn't want a relationship, but he was very clearly having one. Nothing was black and white and things got very complicated and confusing very quickly.

After "she" revealed to him that she was in love with him, he reluctantly admitted it as well, although he continually took it back. One day he loved me, the next day he didn't, the next day he did, the next day he didn't. One day he wanted me, the next day he didn't. It was an insane seesaw of emotions. He repeatedly ended the relationship, swearing he didn't want a commitment. I repeatedly ended the relationship, telling him I wanted a commitment and a sober partner. However, he too would be calling in a few days if she had not called first. His inconsistency only fueled her desire to be with him even more. It soon became clear to me that he was in as much struggle and conflict about this relationship as I was. Both of us knew we shouldn't and couldn't be together, but neither one of us could stay away from the other.

I would say, "I'm looking for a committed relationship," and "I can't be with you unless you get sober," and he would leave for a while. She would get mad at me for continuously driving him away. Then he would come back and engage in a relationship and say he wanted to quit drinking. He'd work on it for a while and after a few days or sometimes a few weeks, he'd once again say he wasn't looking for a "commitment" and he couldn't stop drinking, but he still wanted to be with me. So, I would say, "No, that's not acceptable," and I would leave. She would grieve immensely during the periods that I wouldn't permit contact with him.

Although "she" was undoubtedly addicted to him, her feelings of love for him were real and they were more intense than they had ever been with anyone before. We had a very intense connection emotionally, physically and spiritually. Every now and then there was a glimmer of hope that he would get his act together, but he just couldn't get there. Since he didn't want the same kind of relationship I wanted and was not capable of meeting our needs, I was willing to walk away from the relationship. "She" was not. She could not give up the fight to win his love. It was simply unbearable.

Additionally, we had a sex life that was out of this world, and this became one of the biggest and most powerful aspects of our bond. Neither one of us could walk away from it. Like everything in our relationship, the intensity and passion was overpowering. The amazing thing is that in all the years of my life when I was having all that sex with all the other men in my life prior to this, I almost never had an orgasm. They were pretty rare until I met this man and then I was having orgasms left and right, and they were unlike anything I'd ever experienced before. I did things with this man I never dreamed of doing with anyone. I opened up and let go like never before. I discovered my sexuality in a whole new way and learned how to get my sexual needs met. If you remember, I had always had quite a voracious sexual appetite, so this aspect of the relationship was very strong. It held us together in times when nothing else was working and anyone in his or her right mind would have walked away. We probably broke the Guinness world record for having break-up and make-up sex.

For eight very long years we rode this roller coaster of going back and forth and back and forth before it finally burned itself out. We broke up more times than I can remember and went through a great deal of life experiences together. A couple times he went into treatment for addictions and attempted to change, but it never lasted very long. Like most addicts he had more than one addiction, of which included a sex addiction, so there were other women in his life from time to time that caused me excruciating pain. My first week in graduate school, I showed up for class up with a severely battered face, because he had been on a bender for days and for the first time in our relationship, and also the last, he became violent and took it out on my face. This was very embarrassing, as I didn't know how to explain to my fellow classmates and professors in the mental health counseling program how I had ended up in this situation.

Once again it sounds like I was going backwards rather than forward, but that was not the case. In the past when I was involved in abusive relationships, I accepted their behavior. I never took any steps to let them know it was unacceptable or protect myself. This time I promptly went to the police station and pressed charges against him. He was arrested and eventually sentenced to three months in jail, probation for a year, mandatory counseling and AA meetings.

It was one of the hardest things in the world I had ever gone through. "She" resisted me terribly when we had to testify against him and tried to minimize the situation, but I insisted that she had to let him know that hitting was not acceptable. The district attorney handling the case told me it was the worst black eye she had ever seen, so it wasn't like we were talking about an innocent slap in the face. Michael was extremely angry with me and I assumed our relationship was over, but he wasn't out of jail four hours and he had already called. As a matter of fact, he had already contacted me before the court system alerted me that he was free, which is standard practice in domestic violence cases. We were together another six years and he never touched me in an abusive way again, never even came close to it.

There's a very big difference between someone who engages in an abusive relationship without any awareness and who is not actively working on changing than there is with someone who is aware. The one without awareness is perpetuating the cycle, where the one with awareness is growing and learning and working her way out of the dysfunction. When you let the abuser know that their behavior will not be accepted, then the abuse stops. Just because a man hits you once, does not necessarily mean he will hit you again, if you do something about it. If you don't do anything about it, then you reinforce his behavior and pretty much guarantee that he will do it again. You are essentially saying that this is acceptable behavior. However, if you set a firm boundary the first time it happens by taking the necessary legal steps to protect yourself and force him to face up to it, then you have taken the first steps to break the cycle.

However, our dysfunctional dance continued and so did his inability to meet "her" emotional needs. The better she got at expressing her needs and pointing out his unacceptable behavior, the more he ran; however, he continued to return over and over. His drinking continued and progressed and so, of course, so did his alcoholic behavior. He left her a couple times for his flavor of the week, but would return after it sizzled out. He continued his "I love you, I don't love you" pattern throughout the whole course of the relationship. He'd let her in his life and his heart and kicked her out just as fast. He ripped her heart out, threw it on the ground and stomped it to smithereens more times than I could count, and yet she continually took him back. It seemed her tolerance for pain was an endless pit and her willingness to live with it undying.

On the other hand, as there always are in unhealthy relationships, there were intensely good times as well. I had some of the best times of my life with this man as well as some of the worst, but that's true of all relationships, is it not? We spent many perfect days on country rides basking in the beauty of fall foliage or snow squalls, at the lake making love, connecting with nature and engaging in intimate and intelligent conversation, or cooking meals of spaghetti and meatballs. We shared our lives together and ourselves more deeply than either of us had done before and we had a great deal of fun. He had endured his own unspeakable hell as a child and that is where we connected—two wounded souls reaching out to one another.

To most people, on the surface it looked like I was engaging in an unhealthy abusive relationship, but in reality it was the deepest, most intimate, healthiest relationship I'd ever had. "She" was changing, growing and learning as a result of it. Each year she demanded more from him and he actually learned to give more over the years. There were times I thought we might actually make it. He would take a couple steps forward and then fall back into his old pattern. Every time we broke up and got back together, he came back more willing to meet our needs. For a long time it was the hope that he was going to take those crucial steps necessary to move forward that kept her hooked in the relationship.

"Her" change and growth was a very gradual process and she would often run out of control and engage in behavior that was unacceptable to me. I continually had to undo things that she allowed to happen. Her behavior put me through an immense amount of shame and pain. She would sometimes take him back when he hadn't acknowledged what he'd done wrong and I'd have to end the relationship again, until he did. There were times she didn't stick up for herself when she should have and I would go back and revisit the situation with him and point out how he should not do this in the future.

There were many times that I had to drag "her" kicking and screaming by her hair out of the relationship because he was engaging in unacceptable behavior, but she was willing to put up with it. There were times I ended the relationship and she would sneak a visit with him before I had a chance to step in and I'd have to end it again a few hours later. If I had a nickel for every time I said "it's over" or "we're over," I'd be rich. I thought by saying it with such conviction, it actually made it true. I wanted it to be true. I tried to make it be true, but it wasn't.

However, as the years went by, "she" learned how to do all this for herself and the times I had to step in became less and less. The stronger she got, the more she wanted and expected from him. Each year she was less willing to accept his behavior and more capable of standing up for herself. Each year she learned how to live without him a little better. Each time the relationship ended and she grieved, she realized she could live without him or any man for that matter. It became clear that if we could survive this pain we could survive anything.

Eventually over the years, the line between "her" and "me" began to blur. Slowly this relationship was losing appeal to her as she grew healthier and wanted more from him and accepted the reality that he was not going to change. She began to align herself with me and my values more often and grew less tolerant of his behavior. The times in which she took control and engaged in unhealthy behavior grew less frequent. The internal battles didn't occur as often.

Then the day came, when "she" tried to win his love for the last time. He was no longer fighting with his addictions and had succumbed completely to the addictive lifestyle. It became crystal clear that he wasn't going to get sober and he wasn't able to meet our needs in the manner in which we needed. She no longer had the craving or uncontrollable drive to try and change his mind. It was no longer important to her. Having her needs met was now more important. It was no longer acceptable to be with him if he could not rise to the challenge. She was disappointed in him for the last time.

I can remember the day very clearly in my mind when the final break happened. Once again, it actually felt like something inside broke. It was the same kind of break I felt when I realized that I would never get my needs met with my parents and I let go of them. I was done and it didn't even need to be said out loud. I had said it so many times before when I didn't mean it, trying to make it be real and in the end I didn't feel the need to say it at all. There was no anger, no conflict, no resentment and no drama. We simply walked away calmly and let him go.

However, for the first year, it wasn't a clean break without any struggle. He continued to pursue her. Every now and then she was tempted by his attempts to see her, but would quickly change her mind. She still sexualized herself somewhat with new men in her life for a short period because she had never been in this terrain under these new circumstances. However, things were very different now. She found that the old behavior was no longer comfortable or desirable. It used to fit like a glove, but that was not the case now. Men like my father were still appearing in my life, but I was thrilled to realize that she no longer had a need or uncontrollable drive to be with them. They were unappealing to her. She didn't want to play the game anymore. As soon as it became clear who they were, she would walk away. It took about a year for her to learn how to navigate these waters with her new and healthier behavior, but by the end of that year, her values and mine were pretty much aligned and in harmony most of the time.

I don't think Michael even realized it was over. I guess I wasn't sure either until later. I'm sure he assumed I'd be back as I always was in the past. It's been eight years since we've seen each other and I'm not sure he's still accepted it's completely over. We're on friendly terms and he still calls from time to time. He often asks to see me, but I decline. I don't think he realizes I'm a completely different person now. There are no bad feelings towards him. He wasn't a bad person, just an active addict struggling with his own issues and for some reason couldn't find his way out. He continues to drink and has developed a variety of serious health conditions as a result. I fear he will probably be one of those tragic alcoholism statistics that takes him away before his time.

In all honesty, I can't say that I regret having this relationship. We had a lot of great times, a healing, educational and intensely pleasurable journey through sexuality, and I attained profound emotional healing. I truly believe that it was essential for me to go through this relationship to arrive at the point I'm at today. If I hadn't, I would still be struggling with my attraction to abusive, emotionally unavailable men. I would not be who I am today without it. For this and all that we shared, I still feel connected to him on some level and probably always will, however, there is no desire to spend time with him.

In the end, we were both better people. I don't think he realized this about himself, I don't believe he was aware that he changed and grew in spite of himself, but I could see it. He was a different man, but he just couldn't take those last steps necessary to take the relationship where it needed to go.

The only regret I do have is that I wish I would have been capable of having a loving relationship with a man who could have been a caring role model for my son; because my son's father was an alcoholic and I never had a good stable relationship, my son grew up with a big vacancy in this department, which ultimately affected his development as well.

It would take a whole other book to write about the eight years I spent with this man and all that I went through and learned, so I'll try and summarize it by saying this. It was through this relationship that "she" learned how to set boundaries, to stand up for herself, to not allow abuse, to get her needs met, to stop being used, to communicate, to have intimacy and to stop sexualizing herself.

Like any other skill, the only way to learn something is to do it. Since she had never learned these things as a child, she had to learn them as an adult. She had been programmed by my parents to respond in a dysfunctional, self-abusive manner; I had to reprogram "her." In order to be reprogrammed I had to be exposed to similar situations that simulated the experience I had as a child, and instead of responding in the abusive manner I had been forced to as a child, I had to learn to respond in a healthier manner that protected myself. Additionally, as we learned in the chapter on child abuse, the brain of an adult who was abused as a child has been altered. So we're also talking about changing brain chemistry in this situation as well.

In the past, "her" response to relationships that didn't meet her needs was to have several relationships simultaneously and to bounce back and forth between them. Anytime one of them caused her emotional pain she ran to the other one for comfort. She was afraid to have needs and express them because it would mean that he would leave her. It was this pattern that perpetuated the dysfunctional relationships. That didn't happen this time. Michael was the only man in our life for eight years. There were times when we were broke up that I tried to encourage her to date other people and we tried, but she just couldn't do it. Instead of drinking, drugging or turning to other men, she learned to express her needs to this man and attempt to get them filled. Instead of burying her emotional pain with another man, she learned to grieve, express and feel her pain.

It was this relationship that brought the childhood pain to the surface, which was released with the screaming and pounding of the plastic bat on the mattress, etc., that I talked about in the previous chapter. The emotional pain that this relationship put her through triggered the emotional pain that she endured as a child. However, since she was now feeling and expressing the pain and grief instead of burying, medicating and avoiding it, this relationship allowed, encouraged and incited a purging of the pain, grief, shame and dysfunction of our childhood.

The childhood pain and shame were no longer spinning around inside on an unconscious level as they were all those years perpetuating the vicious cycle of dysfunctional relationships. They were released and this broke their hold on me and her pattern of relating to men. It was the essential tool that helped me integrate or develop my identities and stop wanting men like my father. Through this relationship I really discovered who I was on a deeper level and what I truly wanted and grew strong enough to not be willing to accept less.

Yes, I know it was a pretty unconventional path for recovering from child abuse. It challenges and violates everything the mental health field teaches. I know there will be many people in recovery and counselors who will read this section and shake their head in disbelief or gasp in horror, but it is what worked for me, when everything else had failed.

It took eight years for me to get there, but I learned it's not done until it's done. There were many times throughout the process that I questioned the sanity of both my counselor, Daryl, and myself for believing as we did and allowing this relationship to continue; but every time I reevaluated my position, I still saw no other way. There was nowhere else to go but "through it."

There were times I'd sit in her office and say, "This isn't working, nothing is changing," or "this is crazy."

She would say, "That's not true," and point out all the ways I had changed and grown.

When the pain was so great I thought it would consume me or that I might die, I would cry, "Is it ever going to end?"

Daryl would respond with, "Yes, I believe it will, but I don't know when."

To be honest there were times I wasn't sure it would ever end. There were times the pain was so raw I couldn't think or function at all and the tears were so plentiful I thought I may drown, but the day did come when it ended. I think it was a surprise even to me. When I was finally able to walk away from this relationship, an amazing amount of childhood trauma had been purged and healed. My pattern of being attracted to men like my father was broken and I was much more whole.

Through this process I came to the conclusion that intimate relationships are the main way that we heal our child abuse issues. It is in intimate relationships that our worst issues surface and it is here that they get worked out. We can't just read the recovery books and be healed. Yes, reading the books, attending seminars, groups and workshops, engaging in the written homework, confronting our families, etc., is all an essential step in the process, but it is only the first step. These activities help us become aware of the damage that's been done, they give us the head knowledge of what's healthy and what we want to strive for, but it's a long way from the head to the heart and the only way to get there is through experience.

Adults who were abused as a child can't go immediately from having unhealthy relationships into having healthy relationships. It is a skill that must be learned through practice. There is a process that must run its course. The trauma and all the emotions connected to it must be purged first and this purging is accomplished by reliving the childhood pain through a similar relationship on a conscious level.

The mental health field has been teaching people to avoid dysfunctional, abusive relationships because they cause emotional pain and are unhealthy. That seems like the logical and reasonable conclusion, but ironically it's not the healthy and effective one. We all want to avoid pain, but if the pain is not purged, it will continue to drive the destructive, dysfunctional patterns. The key is to help the individual going through the painful or abusive relationships to become aware and conscious of the process and how to use that process to heal and change. When you engage in the process as an aware individual, here's what happens:

- The one who is aware grows and learns how to assert herself, set boundaries, get her needs met and not allow abuse in her life.

- The abuser is pushed to grow whether they want to or not if they want to remain in the relationship.

- When firm boundaries are set and the abuser understands that abusive behavior is not going to be tolerated, then the abuser is either going to grow or leave.

- Sometimes they leave and never return. Sometimes they leave and come back repeatedly. The big lesson for the aware one is to be able to let them go when they leave. My pattern in the past was to let the abuser do whatever they wanted so they wouldn't leave and that is the way many women who grew up in abusive childhoods interact. It was a huge step when I could take the risk of asserting myself, not allowing abusive behavior, even if it meant he might leave.

- During this process, the interaction between the two individuals brings all the unresolved emotions, shame, pain, and dysfunction from their childhood to the surface. For the person who is aware, this pain and shame is purged. Sometimes even the unaware partner will grow and change in spite of themselves in response to the healthier, more aware partner setting boundaries.

- If the abuser does not grow and change, in time, after purging of the pain and shame and learning to stand up to abuse; the aware individual will want a healthier relationship and will be strong enough to leave.

Yes, we can leave and run away from the abusive men we are attracted to, but until deep healing has taken place we will just find another one and another one and another one. Separating the men and women in these relationships is not the answer, because they will continue to be attracted to one another like magnets. We must work together to heal one another. Deep healing cannot happen without each other.

Unfortunately, the sad truth is that most abusive men are not willing to work on themselves and have no interest in changing, so it's not all that often that this scenario ends with the couple being able to stay together, once her purging has finished. Most of the healing that takes place occurs within the abused, rather than the abuser. To some extent it seems the Universe uses the abuser as a tool to help the abused arrive at a healthier point; and once that has occurred, the abused one moves on.

However, I'm not saying there would never be exceptions to this formula. There are different levels of abuse and abusers. Naturally, if your life is in danger, then you have no choice but to leave, magnet or no magnet. Nor am I suggesting that anyone stay if they feel compelled and capable of leaving. The ultimate goal for the abused is to be attracted to healthier relationships and stay away from abusers, so if one is capable of achieving that goal without going through this process, then by all means they should do so. However, as anyone knows that works with domestic violence victims, keeping the abused and the abuser away from each other is usually pretty difficult, if not impossible.

This is because they are fighting a spiritual force and literally trying to rewire the brain. Each one of them is reenacting their childhood and unconsciously trying to work out the past. They need to become aware of this process and then help each other learn how to do it differently. She, or the abused, needs to learn how to set boundaries and limits. He, or the abuser, needs to learn how to respect these boundaries and limits. They both need to learn how to recognize and communicate their needs and resolve conflict in a healthy manner. She, or the abused, needs to say no to abuse and impose consequences on behavior that is abusive; and he, or the abuser, must learn to face the consequences of his actions. These are the things neither one of them learned in childhood.

Our current approach to stopping domestic violence is not very successful. It only makes the abused individual feel more guilty and shameful for not being able to do what she is told to do. It should be obvious that a new paradigm is called for. We often hear mental health professionals and people like Oprah tell us that if you stay with a man after he hits you then you do so because you feel that you don't deserve anything better. That may be the case sometimes in the beginning, but that is not always true. I had years of counseling, had healed a great deal emotionally, was very outspoken at injustice, had greatly improved my self-esteem, had no trouble standing up for myself, really liked myself and yet couldn't stop being attracted to men like my father. I very much believed that I deserved better than this, but I couldn't be attracted to better. Knowing that I deserved better was what made it so incredibly heartbreaking and filled me with shame because I couldn't achieve it.

I believe we are unconsciously drawn to partners who have the power to heal us. However, we need to be aware and conscious of the process. The reason that Michael was so overwhelmingly irresistible to "her" was because he was, for lack of a better word, our "soul mate." I believe a soul mate is someone who helps you learn and grow. They may be in your life for a season, a year, a decade or an eternity. It all depends on when the lesson is finished and what steps each person has taken in the process.

Your relationship with a soul mate is often passionate, tumultuous and/or filled with conflict. Some people have one soul mate, but some of us have a variety of soul mates. There may be several of them throughout a lifetime. You know someone is your soul mate when the connection you have with each other is so powerful it is much bigger than you are and can't be denied. A soul mate is not always someone you are intimate with; it can be a friend, a mentor, a counselor, etc. For example, I believe that my counselor, Hal, from the drug and alcohol rehabilitation center was a soul mate, and I believe my Scottish lover from rehab was a soul mate, and so were my counselors Stephanie and Daryl, and some of my friends and boyfriends from my drunken years were as well. A soul mate has such a profound impact on your life, it alters its course and you feel connected to them forever, even if you never see them again.

We are a society that expects and demands instant results, so the approach I'm presenting will be very difficult to accept. It took me 14 years after getting sober to heal my child abuse issues enough that I could stop being attracted to abusive, emotionally unavailable men. The truth of the matter is that I don't believe you're ever done healing from child abuse. To some degree it leaves an imprint on your life forever and some pieces are too broken to fix. There are many different levels of damage, and when you heal one level, you move on to the next. As I went through the process of writing this book, many of my childhood feelings and issues resurfaced and were healed again on an even deeper level. The process of my recovery was solidified in a whole new way.

It's been seven years now and I'm happy to report there have been no men like my father in my life during this time and there haven't been any internal battles with "her." There have been more than several opportunities that have presented themselves over the last seven years with married men and other emotionally unavailable men like my father that in the past would have been irresistible to her and immediately called her out to play. She would have been off and running, no matter what the cost, but that didn't happen. I did not have to battle with her in order to turn these men down. She was not interested either. At first I was nervous and worried that it would be an offer she couldn't refuse. I held my breath and listened for a conflicting voice, but didn't hear one. There was no struggle at all. In the past she simply could not resist anyone who showed an interest in her who had the magical dysfunctional qualities of her father, but now she examines the situation, weighs it against what she's looking for and says, "Nope, this is not what I want," and I let out a big sigh of relief. There is no doubt in my mind that, at this point of my life, a relationship with an abuser, a deceitful cheater, a user, a player, or an active alcoholic or addict will not happen again. There is no longer any tolerance for it whatsoever or uncontrollable drive to do so. It seems we are now both attracted to the same kind of man, but as of the date of this writing, we have yet to find him.

Unfortunately, now that I'm a lot pickier in my choices, it's pretty darn hard to find a man. However, that's okay, I really haven't been looking. For the first time in my life, I am completely comfortable without a relationship. I've actually grown to enjoy being alone. I used to be willing to put up with anything and accept any little crumb he threw my way just to have a man in my life, but that is no longer the case. I'm content with my life, not afraid to be alone and no longer willing to settle. If he comes along, that would be great; if he doesn't, that's okay too. I would rather be alone than accept less than what I want and deserve.

Was "she" a whole other personality or just a badly damaged, undeveloped piece of my identity? I think it was the latter, but I don't really know for sure. I came to the conclusion that it's not really important to know. The important thing is that we now live in harmony together.

In some ways I feel like she was absorbed by me and we are one, yet I can still feel her presence inside me. Sometimes I feel her stir, I recognize her thought patterns and feelings, but she doesn't engage in any behaviors that I find unacceptable. It feels as though she was integrated to some degree, but I didn't lose her completely, nor would I want to. She has many beautiful qualities that enhance who I am. Her piece of my identity is incredibly sensual, sexy, loving, free, sensitive, flexible, accepting, adventurous, fun, vulnerable, committed, reliable, loyal, vibrant and full of life. She makes me feel alive. I, on the other hand, am the logical leader. I'm strong, confident, driven, rigid, controlled, guarded, critical, determined, goal focused, responsible, structured and efficient. We balance one another out.

One of the dilemmas we faced in the past was that when I didn't allow her to come out to play, then I also lost all her good qualities. She would feel dead, repressed and stifled and yearned to be allowed to live. Sometimes I would simply let her have her way just so I could feel vibrant and alive, but then I couldn't stand it because she was too needy, inconsistent, irresponsible and didn't know how to set boundaries, and I'd have to fight to reign her back in. I would miss all her wonderful qualities when I suppressed her, but at the time suppressing her was the only way to keep her from engaging in destructive behaviors.

We have now arrived at a place where we work together and she exists alongside me. Her wonderful qualities are now a part of me and she doesn't have to be suppressed. We seem to be striving for the same things in life now, and I no longer feel like there are two me's.

Seventeen
Overcoming Sexual Shame

"Most truths are so naked that people feel sorry for them and cover them up, at least a little bit." ~ Edward R. Murrow

Healing in the area of sex, sexuality, sexual relationships, etc., is a crucial part of recovery for most alcoholics and addicts. They often go hand in hand and if not addressed may lead to drinking or using again. For many it is one of several of addictions, while for others it is an area where maladaptive patterns of interacting result in emotional pain, and conflict abounds.

If one cannot understand their sexual behavior or engages in activities that spur feelings of shame and guilt, this leaves them at high risk of relapse. In the case of sex addiction, if not addressed, it will keep the physiological cycle of addiction active, which could lead back to alcohol or drugs.

Even Bill W. recognized this fact early on, although, he never was able to get the upper hand on his sexual addiction. The topic of sex and the many struggles that alcoholics face in this area are referred to extensively throughout the *Big Book* and the *Twelve Steps and Twelve Traditions*. Here's what he tells us on page 68 of the *Big Book*: "Now about sex. Many of us needed an overhauling there."

The extent of this issue is widespread in those recovering from addictions; however, it is not common knowledge to society, because it is not talked about openly. A lot of people are unaware that their sexual behavior is connected to addiction, some people have no interest in changing their sexual behavior, while others are not willing to be honest about the impact it has on their life; however, for most it's about shame. The pervading attitude towards sex in our society is that of shame and guilt, which is created and perpetuated by religion and the hold it has on the minds of the people. It is considered shameful to not only discuss these matters but to have any kind of issue in this area. So people with sex issues, which are a large part of society, are afraid and uncomfortable to talk honestly about it. Instead they hide it and repress it, which results in an even bigger problem.

As a matter of fact, I had to get past a great deal of shame and fear to share openly everything I have shared in this book. To be completely honest, it was not an easy task and that is the case for most people. Through the process of writing this book I'd sometimes wake up in the middle of the night thinking, "You can't tell the whole world that," and I'd get up and cut pieces out of the book and then get up in the morning and put them back in. I'm aware that any discussion of sex is likely to provoke a variety of feelings, thoughts, sarcasms and judgments; however, I concluded that leaving out these crucial pieces of the journey would not be helpful to anyone, including myself. I'd only be perpetuating the cycle of shame.

Religion encourages an inaccurate perception that sex and spirituality are separate and that in order to be spiritual you need to be asexual and that you are a better person if you divorce yourself from your sexual energy, feelings, desires and needs, and that spirituality is somehow superior to sexuality. As a result of this, many people falsely believe that sex and spirituality are at opposite ends of a continuum. It is incredibly sad that something so beautiful and intrinsic in our nature is so poorly understood and completely obliterated in our society. Most of us are taught from an early age that the body is dirty, sex is bad, sexual thoughts are sinful and that we shouldn't touch our genitals.

These attitudes are in complete contradiction to what is natural and healthy. It is like cutting off one of your legs and trying to run. We are taught to suppress our sexuality and to feel shame for being a sexual being and, therefore, this creates the problematic patterns we see associated with sex in our society such as excessive sex partners, violence, dissatisfaction with one's sex life, sexual confusion, degradation, incest and addiction that are practically an epidemic. We have created a society with two sexual extremes and very few people are able to find a healthy medium. At one end we have people with very few or no limits where meaningless sex, addiction, violence, rape, incest, degradation, etc., occurs, and at the other end we have people with very rigid limits who are afraid of sex, who are uncomfortable even talking about it, who don't know even know what arouses them, who think it is dirty and bad and should be hidden and/or not engaged in. The common thread in both of these extremes is shame. People at both ends of the continuum are experiencing shame but exhibit it in different ways. These are prime examples of what happens when we disconnect our spiritual self from our sexual self.

Sex is not bad, dirty, shameful, unhealthy and the root of these problems. It is the separation of sex from our self and suppression of sexual energy that creates these problems. It is the lack of understanding and awareness of our sexual energy and the ignorance this creates that causes us to act in ways that are troublesome and destructive. Being taught to suppress and divorce our sexual energy separates us from a vital piece of our spirituality. Our whole survival is dependent upon sex, and it is one of the most pleasurable and spiritual experiences one can have when in the context of love and respect.

One of the factors that cause sex to create such great difficulty in our relationships is because sexual energy and spiritual energy feel very similar. Sometimes it is difficult to tell the two apart. They often overlap. Because our society doesn't encourage awareness or understanding of either one of these energies we are left to try and figure them out ourselves, and in our ignorance we develop patterns that don't serve us well. Sex is very spiritual and spirituality can feel very sexual at times. It is one of the factors that make sex addictive, as I believe all addictions are in part really a search for the spiritual. We are not taught that these incredible spiritual feelings can be achieved on a regular basis through developing deep, healthy relationships with ourselves, the Universe and others.

Sexuality is a core ingredient of our spiritual makeup. By continually trying to suppress sexuality we are only throwing fuel on the fire. The solution is to explore and embrace our sexual energy, thoughts, feelings, and fantasies. Reclaim our sexuality and reconnect it to our core self, or souls, as many prefer to call it. Get it out in the open. Part of the reason destructive sexual forces have so much power is because of the suppression and shame. Problems lose their power when brought out in the open and dealt with directly.

Steps to Heal Sexual Shame

So how do we shed ourselves of years of negative conditioning and develop a healthier attitude, reconnect our spiritual self with our sexuality and celebrate our sexual selves? Well to begin with, and to ensure that our next generation will be a more sexually enlightened group of people, we start by teaching our children. From a very early age we help them to develop a healthy appreciation and respect for their bodies and promote a healthy attitude towards masturbation. We talk freely and openly with them about sex and sexuality without shame. We encourage them to talk to us and ask questions. We teach them the difference between healthy and unhealthy sex. We teach them that sex is human, healthy and sacred, and not just a physical act. One of the main reasons we are so messed up sexually as a society is because no one teaches us anything about sex.

When we become an adult, we need to expand on our sexual knowledge base by educating ourselves with high-quality sex education books and videos created by sex experts. We need to understand the differences between men and women's sexuality and needs. Men and women have very different sexual needs, biological sexual responses and attitudes towards sex, and it is the lack of understanding these differences and how to negotiate them that causes a great deal of conflict and dissatisfaction in couples and leads to infidelity and/or the failure of the relationship.

Although most men can have casual sex without any difficulty, that isn't usually the case for most women. Women get into trouble because they frequently get into casual sex relationships even though they don't want them in hopes that the relationship will grow into something more, or that they can change his mind or because they can't find what they're looking for. However, they end up feeling used and disrespected and their self-esteem and self-worth suffer.

I don't believe that having casual sex is a moral issue. If two grown adults make a unanimous decision to engage in an activity for the purpose of pleasure or to fulfill their sexual needs, there is nothing wrong with that in my eyes. Morality is called into the picture when one or both of the parties is not honest with the other or one party manipulates the other party to meet their own needs without taking the other party's needs into account. It's about being true to yourself.

For example, for me it's impossible to have sex without emotions involved. When I would try and "just have sex," it never worked. Once I had sex with someone, then emotions were present. There is no way for me to separate the two. That is the case for many women. It's the way many of us are wired.

I personally feel that sex outside a relationship is not very satisfying or fulfilling emotionally or spiritually. If there isn't any emotion or personal connection involved, then the sexual pleasure is lacking in intensity and depth. Yes, there is physical release and pleasure, but it leaves me feeling empty emotionally and spiritually. Additionally, I am very damaged in this area because of my childhood sexual abuse. Whenever I tried to have casual sex, it triggered all those feelings of shame and made me feel used and cheap, even when it was a conscious choice on my end.

For many years I wasn't aware of these issues and didn't understand all of this about myself. In my attempt to get a man and meet physical sexual needs, I kept engaging in behaviors that went against who I was. Even after I began to recognize these facts about who I was, I betrayed myself by trying to ignore them. Part of my recovery process was accepting these facts about who I am and to stop allowing that part of myself who wanted a man at any cost to engage in behaviors that violated who I was. I had to honor the truth of these aspects in my life.

My personal belief is that the healthiest, most satisfying sex takes place between two people who connect on many levels and care, or are on their way to caring, about each other. In my experience, the deeper the relationship and the deeper the spiritual connection is then the more fantastic and spiritual the sex will be. Healthy spiritual sex can also occur by yourself if you are without a partner by deepening your relationship with yourself. Make love with yourself or have a love affair with nature. I once had one of the most satisfying and pleasurable sexual experiences of my life alone, on a beach, under the moonlight with the wind blowing across my body and the waves crashing against my feet. It was very spiritual and romantic.

For many, meaningless or casual sex usually results in feelings of emptiness, lack of fulfillment, and shame. It takes us further away from our soul or core self and leaves us searching for more in someone else. In my opinion, great sex requires deep spiritual connections, deep intellectual connections, communication and, as the relationship evolves, trust will become an issue.

Although I don't think I believe there is such a thing as a soul. I use the word in this conversation for lack of a better term that everyone can relate to. I believe soul-satisfying sex is the type of sex we should be pursuing.

Any activity that is soul-satisfying is something that nurtures our core, makes us feel whole, complete, satisfied, euphoric, deeply connected with the Universe, God, or whatever your spiritual connections. So, soul-satisfying sex is sex that provides us with these wonderful feelings. Soul-satisfying sex can only occur with people we are connected to emotionally, intellectually, physically and spiritually. This includes our connections to ourselves. If you are connected to that person on all these levels, then the more satisfying the sex will be.

Sure we can have good sex with someone we are only attracted to on a physical level, but that is not fulfilling for our souls or core self. It will only satisfy us physically and leave us empty emotionally and spiritually. We usually feel like we are missing something in our life and are unfulfilled. The thing we are missing is deep connections to another person and spiritual satisfaction.

Although there may be times in your life when you are not able to find a soul-fulfilling connection, and still feel the need to meet your sexual needs, that is okay as long as it is always respectful and both parties are comfortable with that, but I believe striving for deep connections should be the goal.

The deeper our connections with the person we are having sex with, the more exciting, satisfying and ecstatic our sex will be. You will experience sex that takes you to a higher level of consciousness and cements you to your lover. Not only will you have a physical orgasm, but you will have a body, mind and spirit orgasm, which is an orgasm like no other. You will experience total euphoria, complete bliss and heights of passion like you never experienced before. Penetration becomes a union of the souls. The ultimate spiritual high is achieved when engaging in soul-satisfying sex.

Deep connections with other people may be very frightening. It means we can be hurt and we may be afraid to expose our true selves to others. Thus, hopping from partner to partner can become an easy way to avoid intimacy and the risk of being hurt, but ultimately what happens when doing this is that you short change yourself from experiencing the deepest, most passionate, mind-blowing sex one can find as well as profound complete satisfaction and fulfillment emotionally, physically and spiritually. You will prevent yourself from reaching your highest potential sexually and as a human being.

Another component of soul-satisfying sex is communication. In order to really connect with another, we need to communicate. In order to communicate, we need to have some type of a relationship. The more we get to know someone, the more we share of ourselves. Most of us find it difficult to communicate intimately with a stranger. We need to foster a relationship before we communicate too much. Therefore, the deeper our connections with our lover, the freer we will be to communicate our desires, needs, wants, fantasies, etc. Thus, the more two lovers understand each other, the better they will be able to satisfy one another. The more we communicate, the better the sex will be and the connection will deepen. The deeper the connection, the more we will communicate. Therefore, it becomes reciprocal with each feeding the other. The greater the intimacy, the better the sex, and this will create bonds so intense that desires for each other and desire and willingness to please each other will be raging.

One of the most wonderful aspects about soul-satisfying sex is that it has no limits. When two people continue to deepen their intimacy, connections and bonds to one another, they can always reach a new height of ecstasy that was not reached before.

Sometimes we meet someone and have an instant attraction. In this instance great sex can occur quickly, but if deepening of the spiritual and intellectual connection, communication and trust are not nurtured, then this attraction will diminish and die. These things can only be developed over time and, therefore, the deeper the trust, the connection and communication is, the fewer inhibitions we will have and the freer we will become in enjoying our sexual experiences. The sex will become even more explosive and we will be able achieve new heights of passion and fulfillment we didn't know existed. The depth of a relationship has no limit except those that we bring to it with our own fears and issues, and if we allow the relationship to grow and deepen, there will always be another higher level of soul-satisfying sex to be achieved.

However, I realize the scenario I present is an ideal. The problem with this is that life doesn't always unfold in an ideal manner and there may be times in people's lives when they are not able to find a partner to connect deeply with and may still have the need to fulfill their sexual needs. Many people are comfortable with casual sex and there are phases in life especially in adolescents, young adulthood, and phases of adulthood such as after divorce that it may be necessary to experiment, retaliate or be reckless to find one's way and learn who we are. Ultimately, I believe that what we find in the end is that the most fulfilling sex is that which is explored with someone we care about, but we may have to go down many roads and through many experiences to learn this for ourselves. Each person needs to discover who they are sexually and what they're comfortable with and honor that.

While we are on this journey, or when we are with a loving partner, I believe there are some basic principles we should teach our children and abide by ourselves to promote the most spiritual, respectful and ethical sex possible in each circumstance. Those principles are:

- Respect

- Neither party should be hurt physically

- No coercion or manipulation

- Honesty
  - o You should always be clear with your partner about your motivations and expectations.
  - o You should not be getting your sexual needs met outside your primary relationship unless your partner has given you permission.
- Both parties should agree upon the activity engaged in

- Communication

- Mutually pleasurable – Both partners should attempt to meet the needs of their partner and not be selfish, even if the act is purely a physical one.

- Both parties should want the same result – If you are looking for just sex, then you should not have sex with someone you know is looking for a relationship.

Other steps you can take to continue to heal sexual shame may include beginning to tell yourself different messages. Tell yourself that sex is great, wonderful, good and spiritual. Find some good books, videos or websites on healthy sexuality and read, read, read. Do everything you can to educate yourself. Bring sex-positive people into your life. It will probably take a long time to override the old voices in your head and you may need to hear the new messages over and over. It may be helpful to talk to someone like a counselor, advisor or an educator who specializes in sexuality to help validate your new messages. Try to find friends who are on the journey of understanding their sexuality or who are comfortable with sex that you can share this aspect of yourself with freely.

Explore your own body and discover what you like and what you don't. Find what excites you and what doesn't. What feels good and what doesn't. Make love with yourself. Be adventurous. Be aware. Be present in the here and now. Allow yourself to become immersed in the sexual experience. Open yourself up and fully experience each touch, sensation, smell, movement, sound and taste while you are making love with yourself or your lover. Tune into your body and soul and listen to the yearnings of your core; they will guide you. Be willing to try new things even if they feel foreign or scary.

Get naked outside and make wild passionate love. Personally, I believe that there is not anything more arousing and spiritual than to be naked outside and make love with the feel of the elements upon your body. There is something incredibly freeing about it and it elicits uninhibited passions. It takes you back to the primal basics. This can be done either by yourself or with a partner.

Communicate. Communicate. Communicate. This cannot be emphasized enough. Talk to your lover about your feelings, needs, desires and wants. Express your fears, inhibitions and embarrassments as well as your fantasies and expectations. If you are without a partner, then get to know yourself completely from the inside out. Not only will this enhance your sexual experience, but it will make life more fulfilling in general; and if the time comes to be with a partner again, then you will be a better lover and better able to enjoy the experience fully. If you are with a partner, then get to know yourself and your lover from the inside out.

A pattern that I observed in many married men over the years is they marry a "good" girl, which means one or more of the following. She doesn't really like sex; she's sexually inhibited; she's someone who's uncomfortable with or ashamed of sex; has very rigid views about sexuality; she's not willing to give him oral or anal, or if she is willing, she doesn't really enjoy it and complains about it; or she's not willing to try new things. But then he's not happy or satisfied sexually, so they get their sex from the "bad" girl, who is a woman who enjoys sex and is willing to do all the things his wife isn't. They can't put the two together. They don't seem to realize that the woman they marry should be the woman that meets their sexual needs. In their head a "good" girl doesn't like sex, and a woman who likes sex is a "bad" girl. A "bad" girl is not the woman you marry. This struggle doesn't occur in just the man. Many women are socialized in the same way, and carry the exact same views. They are afraid to be sexual beings and enjoy sex because they will be viewed as a "bad" girl.

This scenario is becoming less common in younger generations as this attitude about labeling a woman as "bad" if she enjoys sex is beginning to dissipate and males and females are being socialized a little differently than they were in my day. However, for men from my generation, 40s and older, it is still a common struggle. Many men live a double life and their wife never knows about it. She doesn't have a clue that he is being unfaithful, that he is not satisfied with their sex life or that he has sexual desires he hasn't shared with her. He shares that part of himself with the "bad" girl, but he doesn't share his emotional self with the "bad" girl. That part is shared with the wife. Men like this feel justified in their actions, because they feel their sexual needs have to be met. They think it's okay to betray their wife and use another woman for sex.

So, this is something women should be aware of. I can tell you from personal experience that the wives of almost all the married men that I had a relationship with over the years were completely unaware of his infidelities and would have been or were shocked to find out otherwise. He is very good at hiding this piece of himself. Additionally, I now work as an adult sex educator and I still see this phenomenon happening quite frequently in many of my client's relationships today.

On the other hand, although I hate to say this, and I know it sounds harsh, there are a lot of women who don't want to know the truth and choose to stick their head in the sand and ignore the signs that are right in front of their face. With a little awareness and willingness to face the truth, infidelity is often easy to see. There are many signs and symptoms. Listen to your gut or that little voice in your head. If something doesn't look right or sound right, then it probably isn't, regardless of how much he denies it. If you're not having sex with him and you think he's going without, I urge you to think again. Most men do not go without sex for extended periods of time. If they don't engage in an actual affair, they often turn to phone sex or Internet sex to meet their needs. Phone sex operators report that 50 to 90 percent of their customers are married men. On the other hand, it's also important to note that it isn't fair, realistic or healthy to expect him to go year after year without sex. If there is a problem with sexual desire, then it needs to be addressed. Sexless, or almost sexless, marriages or relationships are not very fulfilling for most people and lead to numerous problems in addition to infidelity or ending of the relationship.

Men, who are not satisfied with the quantity, quality or type of sexual relationship they have with their wife or partner, need to be honest with her instead of turning to someone else. Couples need to get honest with each other and work together to overcome their socialization and develop more satisfying relationships.

In regard to sex addiction, it like alcoholism is complex and multi-faceted with many unique components that should be addressed in depth by the individual, but are beyond the scope of this book. Although this is not a book about recovering from sex addiction, here are a few of the most important aspects to keep in mind. Addiction is addiction. They all operate on the same principles. Sex addiction rarely occurs in and of itself. Like alcoholism and drug addiction, it is mostly about neurotransmitters, often has roots in child abuse and is about filling the void—the black empty pit—that was left inside and perpetuated by shame. If you're taking the steps suggested in this book to heal and recover from alcoholism, it will cover all addictions.

Sex addiction, like all other addictions, is largely the result of an excessively stimulated reward pathway and the euphoria that accompanies it. When you have an orgasm, it releases neurotransmitters and endorphins. This is why it feels so good. Remember neurotransmitters in the reward pathway give us good feelings so that we will repeat a behavior. Since survival of the human race literally depends on having a healthy desire for sex, nature makes it very pleasurable for us to ensure we won't become extinct. Although this is a natural process, it simulates the experience you have when you use drugs and alcohol.

When your neurotransmitters are out of balance, deficient or malfunctioning from drugs, alcohol, diet, environmental toxins, child abuse etc., sex is often one of the activities that we turn to stimulate or soothe them. However, it works the same way as other addictions. Over time the neurotransmitters become more deficient and it takes more sex to achieve the same results. Thus, when you take the necessary steps, outlined in this book, needed to balance the neurotransmitters with amino acids and diet and stop stimulating them with mind-altering substances like drugs, alcohol, cigarettes, caffeine and sugar, then you have taken the first and most important step to address sex addiction.

In chapter 12 we learned that child abuse damages the HPA axis and causes it to malfunction, and that the H in this axis stands for hypothalamus. The hypothalamus is an area in the brain that has a variety of different functions, but the one we're concerned with right now is that it is responsible for regulating the sex drive. You've seen me mention a variety of times in this book that I always had a very high libido. Even after sobriety, sometimes my sexual desire was so intense that it was physically uncomfortable and couldn't be relieved with any amount of orgasms. In my search for answers to this problem, I talked to a physician once about this and he had an instrument that checked my hypothalamus functioning and he told me that my hypothalamus activity was off the chart. I have an overly stimulated hypothalamus and he said this was the cause of my intense desire for sex.

As we learned in chapter four, when you're engaged in active addition, there are large doses of dopamine being released and one of the effects of increased dopamine is an increase in libido. So I already had a high libido from an overactive hypothalamus, but when I was engaged in active addiction, dopamine was making it even higher. When I was inebriated, which was the majority of the time, this lowered my inhibitions and my ability to control behavior and so I engaged in sexual behavior I found distasteful to meet my sexual needs. Once I got sober, then I didn't have the excessive levels of dopamine driving me anymore; and even though my sex drive was still high, it wasn't as high as it was. Since I wasn't inebriated anymore, I was able to stop engaging in behavior that, although fulfilled my sexual needs, left me empty emotionally and spiritually.

Child abuse or any traumatic, high-stress life event that damages the HPA axis is one of the main roots of sex addiction or excessive sex drive. Although I haven't found a solution to stop the high sex drive from occurring completely, because it appears to be permanent damage to the HPA axis for me, just understanding what was happening to me was a big relief and enabled me to deal with it more effectively. Although intense sexual desire still happens to me from time to time even today, the difference is that the emotional work I've done has enabled me to learn to stop acting on the desires in a destructive manner that only incited shame and emptiness and take care of it myself. However, just because my HPA axis has not been able to make a full recovery, does not mean that yours won't.

Just like alcoholism or any other addiction, in addition to balancing neurotransmitters, you must do the necessary emotional work to heal the sexual shame, shine light in the black pit and fill the void. Whether you're dealing with sex addiction or painful maladaptive sexual patterns of relating in your relationships, healing sexual shame is an essential part of the recovery process; and when achieved, brings many benefits into our life.

Sexuality is intricately tied to our mental, physical and spiritual health and can be an amazing tool for spiritual evolution. Through sexual pleasure, connection and energy we can experience one of the most profound spiritual experiences available to us. It promotes feelings of wholeness, harmony and balance. We feel deeply connected to not only our lover, but ourselves and the origin of the Universe as well.

Sexual energy can be used to achieve higher levels of awareness and states of consciousness, thus providing a gateway to finding our true self and deepening that relationship. It becomes a medium for spiritual growth, healing and transformation. We can transcend everyday reality and have a brief rendezvous with Nirvana.

Not only that, the hormones that are released during orgasm and the physical activity of sex provide the following physical benefits: alleviates joint and muscle pain; strengthens the heart; lengthens the life span; relieves stress; boosts energy levels; releases the bodies natural opiates that are an extremely effective pain reliever; stimulates the immune system; lowers blood pressure; improves circulation and flexibility; oils released are good for your skin and hair; strengthens muscles and bones; lowers bad cholesterol and raises good cholesterol; strengthens pelvic muscles; improves quality of sleep; lowers the risk of prostate cancer; burns calories; aids in weight loss; and keeps you physically fit.

Additionally, these same hormones provide the following benefits for our emotional health: relieves depression; improves our mood; we feel closer and more connected to our partner; creates a more satisfying and fulfilling relationship; good sexual energy between couples helps them develop a stronger relationship; it strengthens their bond on all levels and makes them less vulnerable to infidelity; instills inner peace and harmony; enhances overall well-being; releases chemicals that make you feel relaxed and happy; promotes positive feelings about yourself, your partner and your life; instills a sense of contentment; enhances the ability to cope; boosts self-esteem and self-concept.

Sexual pleasure, energy and connection enhance the overall quality of our life.

Eighteen
Spirituality

"The personal life deeply lived always expands into truths beyond itself."

~Anais Nin

There are a variety of reasons that spirituality in alcoholism is an important factor, but not because it is a spiritual illness. As we've learned on the pages of this book, alcoholism is a physiological disease that occurs because of imbalances in brain chemistry, allergy and nutritional deficiencies not a spiritual disease; however, it impacts us on the spiritual level deeply. Yes, when we make biochemical repairs, it heals the physical aspect, but all aspects are interconnected and affect the other. The biochemical impacts the psychological and the spiritual and vice versa.

A rich spiritual life is beneficial not only for recovery from alcoholism, but for living life in general. It brings harmony and balance into our life. It nourishes and feeds the soul, or core self, as I like to refer to it. It provides inner peace and calm during the many storms we face, enhances life and offers comfort. However, before we proceed, we first need to establish what spirituality is and isn't.

There is nothing I hate more than someone trying to shove their religious or spiritual beliefs down my throat or even subtly trying to make me see their ways, so I don't want to do that to you, but I would like to offer you my thoughts on the subject to mull over and explore. Toss it around and see if it resonates for you. It is not my intention to step on anyone's religious toes, so if you're a firm believer in God and are offended by disbelief, then this chapter is probably not for you. Enter at your own risk. This chapter is for those who are looking for an alternate path. However, I believe the spiritual message that I convey can be beneficial to any belief system.

If you've arrived at this page and you're still reading, then you must have a thirst for spiritual knowledge and some questions of your own. Many people struggle with the whole God/religious/spirituality concept in AA and traditional treatment, and for good reason. As we established in the opening chapter of this book; AA and the 12 steps is a religious program based on the principles that came directly from the evangelical Christian cult called the Oxford Group. They operate as a structured religion that is controlling, punitive, shaming, rigid and cult like.

I offer my view to show that you don't have to believe in religion, a Supreme Being or higher power to find spirituality and reap the many benefits it offers. I'm not a religious person at all. I don't believe in a higher power, however, I consider myself to be a deeply spiritual person. I believe perhaps in a higher self or higher consciousness, but not an omnipotent being that is all knowing and powerful. My perception of higher consciousness is not the same as religious or most other spiritual beliefs. In most concepts the "higher power" is superior to, better than, and the human being is not worthy, you are a sinner, etc. I don't subscribe to these shaming views. Instead I see it as the relationship I have with myself and nature.

Spirituality comes in many different forms and can be found on a variety of different paths. It is not synonymous with religion. Yes, religion can be spiritual, but most often it is not. One can consider themselves to be highly religious and be completely out of touch with their spirituality. One can be highly spiritual without being religious at all.

I have known many religious people in my life who didn't have an ounce of spiritual awareness. I grew up with religion and church all around me. My grandfather was a preacher and our family bounced back and forth between being good churchgoers and terrible sinners. In spite of all this religious impact, no one in my family or anyone in our life was very moral or spiritual. Everyone I knew was drinking, lying, beating up their wives, abusing their children and having sex with the neighbors.

Religion can become a haven for dysfunctional people to hide in. When these people become leaders of religion, it gives them a place to abuse their power and fulfill their own interests all in the name of God. A lot of abuse takes place at the pulpit hidden in a deceptive veil of godliness.

It is a place for many sick people to hide behind and mask feelings and thoughts that are considered evil, such as sexual desires for children. Many people use religion to deny and repress large pieces of themselves. When you try and deny a piece of yourself, it comes out in many other different unhealthy ways. We see this very clearly in the chronic sexual abuse that goes on with priests. To make matters worse, everyone interprets religious messages in whatever way they need to for justifying their behavior. I once knew someone that told me their religion told them it didn't matter what they did in this life, as long as they took Jesus Christ as their lord and savior, they were going to heaven. They felt it was okay to lie, cheat, steal, abuse, etc., as long as they believed in Jesus. I see many people maneuvering through life under this belief. What kind of belief system is that?

No wonder our society is so messed up. The Bible, church, religion and the whole God concept are full of cruelty, abuse, violence, shame, dysfunction and contradiction. All structured religions and spiritual paths for that matter claim to be different, but they have at least two primary things in common. They all use shame and guilt to control behavior and they all blame the victim for unfortunate things that happen to them in their life. Each of them breed feelings of shame, worthlessness, self-loathing and hopelessness, which ultimately damage self-esteem and the spirit even more. Religion and the whole God concept are punitive, abusive and shame based. This God does not sound like someone I want to know.

For me, believing in God as a man or an actual omnipotent being is as ridiculous as believing in Santa Claus or the Easter Bunny. It just doesn't resonate for me. I can't see or feel any truth in it at all. I believe that people believe in God because it's just too damn scary to go through life not believing. They need the world to make sense and pain and suffering need to have meaning. It's an attempt to make sense out of a senseless and confusing world, to create a false sense of safety in a dangerous world. Most of all, they're afraid that death means it's over and that's all there is to it. People need something to hold on to and take comfort in and God gives them this. I believe as Christopher Hitchens said in his book, *God is Not Great*, that "God did not create us, we created God,"[1] because we needed him. It is a delusion based on wishful thinking.

There are a lot of people who are afraid to be honest not only with others but themselves when religion doesn't make sense and doesn't feel like a good fit. It's just easier to go along with the flow. We are controlled and conditioned by fear to accept religion out of fear of going to hell. It has been pounded in our head and we're afraid to go out on a limb and do something different from everyone else. To hold a belief system that doesn't include God usually gets you ostracized to some degree and most people want to avoid that. Additionally, many people have grown up with abuse and since it's human nature to be attracted to what's familiar, religion is comfortable for many people.

Without structured religion or God, it leaves so many unanswered questions. There are many gray areas without explanation. What is the purpose of life? Is there a purpose? Is it all random? How did we get here? Where are we going? Do we have a soul? What is the soul? Is there something deeper, bigger and more powerful? It's very uncomfortable to not have clear-cut answers.

It certainly feels like there is something deeper inside of us. What is it? What happens to it when we die? The body is made of energy and energy doesn't die, it changes form. So what does this mean? What form will we take? Maybe we'll just exist as energy suspended in time in oneness with the Universe.

I certainly don't propose to have the answers to all these questions; I am still learning and growing myself. I can only follow what feels true and right at the deepest core of my being. I don't know what is the "absolute truth", and I don't believe anyone can know, but I do know what isn't true for me. I only know what resonates for me and it isn't God, any form of a higher power or religion and I most certainly did not arrive in my current belief system quickly or easily. I struggled for years and went back to religion and God many times to explore it again and again to see if I missed something along the way.

It took a lot of pain, inner exploration and learning to find my truth and deeper self and be strong enough to honor it, regardless of anyone's reaction to it. I was seeking God my entire life, but never found the one that others claim to exist in religion. As a little child, I went to church and lay myself at the altar in tears, completely giving myself to God. Over and over I begged him to come into my life and help me out of the hell I was in. No one came.

As a teenager, I continued to seek God through Bible study, church groups and church attendance several times a week, but never found this omnipotent being. I alternated between feeling angry that I couldn't find him and the desperate yearning to keep searching. I left the church, religion and the search for God and came back, again and again.

I have a very distinct memory of standing in the parking lot of our local ice cream shop with my best friend when I was teenager with tears rolling down my cheek and sobbing, because I read a bumper sticker that said, "Smile. God loves you." I was in terrible distress about life with my family and said, "Yeah, right. Apparently God doesn't love me." In the damaged state of mind I was in at the time, I could only conclude that something was wrong with me. God didn't love me or want me for some reason. I was consumed with guilt and shame for not being good enough or doing the right things.

Ironically, my relationship with God was identical to the relationship I had with my father. With both of them I was always trying to do everything right, but no matter how hard I tried, I was just never good enough in their eyes. I was not worthy of their love and affection. Neither one of them was ever there for me when I needed them. I spent my entire life trying to please them, but I could never get it right. I banged my head against the wall over and over trying to get their love.

They were always wanting more and ridiculing me. Both of them withheld their love and affection and instead inflicted their anger, rage and abuse upon me. Both of them made me feel ashamed for being who I was. They were both selfish, cold, distant and unavailable emotionally. It was a one-sided relationship where I did all the giving and received nothing in return.

As an adult, I asked God over and over to come into my life, to show himself to me in some way. I begged him to help me find him, but again, no one was there. I floundered through life alone like a fish out of water. I tried to have blind faith and trust that he was there and that he would provide and protect me only to fall flat on my face with disappointment. I couldn't find those warm arms of strength to wrap around and comfort me that others claim to have found.

When I found Alcoholics Anonymous, I was so desperate, so beaten, so at the end of the rope, that I put my belief completely into the people and the program. I hung onto my recovery counselor and followed him blindly. Fortunately, he did not lead me astray, but since AA is based on having a relationship with a higher power, I was once again faced with the quest to find my God.

AA and the 12 steps worked for me to some degree for the first year, because I was a prime candidate for this type of program. I grew up in an abusive, rigid, punitive home and shame and guilt were very familiar to me. As I mentioned, my grandfather was a preacher and religion had been a part of my life off and on. I was completely beaten, desperate and at the end of my rope. I was very emotionally unhealthy and easily manipulated. This is why AA works for some people or works temporarily. It's a replacement of the dysfunction they are already familiar with or just the result of pure desperation.

"Normally, happy, well-adjusted persons do not radically change their views; and, especially, they do not normally adopt views that they regard as silly and irrational. On the other hand, when a person is in an emotional crisis, radical alteration in beliefs, including religious conversion, is not unusual. As Drs. Ellis and Schoenfeld point out, a person may be so desperate and beaten that his or her normal beliefs can be temporarily suspended, as in 'there are no atheists in foxholes.' Yes, the drowning may grasp at any straw.'"[2]

When I entered AA, I was not a normal, happy and well-adjusted person by a long shot. I can't say that I'm sorry it worked. It saved my life, but the problem is that after the first year, I hit a wall. Since I was also attending lots of other self-help groups, counseling and activities, I was growing and learning about how to be emotionally healthy and independent, and I was breaking free from my abusive dysfunctional past. The healthier and stronger I got emotionally, the more uncomfortable I became with the shame-based aspects of AA and the 12 Step Program. Eventually the tactics no longer worked on me, because I could no longer be molded. I was no longer comfortable with shame and guilt or the rigid, punitive, controlling structure. Most people in AA are not attending self-help groups, going to counseling, workshops, writing in workbooks and actually healing the many aspects that perpetuate alcoholism, so for many, the 12 steps never become uncomfortable, because they remain enmeshed in the dysfunction.

During this process, I went back to religion, Christianity, God and Bible study again, but again couldn't find that being they called God. There were just too many questions. Too many things that don't make sense or add up. There are too many questions that no one has answered adequately. Throughout my life there was so much pain, hardship, suffering, loss and crises. I repeatedly turned to God for help and comfort in these situations, but there was no one there. There is pain, suffering, cruelty, violence, injustice and horror not only in my life but all through this world that is senseless. The answers that the Bible offers are unacceptable to me and based on fear, illusion and fantasy and it is just too abusive, punitive and rigid, and I couldn't find comfort there.

Even after getting sober and working hard to change my life, I had a lot of horrific things happen to me. Something I struggled to come to terms with immensely as I thought I had already been through enough and that sobriety would be different. Since this is a book about the recovery from alcoholism, I won't go into all those gory details. That's another book in and of itself. However, to sum it up briefly, I have severe and disabling chemical sensitivities that result in extreme limits in my life and a whole list of other chronic health conditions that I have not been able to heal.

The end result of these conditions is that I live with a great deal of physical pain and suffering on a daily basis. As a passionate subscriber to the natural health lifestyle and a liver that can't process drugs, prescription medications are not an option. I use meditation, deep breathing exercises and physical exercise to cope with and manage my symptoms. As a result of these chronic health conditions, there has been a great deal of hardship, financial crises, loss and life-altering struggles over the years. Life can be beautiful, but it can also be difficult, unfair and cruel.

However, don't let this scare you; my situation is not typical for most recovering alcoholics. The combination of the extensive and prolonged child abuse I lived with combined with the damage I did to my body in my addiction and exposure to environmental toxins have left me with some health issues I have not been able to overcome. Sometimes permanent neurological, immune and endocrine system damage can occur from child abuse, Candida toxins, pesticides and other environmental toxins; and that appears to be the case for me, or I have just not found the solution yet. There may be alternative treatment methods that would help me, but like many people in this country, I have never been in a financial position to pursue them. However, I still have hope.

The important point to take away from this is that no matter what I've been through, I never have cravings or desires to drink or drug. If I can stay sober through all of this, you can too. When you do the biochemical, emotional and spiritual work required, then alcoholism is no longer an issue, it's as simple as that. Additionally, no matter how bad life gets, there's not been one day that even comes close in comparison to the emotional and spiritual misery that I lived with during my active addiction years. The inner peace, wholeness and contentment that come with sobriety are always an invaluable gift no matter what you're going through.

On the other hand, these health issues resulted in a great deal of spiritual pain and confusion. I searched desperately for comfort and answers to these issues within God and all the spiritual paths I explored, but couldn't find any.

Every spiritual or religious path I turned to had the same message which was: "If you could just get it right, then everything will be okay." If you are just spiritual enough, godly enough or Christian enough, then bad things wouldn't happen to you and you'll have a good life. If bad things are happening, then you aren't a good enough Christian; you haven't prayed enough; you haven't prayed in the right manner; you didn't think enough positive thoughts; you shouldn't be feeling angry, you attracted it to yourself for some reason; you didn't balance your chakras right; you didn't visualize the right things . . . and so on and so on.

When I went to college, I continued my search for God and truth there. I minored in religion and I've also studied many philosophical beliefs on my own. I tried Buddhism, Hinduism, Taoism, New Ageism and many of the different variations of Christianity, etc. I tried balancing my chakras, positive thinking and creative visualization. I tried it all. When I couldn't accept the teachings of whatever path I was on at the time or things were going wrong in my life, I was continually blamed that I was doing something wrong. I never could get it right, so they all just ended up making me feel worse about myself and pushing me further into despair.

Eventually, I came to realize that the truth of the matter is that even when you're doing everything you possibly can to do it right, sometimes life kicks you in the face, shit happens, bad things happen to good people or whatever you want to call it. God, the Universe, the law of attraction, Buddha, the white light or whatever it is you want to call it is just not always there for you.

I went back to church, Christianity and God a couple more times, but each time I came away even more validated in my feelings that this just was not the right path. This was not the truth. I did not find comfort, peace, joy, contentment, feelings of belonging and oneness with the Universe through religion, Christianity, a higher power or this so-called God. It felt archaic, repressive, patriarchal and abusive. It only deepened the gaping hole inside myself I was trying to fill, reopened old wounds I was trying to heal, and stirred feelings of nausea and shame. You know that feeling you get deep in your gut when you know something is really bad and wrong? That's how the God concept and religion feel to me.

Through this whole process, the one constant thing that I prayed for was this: "Please help me find the truth." Eventually I discovered that I couldn't say that I believe any one particular religion or spiritual philosophy has a corner on "the truth." I see pieces of truth, beauty and serenity here and there in each belief system, but no "absolutes." However, for the most part I don't see any real truth there at all. It just seems like a bunch of fantasy and wishful thinking to me.

Over time my current belief system came together and was clear. I stopped trying to get something I could never get. I stopped looking for something I could never find. I stopped banging my head against the wall. I couldn't find it or him because it doesn't exist, not because something was wrong with me or I wasn't good enough or worthy enough. The only thing that makes any sense at all is there is no God, Supreme Being or higher power.

Ironically once again, this revelation came when I was finally able to stop seeking these things from my parents. My abusive relationship with my parents had tainted, poisoned and altered my spiritual connections. When I was finally able to stop seeking their love and affection, I found my core self.

I did not find the omnipotent, loving being that others claimed to exist. Instead I found myself and learned how to tap into my own higher strength and powers. The only being who can truly be there for me is me. I was shown a very different truth and it was a revelation just as strong as any religious conviction found in the Bible and I could not turn away from this truth.

My turning point came when that gut feeling telling me that God was not truth seemed to consume me when I turned to religion and God. The nausea and shame were overwhelming. My insides were screaming that this was not the place for spiritual fulfillment. Going back to religion or God was no longer an option. I had to honor the convictions that my core self found to be true. I had no choice but to walk away and stay away.

Letting go of the search for God was the same as it was in letting go of my family and the abusive men in my life. There was a break where I finally realized it was futile and I was done. In the beginning, when I first let go of the quest for God, I was terrified, just as I was when I first walked away from AA. Life is very scary without a God to hold on to. Even if you never found him to begin with, you still held on to hope that he was there somewhere. All the fears that had been pounded in my head would rise from time to time. I feared I may be struck down by lightning, the earth may open up and swallow me whole, or some other horrible catastrophe may happen. It was very difficult on many levels. Not believing in God is not a popular stance in our society and makes most people very uncomfortable.

I would occasionally question myself and I repeatedly asked God to correct me and show me if I was wrong, but that didn't happen. I continued to ask to be shown the truth and what continually happens in my life is that my current view becomes clearer and stronger each year. It is validated over and over. My conviction grows stronger and stronger that there isn't a God. It's been about 15 years now with no relapsing back to religion or God.

"What if you're wrong?" I've been asked by others. My response is this: I can only follow my own convictions. I have prayed for truth and this is where I arrived. I left no stone unturned. I have explored all the spiritual paths with an open heart and a thirst for truth, and did not find it in any of them. If I'm wrong, it certainly isn't because of a lack of trying. If there is a God, then God would certainly know my heart and how I have sought him, truth and goodness my entire life. If God is the loving, compassionate being he's supposed to be, then surely he would understand my position.

What is Spirituality?

Spirituality is none of the things that religion and the 12 steps preach. It is not shaming, punitive, controlling, blaming and guilt producing. Instead it incites wholeness, freedom and peace. Spirituality is our roots, it's our core identity. It's about getting in touch with the real and deepest you. The true self that is connected to the origin of creation, whatever that may be. It also involves the connection we have with our self, the people in our life and the world around us. Some people include a relationship with a Supreme Being or a higher power, but that is not intrinsic to spirituality.

All of us are already spiritual, it's not something we have to acquire, it's something we have to become aware of and develop. The spiritual path is the process of finding and getting in touch with this core self or developing an awareness of this self—the deeper you. Engaging in activities that feed and nurture the core identity. The search for truth and climbing to a higher level of consciousness.

When we say something feels very spiritual, what we are saying is that it gets us in touch with our core—our deeper or true self. It feels good because it nourishes and feeds a part of ourselves that we've been cut off from. It's like finding a long lost friend.

Ultimately, the goal is about deepening your relationship with your core self and living an authentic life. To live life as consciously and aware as possible and striving to realize your fullest potential as a human being. Being a moral, decent and honest human being not because you're afraid of the consequences down the road, but because it's what you truly desire in your heart.

Spirituality is a very personal and individualized experience. It is not something you find in a seminar or a building such as a church; it is found by going inward. Spirituality is not a place you arrive at and stay put. It's not stagnant—it is flowing, growing, ever changing and expanding over your lifetime.

The spiritual path is not always smooth and comfortable. As a matter of fact, a lot of times it is painful, difficult and treacherous terrain. Experiencing life completely and consciously even in the midst of great pain and suffering—embracing the whole realm of feelings, both negative and positive—is the essence of spirituality.

Many deep spiritual lessons can be found through some of the following experiences that we often consider unpleasant:

- grieving
- loss
- pain
- death
- sadness
- illness
- conflict

- torment

- emotional and/or physical suffering

- aloneness

- deprivation

Most of us, even those without alcoholism, have lost touch with the core self or never found it to begin with. For the person with alcoholism, the deeper, true or core self has been buried very deep. Over the years of drinking or drugging, the real and true self has been stomped to death, hidden under the rubble somewhere in there. For many of us who lived with child abuse, it was already buried in childhood.

Our culture doesn't really teach us anything about spirituality as a child. No one teaches us as children how to fulfill ourselves spiritually, how to feed our spiritual yearnings. The only thing most of us are taught is religion and this leads us away from ourselves. We're not taught how to be independent thinkers and question things; most people accept blindly what they have been told without ever questioning it. They never examined or explored it.

We are manipulated into conformity and conditioned to believe in God with fear, instead of encouraged to develop a relationship with ourselves. The core self gets lost, stuffed into a model, molded and forced to become what others say is true and what others want us to believe.

Sadly, we are a society that is full of people who are disconnected from themselves and have not been taught to feed their spiritual yearnings in a healthy manner. We see this evidenced in the high levels of alcoholism and other addictions in our communities as well as the extreme prevalence of crime, child abuse, violence, depression, absence of compassion, understanding and respect for each other, and ultimately in the insane destruction of our environment and annihilation of the planet we live. Spirituality is about breaking free from this insanity and getting back on the path to yourself.

So Why is All This Spirituality Stuff Important for Alcoholism Anyhow?

Although the roots of alcoholism are biochemical, there are many secondary issues that contribute to or perpetuate alcoholism that can sabotage recovery. A rich spiritual life protects us from some of these secondary factors.

Nurturing spirituality sustains us and prevents us from becoming stagnant and unfulfilled with life. Most alcoholics talk about a yearning inside them, an emptiness, void or a hole that they tried to fill up with alcohol. They often don't feel complete or connected. We try to fill up that hole with all kinds of unhealthy things.

One could even say that, in part, alcoholism is the search for spirituality— the search for self. All addictive substances and activities simulate that incredible whole, at one with the Universe, complete, euphoric feeling that spirituality makes us feel. I know this was true for me. I was looking for what was missing inside. I longed and ached to belong and connect. I was searching for spiritual food. Drinking and drugs made me feel connected, normal and spiritually euphoric for a short period of time. The problem is that it didn't last and eventually it made the emptiness larger and more consuming, because when achieved with drugs and alcohol, it is artificial and temporary.

If that emptiness inside is not filled with healthy things, it leaves us at risk of returning to alcohol or drugs. Alcoholism, or any addiction for that matter, gives us a feeling of touching the divine and we want more of it. The key in recovery is to find other ways of experiencing this euphoria. Other ways of reaching our true or core self and the bliss that accompanies this connection. Spiritually fulfilling activities give us that same high we experience in addiction, but it is natural and healthy. It doesn't perpetuate the emptiness; it encourages wholeness. The more you engage in spiritual activities, the more it fills you up.

When we have a rich spiritual life that makes life meaningful, gives us purpose and we feel connected to ourselves, our loved ones and the world around us, we don't have the need to seek fulfillment outside ourselves in drugs or alcohol. Since our core or true self is ultimately connected to the origin of creation, whatever that may be, when we strengthen our relationship with our core self, we reach those depths again that we experienced in our addiction and get that same taste of the divine.

On the other hand, as we've seen many times throughout this book, addiction regardless of what substance or activity is involved is mostly about neurotransmitters. The pleasure pathway in the brain is excessively stimulated and then neurotransmitters become depleted. When we get sober we need to engage in activities that stimulate our "happy hormones" in a healthy manner to help balance the neurotransmitters and eliminate the drive to get it through drugs and alcohol. Engaging in activities that are spiritually fulfilling is one of the best ways to do that.

When we pray, meditate, enjoy nature, listen to music, dance, make love, connect deeply with ourselves or others, exercise or any of the activities that bring us spiritual pleasure, they stimulate our "happy hormones." Our neurotransmitters release endorphins that make us feel euphoric and connected, and we experience this thing we call the "divine" or the origin of creation. I think it is entirely possible that the experience of spiritual fulfillment is a result of nothing more than neurotransmitter activity.

In my view, science/biology/physics and spirituality are not on opposite sides of the fence. Science is spiritual, the spiritual is science. I think science, biology, physics, etc., are all very spiritual experiences. What is more spiritual than getting to the roots of who we are, where we came from, what we're made of and how it works? It connects us with our core and so does spirituality. As I see it, they are one in the same.

What is more magical, wondrous and awe inspiring than neurotransmitters, hormones, chemical messengers, neuron receptors, synapses and how it all works together perfectly to let the body and brain communicate with each other when it's given what it needs? What is more complex, miraculous or astounding than the workings of the mind and body, a birth of a child, watching your child grow into an adult and the intricate complexity of the human body and mind?

How amazing and magnificent is a butterfly, a tree, a bug, the sun, water, formation and movement of clouds, a bird looking you in the eyes as it takes food from your fingers, the formation and colors of a rainbow, the face of a chipmunk, a roadrunner, waves crashing against rocks, sea urchins sticking on a rock, the sunset and sunrise, flowers blooming in spring, a bunny wiggling its nose at you, the wing span and soar of a turkey vulture, colors in a rock, energy in a rock, majestic mountains against the sky, or an ant carrying food away from the kitchen.

The way I see it, there is no separation of science/biology and spirituality. It appears the divine source of creation is science/biology, but that doesn't make it any less divine, wondrous or glorious.

Another important aspect for the alcoholic is that nurturing a spiritual life helps keep you moral, honest and decent. It breeds integrity, character and high values. These are important to the alcoholic, because when we engage in behaviors that aren't honest and decent, it promotes feelings of shame, guilt and remorse, and damages self-esteem, which can possibly lead back to the drink in an attempt to cover up the feelings. They are not the cause of alcoholism; however, they can perpetuate it once it is set in motion.

Living a moral life doesn't mean a religious life and it doesn't mean we're perfect, but it means we're always striving to be the best that we can be. Behaving in an ethical and responsible manner, not because someone tells you it's the right thing to do or you fear going to hell, but because it's what feels right inside and it's who you are. It promotes harmony and peace in yourself, the world and people around you.

This does not mean you can't or won't make mistakes, absolutely not. When someone has been drinking for years and/or enmeshed in toxic family dynamics, the brain, emotions and values are saturated in alcohol and dysfunction. As evidenced in my life story, it can take a long time to break out of these patterns and develop a healthy value structure. This may mean falling on our ethical faces several times before we get there.

We are all capable of engaging in behaviors that are shameful, hurtful to others and distasteful. However, we need to keep an eye on our motivations. If we do engage in dishonest or hurtful behavior, then we need to try to understand why and learn from it. We need to make amends to those affected and use it to grow and become a better person because of it. It doesn't happen overnight, but the goal is to always be striving to be as honest and decent as possible.

Care and Feeding of Spirituality

So how do you nurture spirituality without religion, a higher power or God? As I deepened my relationship with my core self and learned how to listen to her needs, I discovered that spiritual fulfillment comes in many different ways. I learned how to fulfill my spiritual yearnings in a healthy and satisfying manner instead of turning to drugs, alcohol, sugar or men. They are the activities that make you feel complete, alive and connected to yourself and the Universe. The ones that give your life purpose and meaning and enable you to know yourself more deeply. They supply you with energy, inner strength, peace, comfort and hope.

One of the best ways to find your spiritual food is to be still and listen to your inner voice. In stillness you connect with your core, its wisdom and euphoria. Follow the path that brings harmony to your life and makes you feel peaceful, whole, connected, and content with life even in the midst of storms.

What is spiritual food for one may not be the case for another. For one person it may be community service or environmental activism, while for another it may be daily meditation or Tai Chi, and yet for another it may be planting a garden, drawing a picture and enjoying the sunrise. It can also be found in dance, making love, exercising, relationships, writing, communing with nature, music, food, sports, reading or walking the dog.

Here are some sources where I find my spiritual food:

Spending time by the lake or ocean, deep stimulating conversation, taking daily walks, country rides, admiring the cloud formations, feeding and watching the birds, feeding a stray cat, listening to music, singing, writing, reading, dancing either with a partner or around my living room by myself, making love, gazing at the stars and moon, the feel of the wind on my body, watching a good movie, and spending time with my son.

I find all the sources I mentioned above to be very nourishing, but my most important spiritual food is nature, walking and time with my son. I can feel as high today from an intimate moment with nature or a deep conversation with my son as I could years ago on a bottle of wine, a big fat joint, a line of cocaine, a bottle of prescription pills or half a dozen beers. Even more so. It's a much richer, deeper and more meaningful experience, and one that I remember in the morning. I'm not hung-over and it stays with me and feeds me for hours or days.

Nature is my lifeline. It rejuvenates me and helps me to go on. It makes me feel alive, full of life and connected to the Universe. There is nothing more nourishing to me than spending a day on a blanket by my favorite lake or ocean shore and being intimate with nature. Spending it with someone I love and engaging in deep conversation is even better. I can feel so euphoric from the stunning colors of nature when the leaves are turning in the fall or a beautiful snowfall, it's almost orgasmic. Intimate time with nature on a daily basis is as important to me as eating three meals a day.

I also find deep breathing exercises, meditation and prayer to be essential methods of spiritual food that I engage in daily. I can reach altered states of consciousness relatively easily through meditation. I believe that's because as a child I was unintentionally entering altered states of consciousness on a daily basis in order to survive the abuse I lived with. Now, I just close my eyes, take a few deep breaths, follow my breath and I'm in spiritual bliss.

Yes, prayer. I know, some people have a hard time understanding why someone who doesn't believe in God or a higher power would pray; and who the heck are you praying too? I don't really have the answer to that. I only know that prayer is a part of who I am, and if I miss it a day or two, I yearn for its connection. When I pray, I talk to the Universe or my higher consciousness. However, I don't really believe anyone is listening to me. I think it's basically just a conversation with the deeper or core self—a form of verbal meditation that connects me with my core and stimulates neurotransmitters that release endorphins and makes me feel good.

Why prayer works or doesn't work is a mystery to me, however, I believe that perhaps some kind of energy in the Universe is available for the taking and you only need to tap into it. When you put your prayers out there, it seems to draw energy towards them or perhaps it's just a psychological trick like the placebo effect. When you pray, it at least feels like you're doing something. I've gotten through some pretty difficult things with the help of prayer, or have I? Perhaps I would have achieved them anyhow if I hadn't prayed. We don't know, because my experience has been that you can't get everything you need with prayer and I have not asked for anything unreasonable, only the basics needed to get through life. There have been times I've been forced to endure unbearable situations for very long stretches, sometimes decades, with no answers or comfort whatsoever. Some prayers are not answered.

Yes, I know all the religious and spiritual explanations for unanswered prayers, such as, "sometimes the answer is no," or "God has his reasons and you don't understand them," or "it's for the higher good," or "you attracted this bad stuff into your life because of your negative thoughts," but those are really unacceptable to me. What kind of being would sit up there and observe all the suffering in this world and ignore it, if they truly have the power to intervene? If that's the truth, then that means that God is a cruel, demented and sick person who gets off on watching people suffer. I don't believe that there's some omnipotent being up there handing out answers to prayers for some people and not to others. Why would one person be privy to grace or blessings and not another? I don't know how anyone can look around at the things happening in this world and believe in a just and loving God.

Throughout my life, even after sobriety, I have had numerous occasions where I have been delivered from one hell only to be thrown immediately into another or I've been given half of a solution. There is no acceptable explanation for this kind of suffering. Have I had blessings and miracles in my life that I am grateful for? Yes, I have, but I don't see that as a sign of God. I see it as perseverance and determination on my part and I believe there are certain laws of nature at work that we don't understand. Not believing in God doesn't mean you don't believe in blessings, gifts and miracles, and when they do arrive, you cherish them greatly.

I don't buy this "everything happens for a reason" crap. I've endured many horrific things in my life that had no possible reason. Was I able to make meaning out of them? Absolutely. It's a choice you must make in order to go on and not be bitter. We must look for the gifts and lessons that may be present in our struggles, pain, challenges and suffering. They can help us learn, grow and become better people. They can also help us clarify our priorities, values and identity, and can sometimes make life more meaningful and richer.

However, to believe that it was meant to happen or God or the Universe put me there for a reason, again, seems like an awfully cruel and demented divinity that is unacceptable to me. There have been many times in my life when a teacher, a solution or direction has been presented at precisely the right moment, which in my view were true miracles and appeared it was meant to happen, however, that is not always the case. I've been in some pretty dire situations where an answer was certainly called for but didn't come. I believe some things happen for a reason, but other things are just random tragedy, synchronicity or serendipity.

I find that statement, "God or the Universe won't give you more than you can handle," insulting and offensive. I've been given more than I can handle many times in my life and one only needs to take a look around the world and you can see many people being given more than they can handle. You either handle it or lie down and die. But, to believe that some omnipotent being or force allowed us to be put in these situations for our own good, or allowed the suffering to continue when they are capable of putting an end to it, doesn't sound like a very loving and kind divinity to me. I see no evidence of a loving protector such as God in my life or anywhere in this world.

However, I continue to pray, because it feels good. It soothes, nurtures and comforts me. I can tap into some Universal wisdom. It brings me closer to my deeper, true or core self. It helps me feel connected to the Universe, life and myself more deeply. Quite frankly, I'm also afraid to attempt to go through life without prayer. Life hasn't been an easy road with it, so I'm afraid to test what it would be like without it. It's one of the pieces of religious/spiritual conditioning/brainwashing that still has a hold on me, but since it brings benefit to my life, I don't try to break it.

Although I don't completely understand the mechanics of prayer, and I feel it has a lot of limits, I do it blindly and faithfully usually during my daily walk. It is one of the great mysteries of life to me that I ponder, analyze and reflect on deeply quite often. Regardless of your spiritual beliefs, prayer and the power it offers is available to anyone. However, prayer does not have to be part of your spiritual path if you choose not to. Many people seem to get by quite nicely without it.

There may not be a clear-cut road for spirituality. As a matter of fact, it will probably be quite curvy, bumpy and contain many untraveled side roads. There will be mountains to climb, oceans to swim and deserts to cross as well as resting spots filled with divine beauty. At times you may feel like you're traveling your path at the speed of an Olympic gold medal track star and at other times you may need to be carried. There may be violent thunderstorms, tornadoes or hurricanes as well as bright and sunny days.

The spiritual path may involve formal methods of exploration such as studying traditional sources like Taoism, Hinduism, or a particular type of meditation with a spiritual guru, etc., but it really does not have to. To truly walk the spiritual path, you must live it. You must experience life. Studying it may be helpful in the beginning to bring about awareness and help you find the truth that is your own, however, there are so many different views and opinions that it can become very confusing about which way to go. It's very easy to get sidetracked by all the intellectual explanations and spiritual activities and miss the real path.

Anyone can claim to be a spiritual guru, and often times there is a lot of ego involved. These people tend to be very charismatic and able to influence others quite easily. Many vulnerable people can fall into a cycle of getting caught in the spiritual leader's path rather than their own. Some people spend years or even a lifetime chasing spirituality by going to one religious or spiritual retreat or event after another, and yet never really follow any internal spiritual journey of their own or achieve any spiritual growth.

Your journey with spirituality is uniquely yours and what you find to be spiritual food may change in response to where you are in life. As you grow and evolve, your spirituality evolves with you. So keep in mind that I am still on my spiritual journey as well. Regardless of where you find your spiritual connections, nurturing your spirituality on a regular basis is as essential as feeding your hungry stomach or quenching your thirst for water. If you neglect this important aspect of your life, you lose touch with your core self and this puts you in danger of looking for spiritual fulfillment in the wrong places like alcohol, drugs, sugar or sex.

Some people are able to see the dysfunction and abuse in religion and walk away, while others are not quite sure why they are uncomfortable with religion, but know they want nothing to do with it. I encourage you to explore, question and find what truly resonates for you. What do you know deep in your core? Find your own truth and follow it, not a truth that you've been conditioned to believe out of fear or because it is the standard that everyone follows. Don't allow yourself to become boxed in or limited by someone else's belief system or even your own. Develop a belief system that is uniquely yours and is always open for growth, change and expansion. Look for validation inside yourself rather than others.

If you have neglected your spirituality, it is never too late to start again. The core self has an amazing ability to recover and flourish in splendor once again.

Nineteen
A Comprehensive and Holistic Plan

"The truth knocks on the door and you say, 'Go away, I'm looking for the truth,' and so it goes away." ~Robert M. Pirsig

A lcoholism is very complex and multi-faceted. A holistic approach that addresses all these intricate facets is what's required for successful recovery. The first and most important step to achieve craving-free sobriety is to stop excessively stimulating neurotransmitters and the pleasure pathway, support the body with a healthy diet that addresses Candida and hypoglycemia and provides essential nutrients, and address all the biochemical traps. Then address any emotional, social or spiritual issue that may apply to you and your situation.

In this book we have examined the biochemical issues that are at the root of alcoholism. Some are root causes and some are root perpetuators. Sometimes it's not clear which came first, however, that's not really important. We would only waste valuable time and energy trying to figure it out. It may actually be different for each individual. The important thing to know is that they are all intertwined and cannot be separated from one another. Addressing these issues is the essential first step in a recovery program that will enable the alcoholic to achieve successful long-term sobriety without cravings. It is the crux of the treatment plan and crucial for everyone.

The biochemistry component provides the foundation for recovery; however, although the roots of alcoholism are biochemical, it is a disease that affects every aspect of an individual's life. It alters personality, cognitive functioning and spiritual connections. It impacts the physical, emotional/psychological, social and spiritual levels deeply.

Although you are not likely to achieve long-term recovery without addressing the biochemical issues, it is equally important to address the social, emotional/psychological, relationship, cognitive and spiritual components as well. They are all interconnected and each one has a profound impact on brain chemistry. If you neglect any of these areas, then you are vulnerable to relapse. I call these issues secondary factors. However, even though they are not the core roots of addiction, if they are not addressed, they have the power to seriously sabotage recovery and perpetuate the addiction cycle once it is set in motion.

For example, I do not believe I would have stayed sober if I had made all the changes in my diet and environment but neglected to heal my childhood abuse issues. The dysfunctional relationship patterns and damage to self that developed as a result of the abuse caused me such immense emotional pain that they were one of my main triggers for using drugs and alcohol. On the other hand, I was struggling to stay sober when I had addressed the emotional and spiritual, but had not yet become aware of the biochemical issues. It was the combination of the three that provided me with all the tools I needed to stay sober.

We learned that the drive to self-medicate is largely based on biochemical factors; however, it can also be triggered by a desire to numb out emotional or spiritual pain and cover up shame. The physical, emotional and spiritual elements are deeply intertwined. The physical impacts the spiritual and the psychological, and vice versa.

The damage that is done on the physical level has a great impact on the psychological and the spiritual. When your brain and body systems aren't functioning properly, it has a profound impact on emotional and spiritual health, which is often exhibited in a variety of negative psychological symptoms and/or intrapersonal conflict. When an individual addresses the biochemical roots of their alcoholism, physical healing begins and deep spiritual and emotional healing can't be complete without it. However, if one only addresses the biochemical and neglects the spiritual and emotional, then they are still at risk of relapse.

Incorporating a comprehensive holistic approach for alcoholism empowers the individual and enables them to heal on all these levels, thus providing them with the strongest defense possible to attain and maintain successful long-term sobriety without cravings.

Depending on individual factors such as each person's background and how long one has been living with alcoholism, there can be a variety of other secondary factors that need to be taken into consideration and addressed, such as relationship issues, childhood sexual or physical abuse and neglect, self-esteem, the impact on marriage, assertiveness and communication, parenting issues, and interpersonal skills. To heal secondary factors, it requires steps like counseling, books, seminars, groups, deep growth on a personal level, self-reflection, inner exploration and time.

Alcoholism is unique from other diseases in that it often destroys marriages or relationships, or alienates family and friends. Family members and friends must often distance themselves from the alcoholic in order to save their own sanity and in some cases protect themselves emotionally and/or physically. When this occurs, the alcoholic is left in a position without a lot of support. For those who stick around, there is usually a great deal of damage done to the relationship and healing is required.

Another unique component to alcoholism is that after one engages in the alcoholic lifestyle for an extended period of time, it then becomes a learned behavior to some degree. They develop many maladaptive patterns for living that must be changed. They learn to respond to stress, pain, sadness, anger, interpersonal and intrapersonal conflicts, etc., by taking a drink or a drug. It becomes a habitual response without thought. These types of behaviors must be unlearned and replaced with healthier behaviors. Habits and routines must be broken. They must relearn how to cope with feelings and emotions and how to interact with self and the world without mind-altering substances. They must learn to allow themselves to feel, to tolerate feelings, and how to ride them out or talk them out. They must learn how to be responsible for their actions.

The only way to unlearn something is through experience—it takes time and you may fumble like a child for a while. The alcoholic must learn new behaviors and put them into action by simply doing them. Instead of reaching for a drink every time in a stressful, sad, angry or painful event, they must learn to replace that with a healthier activity. Over time the new behavior will become the instinctual action instead of medicating.

For many it is truly like learning to live all over again. A whole new lifestyle must be built that not only includes eating healthier but also developing new friendships, hobbies, social activities and, for some, even new employment and place of residence. Hanging out in bars or at the drinking buddy's home must be replaced with healthier activities like meditating, gardening, art, going to counseling, prayer, walking or some other form of exercise. Depending upon the severity of addiction, some people need a protected environment during the early stages of recovery. Avoiding people who drink and drug, and places where alcohol and drugs will be present, is particularly important in the early stages of recovery.

Once you've achieved some biochemical repair and some stability in your sobriety, this probably won't be such an issue, but in the beginning it is essential. After you've been sober for a while, your mind clears, your values and interests change, you find you no longer have anything in common with people who drink and drug, and you'll no longer desire to be around them. However, alcohol and, sometimes even drugs, are found in almost every social function in our culture, so it can be hard to avoid. After making biochemical repairs, it's usually possible to be around alcohol without risk.

After I had some sobriety under my belt, an occasional event such as going dancing in a bar or being around others who were drinking was no problem at all, but this is not something you want to do in the early phases of recovery. If you remember, I dated an active alcoholic for eight years. There was alcohol in my refrigerator nearly every weekend, but I was never tempted even once to touch it. However, I had five years of sobriety under my belt before I became involved in that relationship. I wouldn't recommend this to anyone in early recovery.

Alcoholism is also unique in that there is likely to be a great deal of shame, guilt and remorse for actions and behaviors that the alcoholic engaged in while intoxicated, which must be dealt with in a healthy manner to keep them from interfering in sobriety. Forgiveness of self must occur.

Many people who've lived with alcoholism for a long time may be lacking in a variety of social skills that are necessary to get through life. These factors will not apply to everyone, but for those that they do, this is another area where traditional counseling is called for.

One other factor I want to mention briefly that applies only to women, is PMS or premenstrual syndrome. PMS can be a powerful trigger for relapse. It's not uncommon for women to have cravings during this time or a desire to seek relief from the miserable symptoms they must endure. I didn't write a chapter specifically about this issue because PMS is caused by hormonal imbalances that are caused by a poor diet high in sugar, caffeine and other junk food, Candida overgrowth, nutritional deficiencies, and environmental toxins. Therefore, when you address each of these issues as you've already been instructed to do, your PMS should improve as well.

Additionally, hormonal imbalances are also heavily influenced by neurotransmitters; so, as you address your neurotransmitter issues, this too will improve your hormone balance. Remember that hormonal fluctuations can also cause a drastic drop in blood sugar levels and result in hypoglycemia symptoms, so be sure to adjust your diet accordingly during this time of the month. However, sometimes the hormones can be so off balance that they need to be replaced. The most effective and safest way to do this is through bioidentical hormones, not standard hormone replacement. The most reliable method for testing hormones is through saliva. So, if you suspect hormone imbalance is one of your issues, once again, you'll need to find an alternative medicine doctor who specializes in women's health and is knowledgeable about bioidentical hormones.

During my first year of recovery, before I had changed my diet, cleaned up my environment and stopped smoking, my premenstrual days were always the most miserable and dangerous time. Once I changed my diet, stopped smoking, etc., I no longer felt at risk. However, until you make progress in these areas, you'll want to be aware that when you're premenstrual you're at a higher risk of relapse; so, be sure to stay on guard.

And yet another exclusive aspect of alcoholism is that sometimes the individual goes through a grieving period when they begin recovery. Giving up alcohol is like losing a very good friend or a loved one. Emotional support is needed for those who have this experience.

Although child abuse is extremely common in alcoholics, it doesn't happen to everyone. An individual who lived with childhood abuse or neglect is likely to have more challenges to face than someone who had a loving childhood. Their treatment plan will include a lot more focus on the counseling aspect. Child abuse is a unique factor because it falls in the biochemical category because of the impact on the brain and neurotransmitters; however, it can also be a root perpetuator or secondary factor.

With all these different factors weighing in on the alcoholism equation, to address only one aspect will not lead to successful sobriety. All issues must be addressed or they become possible triggers for relapse and undermine recovery. Let's take a look at my life again as an illustration of the many different facets of alcoholism.

- First of all, I was born with a predisposition to alcoholism because it was in my family. My neurotransmitters were probably out of balance at birth.

- Next, I lived with neglect and severe emotional/physical and sexual abuse as a small child, which resulted in more neurotransmitter damage as well as emotional and spiritual damage.

- I developed nutritional deficiencies from neglect. Somewhere along the line, I developed food allergies and a damaged thyroid.

- Physical and emotional abuse was then carried on by my father throughout my entire childhood. Thus, continuing to whittle away at my biological, emotional and spiritual health.

- In my teens, the combination of neurotransmitter damage and undiagnosed Candida putting out acetaldehyde inflicted my entire body with constant pain which thrust me more into alcohol and drugs to find relief.

- A damaged HPA axis, food allergies and neurotransmitter damage created a variety of problems like anxiety and depression that I needed to medicate with drugs and alcohol. The HPA axis also incited a high sex drive that drove me to engage in activities to fulfill these sexual needs that filled me with shame and drove me to drink and drug even more.

- As a result of the abusive relationships with my parents, I was a very damaged person emotionally who didn't know how to have relationships, which created more emotional pain, so I turned to drugs and alcohol for relief for this pain as well.

- Because of the child abuse in my life, I fell into a very dysfunctional pattern of relating to men sexually, which also caused me immense emotional pain and shame that led to more dependence upon alcohol and drugs to numb out.

- Also as a result of the child abuse, I had severely damaged self-esteem and didn't know how to interact with people unless I was high or drunk.

- Child abuse created a very fragmented identity that caused immense confusion and conflict, which pushed me to drink and use drugs to deal with these feelings.

- All of this combined left me disconnected from my spirituality and a deep emptiness inside that also led to drinking and drugs to fill up the hole.

- After living this life for so long, I literally didn't know any other way. I didn't know how to function without drugs or alcohol.

- Everyone in my life was an addict or alcoholic.

This clearly illustrates to us how complex alcoholism is, how it impacts every area of our life and how they are all interconnected. In my life we see there was a predisposition factor, an abuse factor, food allergies, thyroid issues, nutritional deficiencies, emotional trauma, neurotransmitter depletion, Candida, disconnection from self, maladaptive patterns of interacting, relationship and intimacy factors, a damaged self, spiritual emptiness, deep shame, maladaptive patterns of functioning in the world, sexual dysfunction, and social influence. Each one of these factors was either a root cause or a perpetuator in my addictions. To ignore one of these aspects would have left me at risk of relapse.

A Holistic and Comprehensive Approach to Alcoholism May Look Something Like This:

1. Biochemical repairs that addresses the physical aspect of the illness as well as the psychological.

   The important thing to take note of in this plan is that all the points in the biochemical repairs must be taken for everyone with particular emphasis on the first two points in the list. Points in Step 2 and Step 3 will vary from individual to individual depending upon each person's particular life experience, but that is not the case for biochemical repairs. Although there may be some variance from individual to individual, each of the components listed below must be addressed to achieve successful long-term sobriety without cravings.

   - no mind-altering substances, which includes:

     no nicotine

     no caffeine

     no sugar

   - hypoglycemia diet

   - identify your alcoholic body chemistry

   - restore and balance neurotransmitters

   - identify metabolic disorders

   - nutritional support during detox

   - changes in diet and nutrition

   - isolating environmental factors and chemical sensitivities

   - addressing nutritional deficiencies

   - individualized diet plans

   - dietary and nutritional counseling

   - exercise

- stress management
- identifying food allergies and sensitivities
- Candida diet
- neurotransmitter testing and amino acid supplements
- hormone testing and possible replacement
- heavy metal testing and possible treatment
- adrenal testing and possible nutritional treatment

Optional

- inpatient treatment
- outpatient treatment

2. Counseling, groups, workshops or seminars for social and emotional issues.

- heal childhood trauma (physical, emotional or sexual abuse and neglect)
- dealing with loss and grief of alcoholism
- coping skills
- parenting skills
- lifestyle adjustment
- communication skills
- assertiveness training
- what to do with loneliness, boredom, too much time on your hands
- repairing relationships with children and significant others
- relationship skills
- developing social skills
- dealing with feelings

3. Discovering and nurturing spiritual connections

- developing a relationship with yourself
- connecting more deeply with yourself
- healing relationships

- engaging in spiritually fulfilling activities

- forgiveness of self

- engaging in deep and meaningful activities that make you feel whole, complete and connected

- prayer

- meditation

- time with nature

- art, writing or some other form of creative practice

- yoga, Tai Chi or other similar practice

In my opinion, exercise should be a part of everyone's recovery plan for a variety of reasons. In addition to healthy stimulation of the neurotransmitters, it also boosts the immune system; relieves depression and anxiety; assists in detoxification; improves colon functioning; aids the adrenals, kidneys and other organs to function better; reduces stress; boosts energy; aids in balancing hormones, insulin and blood sugar; enhances sleep; and oxygenates the blood. This does not mean you have to go the gym, join aerobics or participate in a strenuous exercise regimen. A simple, brisk daily walk that consists of 30–35 minutes a day will do the job adequately. Not only that, you'll be exposed to the sunlight, which will also nourish you with vitamin D and stimulate your neurotransmitters as well. However, exercise should be done in moderation. If it is too extreme, it will deplete adrenals and neurotransmitters even more and possibly even perpetuate the cycle of addiction.

It's important to note that in a holistic approach to alcoholism, not everyone's treatment plan will look exactly the same. Treatment is individualized and personalized according to each person's unique needs and issues. Your precise plan depends on what type of alcoholic you are, what your background and childhood were like, when did alcoholism develop, how long you've been entrenched, and how much physical addiction is going on.

If you're a chronic alcoholic who is drinking daily, it can be very dangerous to go through the detox period alone—death is possible. So inpatient treatment, at least for a short period, would probably be called for, or at least supervision by a physician for a few days. While doing it alone may work well for others. Some people who develop alcoholism later in life and don't have as many childhood scars and as much dysfunction in relationships won't need extensive focus on secondary factors. For someone who developed their alcoholism later in life in response to a life event or a biochemical shift, counseling, AA, detox, etc., may not be necessary, because there is no physical danger and not as much to unlearn.

One person may have many secondary issues while another individual may have none or only one or two. One person may need a great deal of counseling and training in areas such as communication and assertiveness while others may be quite competent in these areas. Some people may adjust easier to a new lifestyle while another may struggle a great deal.

Treatment approaches will vary to some degree in the biochemical aspect as well as the emotional and spiritual aspects. One person may need to address Candida, hypothyroidism, food allergies, mold, chemical sensitivities, etc., while another person may only have Candida, food allergies and hypoglycemia. One person may be deficient in Omega 6 or 3 and another may be deficient in a whole string of vitamins and minerals. One person may need to give up corn and another person may need to give up wheat. Some people may get drunk when exposed to gasoline fumes and another may get drunk when exposed to perfume. Someone who has been drinking for 20 years may have a lot more complex biochemical and social issues than someone who became an alcoholic two years ago after their husband died. Each recovery path depends on the biochemical makeup and life circumstances of each person.

All these details need to be taken into account, and the recovery plan is adjusted and tailored specifically for the individual. It's also important to keep in mind that none of these arenas are independent from one another. When you work on the biochemical, it promotes healing in the psychological and spiritual arena; and when you work on the psychological or spiritual, they too promote healing on the biochemical level. Neurotransmitters impact the emotional and spiritual and vice versa. They are not mutually exclusive; it's a loop that feeds into one another. Additionally, I'd like to point out that working on the biochemical issues, at least to some degree, should precede the psychological/emotional and spiritual issues if possible, because you'll then be more stabilized and capable of facing and addressing the psychological and spiritual aspects.

It is my opinion that a 30-day inpatient stay is the best plan for most everyone. For all the same reasons traditional treatment is helpful—it provides you with a protected environment, people who understand what you're going through, a place to rest while you get on your feet and get stronger, connection with others, emotional support, a break from social influences, a place to work on emotional issues, and time to really adopt the necessary lifestyle changes and allow biochemical healing to begin. It's just so hard to accomplish all the changes that must be made while dealing with day-to-day life. This is especially true for those who are in advanced stages of alcoholism. I know for myself I don't believe I would have made it without the protected environment I had for three months.

However, on the other hand, I had no knowledge of the biochemical aspect at that time and was not addressing this issue. If I had been provided vitamins, minerals, amino acids and other nutrients I was deficient in that were needed to support the body through detox, then my rehab experience would not have been as excruciating. If I had learned from day one that I needed to remove sugar, yeast, wheat and refined foods from my diet, I wouldn't have experienced the debilitating hyperventilating and anxiety attacks for a year into sobriety. Recovery would have been a very different experience for me. However, there were still very powerful social and family influences that would have sabotaged me. I didn't know one single person who didn't drink or do drugs, nor did I know how to function in the world without drinking or being high. There were too many temptations and influences, and this is an issue for many people. Even when you're following the biochemical approach, it takes some time for healing to occur and to adopt the crucial diet and lifestyle changes as your own.

One of the things that the alcoholics I work with today struggle with the most is the fact that everyone around them is still eating sugar, drinking coffee, etc. Giving up sugar, caffeine, cigarettes and refined foods can be as difficult as getting off the alcohol for some people. You can't be sitting across the table from someone who is smoking, eating cupcakes and candy bars or have coffee brewing in the kitchen in the morning. Most people just won't make it. All these substances must be removed from the household. The whole family must change and this can be very difficult to achieve. If you're a single parent, it is relatively easy to enforce the rules with your children, but spouses or significant others are a different story. It's very hard to get them to believe that in addition to giving up their evening glasses of wine that they must also give up their donuts, candy bars and Starbucks coffee, and be supportive of this.

Unfortunately, for those wanting to follow the biochemical approach, inpatient treatment is not a realistic option for many people. To my knowledge there are only two treatment centers in the United States that offer complete biochemical recovery to cover all the aspects I've presented to you. One is in Minnesota and is called the Health Recovery Center. It is outpatient only, however, it has a designated apartment complex nearby where you can stay with other patients. The second one is in Colorado and is called Inner Balance Health. It offers inpatient treatment.

There are a handful of treatment centers out there that call themselves holistic, but you must be careful because being holistic is becoming the fashionable thing to do, so a lot of people are picking up the term and applying it to their service even though they are still applying the same old ineffective principles and techniques. Some centers have incorporated a few pieces of the biochemical approach to their program, such as supplementing some of the B vitamins, amino acid therapy or other nutrients and embracing a more spiritual element rather than religious, but they don't yet have the whole picture. Before choosing one of these centers, you'll want to investigate them thoroughly and make sure they are using the whole biochemical approach. However, considering the fact that your other alternative is likely to be mainstream treatment and/or AA, which offer nothing biochemically, a holistic center that has at least incorporated some of the biochemical aspects would be better than nothing.

A major drawback for all treatment centers offering biochemical recovery is that they are all quite costly, with some being more expensive than others and not usually covered by health insurance. Prices can range anywhere from $13,000 to $50,000 for a month. Unfortunately, they are out of reach financially for most common folk.

The way it stands now, anyone who wants treatment that can be covered by their health insurance and be provided with a protected environment and address their emotional issues simultaneously is left with one choice only—a standard 12 step treatment program. They are forced to follow a program that is heavily laden in religion and doesn't offer any attention to the biochemical aspect at all. They are going to be fed sugar, caffeine and other unhealthy foods, and be exposed to environmental toxins, etc., which ultimately perpetuates the addiction cycle and sets you up for relapse.

Some people following the biochemical protocol from home try to go to AA for the social aspect and emotional support, so that's always an option one can try, if you can manage to ignore all the negative aspects. However, the problem they face is that they don't share a common goal or belief system and, once again, they will be exposed to the addictive substances of cigarettes, sugar, caffeine, etc., that they are trying to break free from and it ends up being counterproductive. Additionally, if you don't accept the belief system of AA, you are not truly accepted as one of the crowd.

Ideally, what is needed is for mainstream treatment centers to drop their religious, shaming, blaming, brainwashing approach and adopt the biochemical approach so that all the wonderful benefits they do offer can be combined with an effective treatment plan that addresses the real root of alcoholism and make it easily accessible to everyone. Unfortunately, that does not exist today. So it's quite a dilemma, because there is no way to get all that is needed in one place. Since going to Colorado or Minnesota is probably not an option for most people, they must put a plan together for themselves.

Fortunately, that is entirely possible. The director of the Health Recovery Center in Minnesota is Joan Mathews Larson, the author of the book *Seven*

Weeks to Sobriety that I mentioned earlier, and this makes it possible for you to follow the entire protocol from home. The downside of this is that you have to piece together the other crucial aspects like counseling, spirituality, emotional support, etc., however it can be achieved with a little planning and creativity.

Joan's book outlines in complete detail the protocol she follows at her center. You can follow the same comprehensive treatment plan she uses that will help you identify which type of alcoholic you are, support your body through detox, and then heal the biochemical issues through nutritional supplementation and diet. She tells you exactly which supplements to take and how much, and she even produces and distributes the supplements herself. You can purchase the kit from her directly and the whole program can be done from home.

Here's how I would do it if it were me:

I'd pick up a copy of Joan's book, *Seven Weeks to Sobriety*, then I'd find a reputable alternative medicine doctor who is also an MD who could support me through the process and oversee the physical aspect, in case any problems arise. I'd also be sure to read thoroughly the book in your fingers at this moment and add the information I've presented here to Joan's.

If I suspected that detox would be dangerous or particularly rough, I'd go to a hospital for a few days. You can usually get a three-day detox in the psych ward of most hospitals and it would be covered by health insurance. So you could go through standard detox then come home and begin the true biochemical recovery process.

I'd then find a sobriety coach who was knowledgeable about the holistic and biochemical approach that could assist and guide me through the steps in the *Seven Weeks to Sobriety* book and offer me emotional support. All work with a sobriety coach can be done over the phone, so location is not an issue. (You can find me and my services at my website listed in the back of this book. I also provide testing for neurotransmitters, food sensitivities, nutritional deficiencies, heavy metals, hormones, adrenals and intestinal permeability.)

Depending upon the qualifications and expertise of the sobriety coach, and what other social/emotional issues may pertain to my situation, I may also find a mental health counselor who uses orthomolecular medicine instead of traditional psychiatry to also assist me through the process and help with some of the deeper psychological issues like child abuse. It's becoming more commonplace for mental health professionals to offer their services by telephone as well, so finding one that practices orthomolecular medicine should be possible. You can find them in listings on the Internet or the databases I mentioned to you in the chapters on Candida and nutritional deficiencies.

Additionally, I encourage you to look at the bibliography in the back of this book and to read each one of these sources. The material I have presented to you in this book gives you a good foundation, however, it would be to your benefit if you gain a more thorough and in depth knowledge base of all that I have covered.

Since this is a book about the truth, I must mention that for some people there is one downfall even to the biochemical approach done at home and that is that it too can be very expensive. Since it is not accepted by mainstream medicine, supplements and most testing are not covered by most health insurance companies. The nutritional supplements required during detox and healing are very expensive. However, even if you don't have the financial resources to do all of this, you can still succeed.

To be honest, I lived most of my recovery years below the poverty level because of severe chemical sensitivities that rendered me unable to work. I never had enough money to buy all the supplements that needed to be done at the time it needed done. I often had severe allergic reactions to supplements and was unable to take them. Additionally, remember at the time, I didn't have a resource that taught me everything I presented to you in this book. I was piecing it together over the years.

If you have the financial resources for the supplements, then without a doubt, you should absolutely take them, because it will ensure you have an easier and quicker road to recovery. You won't go through the physical agony and struggle I went through in detox and the first year of sobriety. It's the easiest and quickest way to balance and correct your neurotransmitters, body chemistry and correct deficiencies. They will also help immensely with cravings.

However, in my experience I found that the most crucial changes that I made after removing the alcohol and drugs were to eliminate cigarettes, sugar, caffeine and refined foods from my diet, following the Candida diet, keeping my blood sugar stable, eating organic, and cleaning environmental toxins out of my living space. It was these steps alone that turned my recovery completely around, removed all cravings and struggle to stay sober, and eliminated the anxiety and depression. None of these things except organic food cost money and everyone can do them.

You can usually find a mental health counselor in your community that offers a sliding fee scale, who although may not believe in what you're doing, can still help with the emotional aspect. None of the counselors I worked with over the years had any knowledge of orthomolecular medicine. None of them believed what I believed, but I was able to work on the emotional aspect with them regardless of that.

When you truly want to get sober, you can find a way to do it. I'd like to reinforce something one more time—the most critical steps to achieve craving-free sobriety are to remove sugar, caffeine and nicotine from your life. If you don't remove these three substances, then cravings to drink or drug will continue.

Today I am self-employed as a sobriety coach where I teach people about the biochemical approach to alcoholism and addiction and support them through the process. I use Joan's book as the foundation for my teaching, because it provides you with a step-by-step blue print of exactly what you need to support your body.

Although Joan's work is unprecedented and the most valuable resource on biochemistry and alcoholism you can find, my experience has revealed to me there are a few crucial components for successful recovery that are not included in the biochemical approach, such as child abuse, spirituality, sexuality and relationship issues. As illustrated earlier, it is my opinion that these factors are crucial issues that must be addressed in order to maintain long-term sobriety, because they too are very much part of the biochemical (neurotransmitter) connection.

Additionally, there are some issues in the field of addictive biochemistry, such as neurotransmitters, Candida, environmental toxins, cigarettes, caffeine and sugar that I feel don't receive enough emphasis and need some points expanded and clarified from someone who has lived with it. These are the areas I've covered in this book. Joan's book covers more of the "how," while my book goes more in depth on the "why" and the "what." I wanted to have something to give my clients that put everything I knew into one place for easy access; thus, the book you're reading was born.

Alcoholism treatment that addresses the biochemical issues is a very successful approach. In Joan's Minnesota treatment center she maintains a 74 percent success rate.[1] The center in Colorado claims an 80 percent success rate.[2] It is my hypothesis that those who don't succeed have issues in one or more of the following areas that have not been resolved: extensive neurotransmitter damage, unresolved child abuse issues, undiagnosed Candida and/or environmental toxins that continue to sabotage their recovery, or they don't adhere to dietary restrictions. When I consult with someone who has already tried the biochemical approach without success, what I usually find is that they did not remove sugar, caffeine and other refined foods from their diet and/or there is usually child abuse and environmental toxins that have not been dealt with.

As I've mentioned before, I feel there are many good and valuable aspects that mainstream treatment and psychology have to offer in the recovery of alcoholism, however, they are missing the biochemical aspect. The biochemical approach is missing the emotional/psychological and spiritual facets.

My goal in this book has been to bring the best of all three worlds together. To expand on and fill in the gaps of the wonderful biochemical approach and enhance your chances of success even further. It is my opinion that if you follow the instructions in something like the *Seven Weeks to Sobriety* book and combine that with the information I've presented here, that you have the most powerful recovery plan that can be found to achieve craving-free sobriety. Last but not least, I think it is a crime that this life-changing information is not widely known and accessible. I feel it is my duty to call more attention to the biochemical approach and give testament to the fact of how successful it is. The truth must be told.

There are a couple things we need to clarify with the biochemical approach. Although I consider myself a recovered alcoholic and the word cure may be used in this field of thought, it's very important to clarify that when using the word cure in relation to alcoholism, we are not talking about arriving at a place where the individual can drink normally.

If your body chemistry predisposes you to alcoholism or the process of addiction has been activated, once an alcoholic, always an alcoholic. Social drinking or controlled drinking is not a possibility. Complete abstinence is required. Recovery from alcoholism means arriving at a place where you no longer crave alcohol and your life is no longer controlled and destroyed by it. You no longer struggle to stay sober.

It's important to understand that the changes in lifestyle, diet and environment must be a permanent change. It must become "your" lifestyle. It isn't something you do for a couple weeks and be done with it. You must always follow a diet that maintains healthy blood sugar, provides the body with essential nutrients and discourages Candida overgrowth, and should be free of sugar, caffeine and other refined junk foods, and avoid environmental toxins. If the individual returns to a diet or lifestyle that includes sugar, cigarettes and caffeine, and one that promotes hypoglycemia, they put themselves at high risk of craving alcohol and/or drugs again and relapse, because of excessive stimulation of neurotransmitters and the reward pathway. It is my opinion that personal, emotional and spiritual growth and change should be an ongoing process as well. Even with 21 years of sobriety, I am still a work of art in progress, and probably always will be.

After writing this book, I would recommend to everyone that you write the story of your life, even if you never let anyone read it. The process is incredibly healing and something I didn't expect. It released a lot of shame I was still holding onto in a variety of areas, and I achieved deeper forgiveness and understanding for my choices and myself. I worked through some issues I wasn't even aware I still had.

We experience life in segments, however, when you put all those segments on paper, you can see it all at one time and connect all the dots. Events, actions and choices flow together and match up so that you see a clear and cohesive picture. Actions that I sometimes second-guessed myself on as years went by were clarified as the only possible choice at the time. It all makes sense in a way that it didn't before and I could see clearly how I got from point A to point B and why. The truth in my life was solidified.

It's also important to be aware that change is a process, not an event, and recovery from alcoholism or any addiction requires great change. That is true regardless of which treatment path you follow. Most people do not change unless circumstances in life literally force them, and it usually requires a great deal of pain, suffering and loss before seeing the light. This seems to be human nature. Even with a holistic and biochemical approach, change is not something that usually happens immediately or easily. There are phases you will go through. We'll call them early, middle and final.

Phases of Change

- **Early** – In the early phase of change you begin to recognize that there might be a problem, and you start exploring the possibility of change and gathering information. You probably aren't ready yet to make significant changes, but you might take a couple baby steps and then go backwards. You think you want to change, but you're not sure. You're likely to waver back and forth from day to day or hour to hour.

- **Middle** – In the middle phase of change you have gathered some information and know which direction you want to go. You may try several different methods before finding your way. You want to change, but you may face some resistance with yourself as you attempt to make changes. It may feel too frightening, overwhelming or challenging, and you may abandon your attempts to change for a period of time. You may question whether the problem is really that bad and whether you really want to change. You may go back to gathering more information and reassess which path you want to follow.

- **Final** – In the final phase of change you are no longer resisting yourself. You've identified the problem completely and are certain you want to change. You're ready to do whatever it takes to achieve your goal, no matter how difficult. Not changing doesn't seem like an option anymore.

You may circulate through these phases of change several times before succeeding. All of this is a normal and natural part of change. If you don't succeed at first, don't beat yourself up. It doesn't mean you can't make it next time. t's an opportunity to learn more and become stronger. You'll be more determined and prepared next time. However, in order to stay sober, you must want and be ready to change.

The big difference within the phases of change when using a holistic approach that includes addressing biochemistry is you are less likely to circulate though the phases as many times as you do with the traditional 12 step treatment program because you are actually addressing the root of the problem.

Many people arrive at the doors of AA or a 12 step treatment program and are ready to change, but are not able to succeed because they are given the wrong tools. With AA and 12 step treatment programs most people tend to circulate through these phases repeatedly and never succeed in sobriety.

A lot of people reach the final phase and are completely ready to change, but they can't fight their cravings or live with the other unbearable symptoms like anxiety and depression that so often accompany recovery. Since AA or traditional treatment doesn't address these issues, the alcoholic is at high risk of relapse and then going back to phase 1.

With a holistic approach that addresses biochemistry, when you're ready to change, you are given effective tools that will enable you to fight the battle adequately.

Since your cravings to drink or drug will disappear, there will no longer be any struggle. You may even succeed if you are in the early or middle phase of change because you'll see results and feel better, which will motivate you to keep moving forward. These results can actually push someone who is in phase 1 or 2 into the phase 3. With AA and traditional treatment programs the exact opposite is true. They tend to push people backwards to phase 1, repeatedly.

A holistic and biochemical approach gets to the root of alcoholism and provides you with all the tools needed for success. However, this does not mean that it is an easier path or a shortcut without any work. No one chooses to be an alcoholic, it is a result of biochemistry; however, achieving and maintaining long-term sobriety does require making a choice. Success in recovery requires a great deal of commitment, determination, self-discipline and perseverance. There must be a true desire to stop drinking and drugging, a commitment to self, a great deal of inner strength and the willingness to do whatever is required to reach the goal.

Additionally, it's important to have realistic expectations about life after recovery. When you do the biochemical, emotional and spiritual work required, then alcoholism is no longer an issue, it's as simple as that. However, a life of sobriety does not mean that it will be easy and life will be grand. There is not a fairy-tale ending. Life is a mixture of pain, beauty, sadness, joy, peace, conflict, grief, loss, happiness, etc. Sobriety doesn't change that, it changes how you respond to it. It's learning to embrace the whole spectrum of emotions and experiences that comprise life.

In the summer of 2009, I achieved 21 years of uninterrupted sobriety by following the path I have presented to you in this book. Drinking or drugs is a non-issue in my life. I continue to be completely craving free and there has not been the slightest struggle to remain sober and clean. Drinking or drugs is not something I ever think about. I finished my college education and now hold a bachelor's in psychology and a master's in counseling. In addition to my work as a sobriety coach, I'm also a self-employed adult sex educator helping couples improve their sex life and maintain fidelity. After I worked through my sex issues, I arrived at a place where I despise infidelity and dishonesty. Now, in an ironic karmic twist of fate, I am passionate about teaching couples how to prevent it. Additionally, I'm also a holistic health counselor helping individuals living with chronic illness or chronic pain to cope, manage and live life more fully.

I write a variety of self-help publications and articles in the areas of sex life improvement, holistic health, natural health, environmental health, chronic illness, alcoholism and addiction that can be found widely across the Internet as well as my own websites. I have a variety of different websites on each of these topics where my services, which are offered by telephone, and books can be found. My life is dedicated to teaching others about the role of nutrition, diet and environmental toxins related to not only addiction but to mental and physical health in general and helping couples to have healthy and satisfying relationships.

My son is a beautiful young man and an all around great person, who is also clean and sober without cravings and just finished his college degree in web design. We have a great a relationship that is the most important, valuable and richest part of my life. Now that he is an adult, he is not only my son, but also a great friend.

As you can see, the person I am today is very different from the person you met in chapter two of this book. There has been a great deal of transformation. My life is not riddled with the insanity of alcoholism or addiction. I know who I am. I like who I am. I'm complete, whole, content and comfortable in my own skin. There's not a vast and empty hole inside me anymore, and I have a deep and rich inner life. I don't feel dead, empty or trapped in the bottomless black pit that accompanies addiction, and I find pleasure and joy in the simplest things of life. All of this is, as they say, truly "priceless."

I am a truth seeker and I'm in the business of telling the truth when I find it to enable others to improve their life. I'm not the type of person who can buy an idea or pass information along if I don't know it to be true on the deepest level. Although I did receive a lot of the knowledge I have shared with you from books and schooling, it was because I was searching for answers that fit with what I was going through. I don't recommend book knowledge unless it has also become heart knowledge. There is nothing in this book that I have not experienced firsthand and found it personally to be effective and essential in the recovery process. The information I have presented to you is the truth as I know it today. For me it was profound and life altering. I hope that it will be for you as well.

"Men occasionally stumble over the truth, but most of them pick themselves up and hurry off as if nothing had happened." ~Winston Churchill

Notes

The following is an overview of all the sources cited within this book. You will find the full details of all cited references as well as other recommended reading in the bibliography.

Chapter One

1. *MMWR* Weekly, "Alcohol-Attributable Deaths"
2. Cheever, *My Name is Bill*, 145
3. Ibid., 178
4. Ibid., 225
5. Hartigan, *Bill W.*, 171–173
6. Hartigan, *Bill W.*, 192; Cheever, *My Name is Bill*, 225
7. Cheever, 231
8. Ibid., 231–232
9. Ibid., 227
10. Hartigan, *Bill W.*, 173
11. *Alcoholics Anonymous*, 135 (also known as the *Big Book*)
12. Cheever, *My Name is Bill*, 246
13. Ibid., 248
14. *Alcoholics Anonymous*, 111
15. Cheever, *My Name is Bill*, 233
16. Ibid.
17. Ibid., 232
18. *Alcoholics Anonymous*, 69–70
19. Ibid., 81
20. Mathews Larson, *Seven Weeks to Sobriety*; Ketcham and others, *Beyond the Influence*
21. Bufe, "How Effective is AA?" in *Alcoholics Anonymous: Cult or Cure?*
22. Orange, "The Effectiveness of the Twelve-Step Treatment" in *The Orange Papers*
23. Bufe, "The 12 Steps" in *Alcoholics Anonymous: Cult or Cure?*
24. *Alcoholics Anonymous*, 59–62
25. Bufe, "The 12 Steps" in *Alcoholics Anonymous: Cult or Cure?*
26. Wikipedia, http://en.wikipedia.org/wiki/Cult
27. Wordnet Search, http://wordnet.princeton.edu/perl/webwn
28. Wikipedia, http://en.wikipedia.org/wiki/Brainwashing
29. Mathews Larson, *Seven Weeks to Sobriety;* Ketcham and others, *Beyond the Influence*
30. Health Recovery Center, http://www.healthrecovery.com; InnerBalance Health, http://www.innerbalance.com

Chapter Four

1. The University of Utah, Learn Genetics, "Drugs Alter the Brain's Reward Pathway"; National Institute on Drug Abuse, "The Neurobiology of Drug Addiction"; Canadian Institutes of Health Research, "The Brain from Top to Bottom"
2. Rogers, *Depression Cured at Last*
3. The University of Utah, Learn Genetics, "Drugs Alter the Brain's Reward Pathway"; National Institute on Drug Abuse, "The Neurobiology of Drug Addiction"
4. The University of Utah, Learn Genetics, "Drugs Alter the Brain's Reward Pathway"; National Institute on Drug Abuse, "The Neurobiology of Drug Addiction"

Chapter Five

1. Mathews Larson, *Seven Weeks to Sobriety*
2. Intelegen, Inc., "Acetaldehyde: A common and Potent Neurotoxin"
3. Ibid.
4. Ibid.
5. Ibid.
6. Trowbridge and Walker, *The Yeast Syndrome*

Chapter Seven

1. Veracity, "The Politics of Sugar "
2. Adams, "Sugar Addicts"
3. Merola.com, "Is Sugar More Addictive than Cocaine?"
4. Adams, "Sugar Addicts"
5. Norwood, *Women Who Love Too Much*
6. DeAmicis, "Alcoholism, Candia, Diabetes & Hypoglycemia"
7. Medicolegal.tripod.com, "Prevent Alcoholism"
8. NIDA for Teens. "Facts on Drugs,"
   http://teens.drugabuse.gov/facts/facts_nicotine1.asp
9. Medicolegal.tripod.com, "Prevent Alcoholism"
10. NIDA for Teens. "Facts on Drugs,"
   http://teens.drugabuse.gov/facts/facts_nicotine2.asp
11. New South Wales Government Department of Health, "Nicotine and Other Poisons"
12. Ibid.
13. Pierce-Davis, "The Biochemistry and Physiology of Smoking"
14. Wikipedia, "Caffeine," http://en.wikipedia.org/wiki/Caffeine

15. Veracity, "The Hidden Dangers of Caffeine"
16. Ibid.

Chapter Eight

1. Randolph, *An Alternative Approach to Allergies*
2. Mathews Larson, *Seven Weeks to Sobriety*
3. Null, *Nutrition and the Mind*
4. Schuitemaker, "Nutrition and Behavior"

Chapter Nine

1. Werbach, "Nutritional Influences on Aggressive Behavior"; Rogers, *Depression Cured at Last*
2. Tuormaa, "The Adverse Effects of Food Additives on Health"
3. Null, *Nutrition and the Mind*
4. Kane, *Food Makes the Difference*
5. Intelegen, Inc., "Acetaldehyde: A common and Potent Neurotoxin"

Chapter Ten

1. U.S. Environmental Protection Agency, http://www.epa.gov
2. U.S. Environmental Protection Agency, "Identification of Polar Volatile Organic Compounds"
3. Ibid.
4. Ibid.
5. Ibid.
6. Rogers, *Depression Cured at Last*
7. Ibid.
8. Ibid.
9. Ibid.
10. World Health Organization, http://www.who.int
11. Rogers, *Depression Cured at Last*
12. Ibid.
13. Cullin, "Workers with MCS"
14. Miller, "Toxicology and Industrial Health"
15. Rea, *Chemical Sensitivities*; Leviton, "Environmental Illness"
16. Rea, *Chemical Sensitivities*
17. U.S. Department of Health and Human Services, "Multiple Chemical Sensitivities"
18. Mathews Larson, *Seven Weeks to Sobriety*
19. Duehring, "Screening for Nervous System Damage"

20. Leviton, "Environmental Illness"

Chapter Eleven

1. Barnes, *Hypothyroidism*
2. Information obtained from a Patient Handout provided by Dr. Roy E. Kerry, Greenville, PA.

Chapter Twelve

1. Teicher, "Scars That Won't Heal"; Briere, *Child Abuse Trauma*
2. Briere, *Child Abuse Trauma*
3. Teicher, "Scars That Won't Heal"
4. Ibid.
5. Teicher, "Scars That Won't Heal"; Kendall, "How Child Abuse and Neglect Damage the Brain"
6. Teicher, "Scars That Won't Heal"; Perry, "Child Trauma"
7. Teicher, "Scars That Won't Heal"; Perry, "Child Trauma"
8. ScienceDaily, Low Levels of Neurotransmitter Serotonin
9. Kendall, How Child Abuse and Neglect Damage the Brain
10. Mukerjee, "Hidden Scars"
11. Bremner, *Does Stress Damage the Brain*; Kirmayer, Lemelson, and Barad, eds., *Understanding Trauma*
12. Perry, "Child Trauma"
13. Ibid.
14. Ibid.
15. Herman, *Trauma and Recovery*; Middleton-Moz, *Children of Trauma*
16. Herman, *Trauma and Recovery*; Middleton-Moz, *Children of Trauma*; Briere, *Child Abuse Trauma*; Farmer, *Adult Children of Abusive Parents*
17. Middleton-Moz, *Children of Trauma*; Briere, *Child Abuse Trauma*
18. Blume, *Secret Survivors*
19. Wadsworth, Spampneto and Halbrook, "The Role of Sexual Trauma in the Treatment of Chemically Dependent Women"

Chapter Thirteen

1. Mathews Larson, *Seven Weeks to Sobriety*
2. Holister, "Is Cancer Caused by the Candida Fungus?"

Chapter Fifteen

1. Dictionary.com, http://dictionary.reference.com/browse/forgive; The Free Dictionary, http://www.thefreedictionary.com/forgive

Chapter Sixteen

1. Hendrix, *Keeping the Love You Find: A Guide for Singles*

Chapter Eighteen

1. Hitchens, *God is Not Great*
2. Bufe, The 12 Steps in *Alcoholics Anonymous: Cult or Cure?*

Chapter Nineteen

1. Health Recovery Center, http://healthrecovery.com
2. InnerBalance Health, http://innerbalancehealth.com

Bibliography

The works listed here are a starting point for those interested in more information about topics covered in the book. The list includes all the works cited in the text as well as recommended reading. All websites listed were last accessed in December 2008.

Adams, Mike. "Sugar Addicts." Natural News.com, 2006. http://www.naturalnews.com/020795.html

Alcoholics Anonymous: Big Book. 4th ed. Alcoholics Anonymous World Services, Inc., 2002. Also available online at http://www.aa.org/bigbookonline

Alcoholics Anonymous Comes of Age: A Brief History of A.A. Alcoholics Anonymous World Services, 1957.

Allen, Colin. "Does a Sweet Tooth Mean Alcoholism?" Psychology Today, 2003. http://www.psychologytoday.com/articles/pto-20031120-000003.html

Barnes, Broda O., M.D. *Hypothyroidism: The Unsuspected Illness.* Harper Collins, 1976.

Blume, E. Sue. *Secret Survivors: Uncovering Incest and its Aftereffects in Women.* Ballantine Books, 1991.

Bremner, J. Douglas, M.D. *Does Stress Damage the Brain: Understanding Trauma Related Disorders from a Neurological Perspective.* W.W. Norton & Company, 2002.

Briere, John N. *Child Abuse Trauma: Theory and Treatment of the Lasting Effects.* Sage Publications, Inc., 1992.

Bufe, Charles. *Alcoholics Anonymous: Cult or Cure?* 2nd ed. Sharp Press, 1998. Also available online at http://www.morerevealed.com/library/coc

Canadian Institutes of Health Research. "The Brain from Top to Bottom." http://thebrain.mcgill.ca/flash/i/i_03/i_03_m/i_03_m_par/i_03_m_par_alcool.html

Cheever, Susan. *My Name is Bill: Bill Wilson—His Life and the Creation of Alcoholics Anonymous.* Simon & Schuster, 2004.

Child Trauma Academy. http://www.childtraumaacademy.com

Crook, William G., M.D. *The Yeast Connection: A Medical Breakthrough.* Revised ed. Vintage Books, 1986.

Cullin, M.R. ed. "Workers with MCS." *Occupational Medicine State of the Art Reviews* (1987).

DeAmicis, Ralph, Dr., and Lahni DeAmicis, Dr. "Helpful Herbal Hints from Drs. Ralph & Lahni DeAmicis: Alcoholism, Candida, Diabetes & Hypoglycemia." Space and Time Designing, Inc. http://www.spaceandtime.com/01HerbEnglish/04hints014.html

Deutsch, Roger & Rivera Rudi M.D. *Your Hidden Food Allergies are Making You Fat.* 1st ed. Prima Lifestyles, 2002.

Dictionary.com. http://dictionary.reference.com/browse/forgive

Duehring, Cindy. "Screening for Nervous System Damage." Environmental Access Research Network, 1993.

Eberhardt, Sarah. "What Doesn't Kill You Makes You Stronger: True or False? A Discussion of the Effects of Child Abuse." Available online at http://serendip.brynmawr.edu/bb/neuro/neuro02/web2/seberhardt.html #6

EurekAlert. "Both Alcoholism and Chronic Smoking Can Damage the Brains Prefrontal Cortex." http://www.eurekalert.org/pub_releases/2006-04/ace-baa041506.php

Farmer, Steven, M.A., M.F.C.C. *Adult Children of Abusive Parents: A Healing Program for Those Who Have Been Physically, Sexually, or Emotionally Abused.* Ballantine Books, 1990.

Fraser, Jessica. "American Diabetes Association Peddling Nutritional Nonsense While Accepting Money From Manufacturer of Candy and Sodas." Natural News.com, 2005. http://www.naturalnews.com/008164.html

Hartigan, Francis. *Bill W.: A Biography of Alcoholics Anonymous Co-Founder Bill Wilson.* St. Martins Griffin, 2001.

Health Recovery Center. http://www.healthrecovery.com

Hendrix, Harville. *Keeping the Love You Find: A Guide for Singles.* Atria, 1993.

Herman, Judith. *Trauma and Recovery.* Basic Books, 1992.

Hitchens, Christopher. *God Is Not Great: How Religion Poisons Everything.* Twelve Books, Hachette Book Group, 2007.

Holister, Emma. "Candida: An Introduction." Candida International, 2004. http://www.newmediaexplorer.org/emma_holister/2004/09/11/candida_an_introduction.htm

————. "Is Cancer Caused by the Candida Fungus?" Interview with Doctor Tullio Simoncini. Candida International, 2007. http://candida-international.blogspot.com/2007/03/is-cancer-caused-by-candida-fungus.html

InnerBalance Health. http://www.innerbalance.com

Intelegen, Inc. "Acetaldehyde: A Common and Potent Neurotoxin How to Prevent the Damaging Effects of Smoking, Alcohol Consumption, and Air Pollution." http://intelegen.com/nutrients/prevent_the_damaging_effects_of_.htm

Kane, P., Ph.D. *Food Makes the Difference.* New York: Simon & Schuster, 1985.

Kendall, Josh. "How Child Abuse and Neglect Damage the Brain." *The Boston Globe*, 2002. Also available at http://www.snapnetwork.org/psych_effects/how_abuse_andneglect.htm

Ketcham, Katherine, William F. Asbury, Mel Schulstad, and Arthur P. Ciaramicoli. *Beyond the Influence: Understanding and Defeating Alcoholism.* Bantam Books, 2000.

Kirmayer, Laurence J., Robert Lemelson, and Mark Barad, eds. *Understanding Trauma: Integrating Biological, Clinical, and Cultural Perspectives.* Reprint ed. Cambridge University Press, 2008.

Leviton, Richard. "Environmental Illness: A Special Report." *Yoga Journal* (1990).

Mathews Larson, Joan, Ph.D. *Seven Weeks to Sobriety: The Proven Program to Fight Alcoholism through Nutrition.* Revised ed. (Fawcett Columbine, 1992; Ballantine Books, 1997). Citations are to the Fawcett Columbine edition.

Medical College of Georgia. Online videos on trauma and women's health available online at http://fammed.mcg.edu/residency/modules/trauma/Web%20Trauma%20 video%20powerpoint.htm

Medicolegal.tripod.com, "Prevent Alcoholism: Here's How." http://medicolegal.tripod.com/preventalcoholism.htm

Merola.com. "Is Sugar More Addictive than Cocaine?" http://articles.mercola.com/sites/articles/archive/2007/08/06/is-sugar-more-addictive-than-cocaine.aspx

Middleton-Moz, Jane. *Children of Trauma: Rediscovering Your Discarded Self.* HCI, 1989.

Miller, Claudia (1994) *Toxicology and Industrial Health* Vol 10 number 4/5 July-Oct.

MMWR Weekly. "Alcohol-Attributable Deaths," http://www.cdc.gov/mmwr/preview/mmwrhtml/mm5337a2.htm

Mukerjee, Madhusree. Hidden Scars: "Sexual and Other Abuse May Alter a Brain Region." *Scientific American* (1995). Also available online at http://www.nospank.net/mkrjee.htm

Nakken, Craig. *The Addictive Personality: Understanding the Addictive Process and Compulsive Behavior.* 2nd ed. Hazelden, 1996.

National Institute on Drug Abuse. "The Neurobiology of Drug Addiction." http://www.nida.nih.gov/pubs/teaching/teaching2/Teaching2.html

NeuroScience. http://www.neurorelief.com

New South Wales Government Department of Health. "Nicotine and Other Poisons." http://www.health.nsw.gov.au/factsheets/general/nicotine.html

NIDA for Teens. "Facts on Drugs." http://teens.drugabuse.gov/facts/facts_nicotine1.asp and http://teens.drugabuse.gov/facts/facts_nicotine2.asp

Norwood, Robin. *Women Who Love Too Much.* Pocket, 1990.

Null, Gary, Ph.D. *Nutrition and the Mind.* New York: Four Walls Eight Windows, 1995.

Pick, Marcelle, OB/GYN, NP. "Anxiety in Women: Causes, Symptoms, and Natural Relief." Women to Women.

http://www.womentowomen.com/depressionanxietyandmood/anxiety. aspx

Orange, A. *The Orange Papers: One Man's Analysis of Alcoholics Anonymous.* http://www.orange-papers.org/orangeeffectiveness.html#Harvard_Mental

Perry, Bruce D., M.D., Ph.D. "Neurobiological Sequelae of Childhood Trauma: Post-traumatic Stress Disorders in Children." Child Trauma Academy. http://www.childtrauma.org/ctamaterials/ptsd_child.asp

Pierce-Davis, Carol, Ph.D. "The Biochemistry and Physiology of Smoking." Texas Department of Health Bulletin, 2005. Also available online at www.carolpiercedavisphd.com/files/The_Biochemistry_and_Physiology_ of_Smoking.pdf

Psycheducation.org. "Details of the Thyroid Story." http://www.psycheducation.org/thyroid/details.htm

Randolph, Theron G., M.D., and Ralph W. Moss, Ph.D. *An Alternative Approach to Allergies: The New Field of Clinical Ecology Unravels Environmental Causes of Mental and Physical Ills.* Lippincott & Crowell, 1980.

Rea, William J., M.D. Chemical Sensitivities. CRC Press Inc., 1992

Reed Gibson, Pamela, Ph.D. *Multiple Chemical Sensitivity: A Survival Guide.* New Harbinger Publications, 2000.

Rivers, Kaiten, N.D. "Neurotransmitters: They Run More Than Your Emotions." http://www.tacomanatural.com/articles6.html

Rogers, Sherry A. *The E.I. Syndrome: An Rx for Environmental Illness.* Prestige Publishing, 1986.

———. *Depression Cured at Last.* Prestige Publications, 1997.

Schuitemaker, G. E., Dr. "Nutrition and Behavior." *Journal of Orthomolecular Medicine* 3, no. 2 (1988): 57-61.

ScienceDaily. "Low Levels of Neurotransmitter Serotonin May Perpetuate Child Abuse Across Generations." ScienceDaily, 2006. http://www.sciencedaily.com/releases/2006/11/061102092229.htm

Stamford Center for Natural Health. http://www.stamfordnaturalhealth.com/services_brainchemistry.htm

Strubbe Wittenberg, Janice, R.N. *The Rebellious Body: Reclaim Your Life from Environmental Illness or Chronic Fatigue Syndrome.* Da Capo Press, 1996.

Teicher, Martin H. "Scars That Won't Heal: The Neurobiology of Child Abuse." *Scientific American* 286.3 (2002): 68-75.

The Free Dictionary. http://www.thefreedictionary.com/forgive

Trowbridge, John P., M.D., and Morton Walker, D.P.M. *The Yeast Syndrome: How to Help Your Doctor Identify and Treat the Real Cause of Your Yeast-Related Illness.* Bantam, 1986.

Truss, C. Orian, M.D. *The Missing Diagnosis.* Missing Diagnosis, 1985.

Tuormaa, T.E. "The Adverse Effects of Food Additives on Health: A Review of the Literature with Emphasis on Childhood Hyperactivity." *Journal of Orthomolecular Medicine* 9, no. 4 (1994): 225-43.

U.S. Department of Health and Human Services. "Multiple Chemical Sensitivities." 1996

U.S. Environmental Protection Agency. http://www.epa.gov

U.S. Environmental Protection Agency. "Identification of Polar Volatile Organic Compounds in Consumer Products and Common Microenvironments." EPA Study, 1991.

The University of Utah, Learn Genetics. "Drugs Alter the Brain's Reward Pathway." http://learn.genetics.utah.edu/units/addiction/drugs

Veracity, Dani. "The Hidden Dangers of Caffeine: How Coffee Causes Exhaustion, Fatigue and Addiction." Natural News.com, 2005. http://www.naturalnews.com/012352.html

Veracity, Dani. "The Politics of Sugar: Why Your Government Lies to You About This Disease-Promoting Ingredient." Natural News.com, 2005. http://www.naturalnews.com/009797.html

Wadsworth, R., Spampneto, A.M., & Halbrook, B.M. "The Role of Sexual Trauma in the Treatment of Chemically Dependent Women: Addressing the Relapse Issue." *Journal of Counseling and Development* 73 (1995): 401-6.

Werbach, M.R. "Nutritional Influences on Aggressive Behavior." *Journal of Orthomolecular Medicine* 7, no. 1 (1992): 45-51.

Wikipedia, The Free Encyclopedia. Bill W. http://en.wikipedia.org/wiki/Bill_W

————. Brainwashing. http://en.wikipedia.org/wiki/Brainwashing

————. Caffeine. http://en.wikipedia.org/wiki/Caffeine

————. Cult. http://en.wikipedia.org/wiki/Cult

Wordnet Search. Cult definition. http://wordnet.princeton.edu/perl/webwn

World Health Organization. http://www.who.int

About the Author

Cynthia Perkins, M.Ed., is a sobriety coach and a recovered alcoholic and drug addict with 21 years of uninterrupted and craving-free sobriety. She holds a bachelor's degree in psychology and a master's degree in counseling. Cynthia's alcoholism and addiction services can be found by visiting her website at Alternatives for Alcoholism:

http://www.alternativesforalcoholism.com

Cynthia is also an adult sex educator and holistic health counselor. Services for these topics can be found at these websites:

Helping Couples Have Great Sex
http://www.smolderingembers.com

Holistic Help
http://www.holistichelp.net

Cynthia makes herself available for general holistic health questions and advice at no cost on her blog, Holistic Health Talk.

http://www.holistichelp.net/blog/

Special Offer

As the owner of this book, you are entitled to a $20 discount on an initial phone consultation for sobriety coaching. To take advantage of this discount, visit me at my alcoholism website listed above or give me a call at (866) 343-7714.

LaVergne, TN USA
19 May 2010
183336LV00004B/136/P